Law, Technology and Cognition

This book considers a new approach to online copyright infringement. Rather than looking at the subject within a purely technological context, it provides legal analysis from a human perspective. This book highlights that there are three key instances in which the capacity of a human mind intersects with the development of copyright regulation: (1) the development of copyright statutory law; (2) the interpretation of the copyright statutory law the judiciary; and (3) human interaction with new technology.

Using a novel framework for constructing digital perspectives, the author, Dr Hayleigh Bosher, analyses the laws relating to online copyright infringement. She provides insights into why the law appears as it does, shedding light on the circumstances of how it came to pass and demonstrates a clear malfunction in the interpretation and application of copyright law to online activities that derives from the disconnect between the technological and the human perspectives. The book proposes putting the human element back into copyright analysis to enable the return of reason where it has been lost, and provide a clearer, more consistent and fair legal regulation of online copyright infringement.

Law, Technology and Cognition: The Human Element in Online Copyright Infringement will be of interest to students, academics, researchers, as well as practitioners.

Dr Hayleigh Bosher is a Lecturer in Intellectual Property Law at Brunel University London, as well as Visiting Research Fellow at the Centre for Intellectual Property, Policy and Management. She is also Book Review Editor for the specialist IP blog, IPKat, Director of the Intellectual Property Awareness Network (IPAN), Deputy Editor of the *European Trade Mark Reports*, founder of the World IP Women (WIPW) network and an Intellectual Property & Entertainment Law consultant.

Routledge Research in Intellectual Property

Available:

Contemporary Issues in Pharmaceutical Patent Law
Setting the Framework and Exploring Policy Options
Edited by Bryan Mercurio and Daria Kim

Intellectual Property, Finance and Corporate Governance
Janice Denoncourt

Protecting Intellectual Property in the Arabian Peninsula
The GCC States, Jordan and Yemen
David Price and Alhanoof AlDebasi

Biodiversity, Genetic Resources and Intellectual Property
Developments in Access and Benefit Sharing
Edited by Kamalesh Adhikari and Charles Lawson

Pharmaceutical Patent Protection and World Trade Law
The Unresolved Problem of Access to Medicines
Jae Sundaram

Patent Pools, Competition Law and Biotechnology
Devdatta Malshe

Copyright Law and Derivative Works
Regulating Creativity
Omri Rachum-Twaig

The Patentability of Software
Software as Mathematics
Anton Hughes

Annotated Leading Trademark Cases in Major Asian Jurisdictions
Edited by Kung-Chung Liu

SEPs, SSOs and FRAND
Asian and Global Perspectives on Fostering Innovation in Interconnectivity
Edited by Kung-Chung Liu and Reto M. Hilty

For more information about this series, please visit https://www.routledge.com/Routledge-Research-in-Intellectual-Property/book-series/INTELLPROP

Law, Technology and Cognition

The Human Element in Online Copyright Infringement

Dr Hayleigh Bosher

Routledge
Taylor & Francis Group
LONDON AND NEW YORK

First published 2020
by Routledge
2 Park Square, Milton Park, Abingdon, Oxon OX14 4RN

and by Routledge
605 Third Avenue, New York, NY 10017

First issued in paperback 2021

Routledge is an imprint of the Taylor & Francis Group, an informa business

Publisher's Note
The publisher has gone to great lengths to ensure the quality of this reprint but points out that some imperfections in the original copies may be apparent.

British Library Cataloguing-in-Publication Data
A catalogue record for this book is available from the British Library

Library of Congress Cataloging-in-Publication Data
A catalog record has been requested for this book

ISBN 13: 978-1-03-223972-9 (pbk)
ISBN 13: 978-0-367-33833-6 (hbk)

Typeset in Galliard
by Taylor & Francis Books

For Vikki

Contents

Preface

> The country here is rich and pleasant but you must pass through rough and dangerous places before you reach the end of your journey.
>
> *The Wizard of Oz*[1]

This book is based on my PhD research that I undertook at the Centre for Intellectual Property Policy and Management (CIPPM) at Bournemouth University, under the supervision of Professor Dinusha Mendis and Professor Martin Kretschmer, thanks to Bournemouth University's Vice Chancellor's Scholarship and a Funds for Women Graduates award.

In my experience, undertaking a PhD is not unlike the story of *The Wizard of Oz*. The road is long, sometimes pleasant and sometimes treacherous. It takes brains, heart and courage! Ultimately, it is a journey of self-discovery. However, it cannot be taken alone. So, thank you to those who stood by my side whilst I undertook this research journey.

1 Baum L. F., *The Wizard of Oz* (New York: Puffin Books, 2013) p. 21.

Introduction

The power of technology as a threat to mankind has been a popular science-fiction theme for a very long time, from classics such as George Orwell's *1984* to more recent endeavours such as the haunting TV series *Black Mirror*. Perhaps the reason for the popularity of this subject is that these stories act as a catalyst to explore the future possibilities of the relationship between humans and technology. Based on our current experience we project into the future expecting technological advances to escalate at an advanced rate. Although technology of itself is neutral in the sense that it can be used for positive or negative purposes, the development of technology is quickly progressing and more than ever we are replacing human services with machines and apps. In the high-tech society within which we currently dwell, it is easy to focus on and rely upon technology.

However, this book aims to bring back the human element in the discussion of online copyright infringement at three crucial junctures: the drafting of the law; the interpretation and application of the law; and the cognitive understanding of new technologies. It is argued that putting the human element back into copyright analysis can return reason where it has been lost in technological specifics. It considers the mapping of copyright law online, with key themes of the human element in the development of copyright law and the cognitive perspective of the human experience with new technologies. The moral of the story is the reminder that you cannot forget, or worse exclude, the notion of the human in the law-making process, in the application of the law or in the regulating of those who make use of copyright works online. It is people who make and enforce copyright law, people who create copyright works and people who use those works on the internet. As Tim Berners-Lee stated: "The … Web … it's really a system of people. Yes, it is enabled by technology. So, as time went on, we stopped thinking about the internet as the collection of computers and we stop thinking about the Web as the collection of connected pages and now we think of the Web as humanity connected."[1]

1 Berners-Lee T., Speech at the announcement of the World Wide Web Foundation, 14 September 2008, the Newseum Washington, DC: http://webfoundation.org/about/community/transcript-of-tim- berners-lee-video/.

Overview

This research investigates online copyright infringement through the lens of Professor Orin Kerr's "internal" and "external" perspectives of the internet,[2] which are developed into a framework for analysis, referred to as the Framework for Constructing Digital Perspectives. The Framework is applied to the copyright statutory law and case law relating to reproduction and communication to the public.

Chapter 1 introduces the key concepts and themes which underlie the rest of the book. It captures the perpetual symbiotic relationship between copyright and technology, in particular considering the impact of the internet. It serves to introduce vital concepts that are relied upon throughout the book such as the internal and external perspectives that apply to copyright online, as well as judicial interpretation rules such as the literal and mischief rules.

Chapter 2 undertakes a detailed analysis of the internal and external perspectives and grounds these concepts in the theoretical basis of metaphor and literalism. Thereafter, these concepts are developed into the Framework for Constructing Digital Perspectives and the method of application for the Framework is set out.

Chapters 3 and 4 address copyright infringement by way of reproduction. Chapter 3 analyses section 17 of the Copyright, Designs and Patents Act 1988 (CDPA 1988); looking at the historical development of the law from the 1952 Gregory Committee. It looks specifically at the factors which affected the wording of the clauses within the section and provides context and understanding to the way that the law appears today. Following that, the chapter considers section 17 in detail, looking at each subsection with the view to evaluating its intended meaning, its current policy purpose and whether or not it suggests either an internal or an external perspective.

Based on the findings of Chapter 3, Chapter 4 considers the case law relating to section 17(2) of the CDPA 1988 copying by storage and section 17(6) making transient or incidental copies. It considers in detail the origin of storage, the application and interpretation of the law, looking in particular at cases of caching and browsing.

Chapters 5 and 6 mirror Chapters 3 and 4 in structure but are concerned with copyright infringement by way of communication to the public. Chapter 5 considers the development of section 20 of the CDPA 1988 in order to determine the intended meaning and policy purpose of the section. It looks at the origin of the communication right, the statutory developments and challenges in transposing EU Directives into UK legislation. The chapter then focuses on the key elements of communication – the subject matter, the public and electronic transmission.

Chapter 6 undertakes an analysis of the case law relating to copyright infringement by way of communication of the public. This analysis compares the case law after the Copyright and Related Rights Regulations 2003[3] that amended section 20 of the CDPA 1988 from a broadcasting right to a right of communication to

2 Kerr O. S., The Problem of Perspective in Internet Law (2003) 91 *Georgetown Law Journal*, pp. 357–405.

3 Copyright and Related Rights Regulations 2003 (SI 2003/2498).

the public, in light of the European influence on UK case law. It looks in detail at the jurisprudence defining the factors of communication and public in the assessment of online infringement.

Chapter 7 brings together the findings of research, highlighting the tensions between copyright law and internet technologies.

1 The human element in the story of online copyright infringement

Introduction

The title of this chapter points to a key thread that runs throughout this book, the human element in the application of copyright infringement online. Three key instances in which the human mind intersects with the development of copyright regulation on the internet are addressed in this chapter.

The first instance that is considered is the drafting of the statutory law. The statute is a product of its time,[1] it reflects the economic and political status of the legislator and can only be as informed as those contributing to its construction.[2] Through the debates in the House of Lords and House of Commons and a consideration of the circumstances within which the law was drafted the true intended meaning of the law be understood. Thus, the human element involved in the development of copyright law comes from the thinking and intention of the legislators. As such, the historical context and development of the law is considered in order to establish the intended meaning and policy purpose of the relevant sections of the Copyright, Designs and Patents Act 1988 (CDPA 1988).

The second instance is the interpretation of the copyright statutory law by the judges. The role of the judge is to apply the law to the facts of the case.[3] In order to do this, the judge must interpret the meaning of the statutory law and of the facts. As such, the reasoning of the relevant judgments are considered to ascertain the judge's interpretation of the law.

The third instance is the cognitive interaction with new technologies by all humans. The way in which people respond to and understand new technologies from a cognitive perspective is the same way that humans respond to any new situation – by applying previous knowledge.[4] This often means that in order to be

1 Whitford Committee, *Copyright and Designs Law, Report of the Committee to Consider the Law on Copyright and Designs* (London: Her Majesty's Stationery Office, 1977) Cmnd 6732, para 15 (hereafter, the Whitford Committee Report).

2 Dworkin G. and Taylor R. D., *Blackstone's Guide to the Copyright, Designs and Patents Act 1988* (London: Blackstone Press Ltd, 1989) p. 15.

3 Levi E., *An introduction to Legal Reasoning* (Chicago: University of Chicago Press, 1949) pp. 1–3.

4 Larsson S., *Metaphors and Norms: Understanding Copyright Law in a Digital Society* (Sweden: Lund University, 2011) see discussion in Chapter 2.

able to understand experiences online, the mind will relate the experience to something already known. As such, if a person is looking at a website, what they are actually doing is viewing a set of pixels reflecting the 0 or 1 state of the binary digits that collate to form images on a screen. However, the human mind experiences this technology as shopping online, for example. Human interaction with new technology has become far-reaching, almost in fact, an extension of the self.[5] This can be on a small scale, from using a phone memory to store information that might otherwise have been retained in the mind. Or, on a larger scale, the extension of the personality through social media, online games and virtual realities.[6]

In light of this, the book considers how the internet has introduced a new phenomenon for the application of copyright law. The nature of the internet and the way that humans cognitively digest their experience online means that there are two ways in which the facts of the internet can be interpreted. This is because the facts of the case can be determined by either the technological function of the hardware and software or the cognitive perspective. These two ways to understand online activity are known as the internal and external perspectives.[7]

The focus of this book is digital copyright infringement by way of reproduction and communication to the public, in light of the development of the internet and online technologies. This analysis is undertaken through the lens of the internal and external perspectives, which takes into account the human element in both the development and application of the law in relation to the internet. As Aiken stated: "For too long technology has been about data, devices and tech experts. Now it is time to turn our focus to the greater socio-technological implications … In other words, it's time to factor in the human."[8]

This chapter introduces the main themes and concepts that are built upon throughout this book. It begins by considering the interpretation of online activity through the internal and external perspectives. Thereafter, the application of copyright infringement to online activity by way of copying and then by communication to the public is considered.

Copyright and the internet

Copyright regulation and technology are entwined and bound together in a perpetual symbiotic relationship. This is seen by "every major leap forward in the history of copyright law is linked to a technological leap forward."[9]

5 Shaw J. A., From Homo Economicus to Homo Roboticus: An Exploration of the Transformative Impact of the Technological Imaginary (2015) 11(3) *International Journal of Law in Context*, pp. 245–264, p. 246.

6 *Ibid.*, p. 246.

7 Kerr O. S., The Problem of Perspective in Internet Law (2003) 91 *Georgetown Law Journal*, pp. 357–405.

8 Aiken M., *The Cyber Effect* (London: John Murray Publishers, 2016) pp. 18–19.

9 Groves P., *Copyright and Designs Law: A Question of Balance* (London: Graham and Trotman Ltd, 1991) p. 1.

Copyright law adapts in response to new technologies and so changes in the law could "be seen as attempts to modernise the law, to bring it in to line with the cultural and technological changes".[10] Each major development in copyright law can be associated with the development of a new technology; from the first Copyright Act 1710[11] which was adapting to the challenges of printing press technology.[12] Thereafter, sound recordings,[13] films,[14] broadcasts[15] and computer programs[16] have all left their marks on the development of copyright law.

Copyright law is thus a product of its time; the Whitford Committee likened the amending of the Statute of Anne to "a modest Queen Anne house to which there have been Georgian, Victorian, Edwardian and finally Elizabethan additions, each adding embellishments in the style of the times."[17] As new technologies have been developed, copyright law has always adapted to encompass them.[18]

At every advent of a new technology a fear rises in stakeholders that copyright is under threat; copyright law is claimed to be out of date and if immediate action is not taken, copyright will become obsolete. For example, at the introduction of the photocopier, the technology that enabled quicker and cheaper copying of books was considered a serious threat to copyright holders at the time.[19] It was claimed that the photocopying technology threatened a complete breakdown of copyright observance with which the copyright laws were inadequate to cope.[20]

As a result, the Gregory Committee was set up in order to consider how the law should evolve in response to this technology.[21] The consultation highlighted the need for copyright to respond and adapt to new technologies, whilst also upholding a fair balance between stakeholders. For example, publishers insisted that the law could not allow large-scale copying, but scholars wanted to be able to make copies for their research, and librarians required clarity on which they to

10 Sherman B. and Bently L., *The Making of Modern Intellectual Property* (Cambridge: Cambridge University Press, 1999) p. 65.
11 An Act for the Encouragement of Learning, by vesting the Copies of Printed Books in the Authors or Purchasers 1709, commonly referred to as the Statute of Anne.
12 Jones R., Intellectual Property Reform for the Internet Generation: An Accident Waiting to Happen (2010) 1(2) *European Journal of Law and Technology*, pp. 1–17, p. 2.
13 CDPA 1988, section 1(1)(b).
14 *Ibid.*, section 1(1)(b).
15 *Ibid.*, section 1(1)(b).
16 *Ibid.*, section 3(1)(b).
17 Whitford Committee Report, para 15.
18 Bracha O., Copyright History as History of Technology (2013) 5(1) *The World Intellectual Property Journal*, pp. 45–53, p. 45. See also, Sherman B. and Bently L., *The Making of Modern Intellectual Property* (Cambridge: Cambridge University Press, 1999).
19 Feather J., *Publishing, Piracy and Politics: An Historical Study of Copyright in Britain* (London: Mansell Publishing, 1994) p. 205.
20 Dworkin G., Reports of Committees; the Whitford Committee Report on Copyright and Designs Law (1977) 40 *Modern Law Review*, pp. 685–700, p. 696.
21 Gregory Committee, *The Board of Trade Report of the Copyright Committee* (London: Her Majesty's Stationery Office, 1952) Cmnd 8662, Preliminary to the Report, p. 1.

base their practice.[22] In order to address these conflicting interests the Gregory Committee suggested an extension of fair dealing that would allow reproduction by mechanical or photographic means, but only of extracts up to a certain length for the purpose of private study.[23] Feather described this balancing act as an "important conceptual innovation … an ingenious compromise."[24]

In this respect, copyright is seen to respond to technology development. In the same way, the current statutory legislation, the CDPA 1988, was drafted in response to new technologies by recognising copyright protection in computer programs,[25] and cable and satellite broadcasting,[26] which did not appear in the previous Act.

The reason, perhaps, that the internet is considered different to other technological developments is due to the increased pace of technological advance. Moore's Law forecasts that the rate of technological power doubles every two years and lowers in price accordingly.[27] As Lessig noted, technological changes have previously been gradual and the enabling of cheaper and easier copying had been only by degrees and over an extended period of time.[28] This allowed the legislator time to react by slowly modifying the regulation protections and extending them where technology seemed to be eroding them.[29] However, some believe that current online technologies[30] increased at such a rate of accessibility[31] that cultural and behavioural changes occurred too fast for the law to keep up.[32] Some argued that copyright law is rendered obsolete in the face of the internet, for example suggesting that copyright is challenged by internet technologies that allowed multiple copies of copyright works, of equal quality, to be copied instantly at an almost zero cost.[33]

22 *Ibid.*, p. 1.

23 *Ibid.*, para 52.

24 Feather J., *Publishing, Piracy and Politics: An Historical Study of Copyright in Britain* (London: Mansell Publishing, 1994) p. 206.

25 CDPA 1988, section 3(1)(b).

26 CDPA 1988, sections 1(1)(b), 6(4).

27 Mollick E., Establishing Moore's Law (2006) 28(3) *IEEE Annals of the History of Computing*, pp. 62–75: Gordon Moore's forecast has been upheld for 40 years.

28 Lessig L., *Code and Other Laws of Cyberspace* (New York: Basic Books, 1999) p. 125.

29 *Ibid.*, p. 125.

30 Hardy T., Computer RAM Copies: A Hit or a Myth? Historical Perspectives on Caching as a Microcosm of Current Copyright Concerns (1997) 22 *University of Dayton Law Review*, pp. 423–621, p. 425. See also Hargreaves I., *Digital Opportunity; A Review of Intellectual Property and Growth* (May 2011) para 8.5.

31 Van Santen R., Khoe D. and Vermeer B., *2030 Technology That Will Change The World* (Oxford: Oxford University Press, 2010) pp. 111–112: "Digital assistants in our pockets … provide at any time and any place a gateway to all people and information in the global village."

32 Peitz M. and Waldfogel J., *The Oxford Handbook of The Digital Economy* (Oxford: Oxford University Press, 2012) p. 491; Lessig L., *Code and Other Laws of Cyberspace* (New York: Basic Books, 1999) p. 125; Davis G., *Copyright and the Public Interest*, 2nd edition (London: Sweet & Maxwell, 2002) p. 326.

33 Landes W. and Posner R., An Economic Analysis of Copyright Law (1989) 18 *Journal of Legal Studies*, pp. 325–364, p. 326.

It has also been argued that attempting to map copyright law onto online activity simply does not work,[34] and that copyright law is unable to embrace the future of the internet.[35] For example, John Perry Barlow stated: "real world conditions will continue to change at a blinding pace, and the law will get further behind and more profoundly confused."[36] Furthermore, Murray argued that "the move from physical to digital distribution models and the development of the internet are two of the most disruptive events of the twentieth century."[37]

Needless to say, the advent of internet technologies has introduced new challenges to copyright regulation. Copyright infringement may have occurred pre-internet, but the internet has created the phenomenon of online copyright infringement. These technologies allow users to easily access and replicate copyright material,[38] and limit the ability of copyright holders to control the use of their work.[39]

Some have argued that the internet offers nothing new and that applying copyright regulation online is the same as applying the law to any new set of facts.[40] For example, Goldsmith suggested that whilst it is a challenge to apply traditional legal doctrine to the novel internet context, it is manageable.[41]

The word "internet" is used every day, mostly without a thought to what it actually means. "Inter" is from the Latin root meaning between or among, and "net" is an abbreviation of network. So the internet is a system that connect individual computer networks to allow for the transfer of data across the network.[42] For the avoidance of doubt, what is meant by the internet for the purposes of this book is not the components that create an online experience such as email or a website, but instead it refers to the network or networks[43] upon which these online technologies and components are built. The internet is regarded, within this book, as the network system that encompasses online technologies to which copyright law is applied.

34 Davis G., *Copyright and the Public Interest*, 2nd edition (London: Sweet & Maxwell, 2002) p. 326.

35 Ploman E. W. and Hamilton L. C., *Copyright: Intellectual Property in the Information Age* (London: Routledge and Kegan Paul, 1980) p. 148. See also Patterson L. R., *Copyright in Historical Perspective* (Nashville: Vanderbilt University Press, 1968) p. 214.

36 Barlow J. P., The Next Economy of Ideas, After the Copyright Revolution, 1 October 2000: http://www.wired.com/2000/10/download/

37 Murray A., *Information Technology Law: The Law and Society* (Oxford: Oxford University Press, 2013) p. 252.

38 Lessig, L., *Code and Other Laws of Cyberspace* (New York: Basic Books, 1999) p. 124.

39 *Ibid.*, p. 125.

40 Sommer J. H., Against Cyberlaw (2000) 15 *Berkeley Technology Law Journal*, pp. 1145–1232, p. 1148.

41 Goldsmith J. L., Against Cyberanarchy (1998) 65 *University of Chicago Law Review*, pp. 1199–1250, p. 1218.

42 Murray A., *Information Technology Law: The Law and Society* (Oxford: Oxford University Press, 2016) p. 16.

43 Vitoria M., et al (eds), *Laddie, Prescott and Vitoria: The Modern Law of Copyright and Designs*, 4th edition (London: Butterworths Law, 2011) 37.2: *"Physically, the Internet consists of many networks which interconnect many individual computers (hundreds of millions)."*

The original intention for the development of the technology that has now become the internet was for military communication, commissioned by the US Department of Defence.[44] However, in the first recorded description in 1962, J. C. R. Licklider of MIT envisioned a globally interconnected set of computers through which everyone could quickly access data and programs; naming the concept the "Galactic Network."[45] Subsequently, in March 1989, Tim Berners-Lee proposed the idea of a linked information management system[46] which ultimately led to the development of the World Wide Web. Berners-Lee has revealed how it took 18 months to persuade his company that the technology he was building should be royalty free for anybody to use and has expressed his aspirations for "one web that is free and open."[47] However, he has also recognised the importance of intellectual property as: "an important legal and cultural issue. Society as a whole has complex issues to face here: private ownership versus open source and so on."[48] Ultimately, the nature of the internet was intended to be an open, sharing network.[49]

The internet has been recognised by many as a radical departure from previous technologies and therefore within a legal context is vastly different from that of the past.[50] This is because the nature of the internet presents challenges "of an entirely different order."[51] As Ola stated: "The switch from the Advanced Research Project Agency Network (ARPANET) to Transmission Control Protocol/Internet Protocol (TCP/IP) marked the birth of the internet, and the world has not been the same ever since."[52] It can be set apart from previous technological developments for a number of reasons. As Epstein stated: "Nowhere is this task of reconciliation more daunting than with cyberspace, where the speed and spread of information has been ratcheted up to levels that were unimaginable even a generation ago."[53]

44 Leiner B. M., Cerf V. G., Clark D. D., Kahn R. E., Kleinrock L., Lynch D. C., Postel J., Roberts L. G. and Wolff S., Brief History of the Internet: http://www.internetsociety.org/internet/what-internet/history-internet/brief-history-internet

45 *Ibid.*

46 Berners-Lee T., Information Management: A Proposal, March 1989, May 1990: https://www.w3.org/History/1989/proposal.html

47 Berners-Lee T., Speech at the Newseum in Washington at the announcement of the World Wide Web Foundation, 14 September 2008, Washington, DC: http://webfoundation.org/about/community/transcript-of-tim-berners-lee- video/

48 BCS The Chartered Institute for IT, *Leaders in Computing: Changing the Digital World* (Swindon: British Informatics Society, 2011) p. 44.

49 The concept of the internet as a communication device is developed further in Chapter 6 in relation to communication the public.

50 Reed C., *Making Laws for Cyberspace* (Oxford: Oxford University Press, 2013) p. 26.

51 Edward L., Rules and Standards for Cyberspace (2002) 77 *Notre Dame Law Review*, pp. 1275–1372, p. 1279.

52 Ola K., Fundamentals of Open Access (2014) 36(2) *European Intellectual Property Review*, pp. 112–123, p. 116.

53 Epstein R. A., Privacy, Publication, and the First Amendment: The Dangers of First Amendment Exceptionalism (2000) 52 *Stanford Law Review*, pp. 1003–1048, p. 1004.

Firstly, the internet allows data to be in multiple places at once, whereas previously data could only be in one place at one time.[54] This means that copyright material is no longer subject to scarcity. It also means that there is a lack of proximity between cause and effect which therefore makes enforcing copyright more challenging.

Secondly, bandwidth is infinite compared to the physical limitations of real space. Online technologies facilitate instantaneous transmission of perfect reproductions of copyright works at almost zero costs.[55] This makes copyright infringement much easier and cheaper on an unlimited scale, therefore challenging the copyright owner's ability to control the distribution of their work.

Thirdly, online technologies disconnect copyright works from their original format.[56] Previously, technological developments had an effect on a specific type of copyright work, such as the photocopier and literary works. Digitalisation, on the other hand, applies to almost all types of copyright works, making the impact much larger. The technology is increasingly subsuming all media into itself.[57] Communications such as mail and telephoning, and entertainment such as film, television, music, photography and radio have all been translated into digital form.[58] Therefore, the exclusive rights that attach to such creative works are more frequently defined in technical terms.[59] These technological parameters are largely prompted by lobbying on the part of entertainment industries in response to new technologies that allow novel ways to reproduce and share creative content.[60] As we have seen most recently in the Copyright in the Digital Single Market Directive[61] where, for example, Article 13 – now Article 17 – was intended to remedy the alleged mismatch between the value of content uploaded by users on YouTube and the remuneration of the rightsholders of that content.[62] This notion, coined the "value gap" is highly controversial and argued by some to be based on content industry assumptions

54 Lemley M., Place and Cyberspace (2003) 91(2) *California Law Review*, pp. 521–542, pp. 525– 526.

55 Yan M., The Law Surrounding the Facilitation of Online Copyright Infringement (2012) 34(2) *European Intellectual Property Review*, pp. 122–126, p. 122.

56 Reed C., *Making Laws for Cyberspace* (Oxford: Oxford University Press, 2013) p. 154.

57 Reed T. V., *Understanding Our Digitized World: Culture, Power, and Social Change in the Internet Era* (Oxford: Routledge, 2014) p. 2.

58 *Ibid.*, p. 2.

59 Burk D. L., Copyright and the Architecture of Digital Delivery (2014) *University of California Irvine School of Law, Research Paper No. 2014–57*, p. 4.

60 *Ibid.*, p. 4.

61 Directive (EU) 2019/790 of the European Parliament and of the Council of 17 April 2019 on copyright and related rights in the Digital Single Market and amending Directives 96/9/EC and 2001/29/EC [2019] OJ L 130/92 (hereafter the DSM Copyright Directive). For background, see Kivistö M., The DSM Directive: A Package (Too) Full of Policies in Pihlajarinne T., Vesala J. and Honkkila O., *Online Distribution of Content in the EU* (Cheltenham: Edward Elgar, 2019) pp. 5–24.

62 Rosati E., *Copyright and the Court of Justice of the European Union* (Croydon: Oxford University Press, 2019) p. 200.

rather than independent empirical evidence,[63] and merely a rhetorical device almost exclusively fabricated by the music and entertainment industry.[64]

Fourthly, as a result of the development of internet technologies, consumption behaviours have altered, changing the value of copyright works due to unlimited unauthorised dissemination.[65] Online technology has enabled users to share and connect with the 4,383,810,342[66] other people online and sharing thus has become an established part of modern culture.[67] For example, Facebook statistics state that it has 1.56 billion active users[68] and over 100 million photos and videos are shared on Instagram per day.[69] Sharing has now become a complete functionality of web pages[70] and social media platforms, allowing endless possibilities of broadcasting any information on any portable device.[71] It has become impossible to control the spread of information on the internet; as soon as content is online, it is accessible and sharable.[72]

The nature of online sharing and copyright infringement in general has been explored through academic research, particularly focusing on how much sharing is done, by whom and why. A brief overview of this research is considered below in order to demonstrate the impact of internet technologies on the consumption of copyright works.

Since 2003 there have been at least 200 empirical studies on the user's decision to engage in online copyright infringement.[73] These studies have examined end-user motivations using the following frameworks: cost benefit analysis, legal deterrence, value of the goods in question, technical ability, social influence and moral associations.[74] However, there is no overwhelming evidence to suggest that one, any or all of these motivations have a casual effect on a user's decision to infringe.

63 Giancarlo F., From Horizontal to Vertical: An Intermediary Liability Earthquake in Europe (2017) 12(7) *JIPLP*, pp. 565–575, p. 568.

64 Giancarlo F., To Filter, Or Not To Filter? That Is The Question In EU Copyright Reform (2018) 36(2) *Cardozo Arts & Entertainment Law Journal*, pp. 331–368, p. 136.

65 Lessig L., *Code and Other Laws of Cyberspace* (New York: Basic Books, 1999) p. 125.

66 This represents about 56.8% of the population worldwide and a 111.4% growth from 2000 to 2019, Internet World Stats: http://www.internetworldstats.com/stats.htm

67 Levine R., *Free Ride, How the Internet is Destroying the Culture Business and How it Can Fight Back* (London: Vintage, 2012) p. 9.

68 For March 2019: http://newsroom.fb.com/company-info

69 Omnicore: https://www.omnicoreagency.com/instagram-statistics/, see also Instagram: https://business.instagram.com/getting-started/#why-instagram

70 Tapscott D. and Williams A. D., *Wikinomics How Mass Collaboration Changes Everything* (London: Atlantic Books, 2008) pp. 300–301.

71 Van Santen R., Khoe D. and Vermeer B., *2030 Technology That Will Change the World* (Oxford: Oxford University Press, 2010) pp. 111–112.

72 Lessig L., *Free Culture* (New York: Penguin Book Press, 2004).

73 Watson S., Zizzo D. and Fleming P., Determinants and Welfare Implications of Unlawful File Sharing: A Scoping Review (2014) *CREATe Working Paper 2014/05*, p. 2. This paper carried out a scoping review to investigate the extent and nature of research into the welfare implications and determinants of unlawful file sharing, 54,441 sources were initially found with a wide search and were narrowed down to 206 articles which examined human behaviour, intentions or attitudes.

74 *Ibid.*

Twelve of these studies considered legal awareness. Although no causation could be shown, the evidence from these twelve studies strongly suggested that people were unaware of whether their activity online was legal.[75] For example, the Palfrey *et al* [76] study revealed that when students were asked "do you know what copyright means?" 84% responded "yes", but their subsequent description of copyright was either wholly or partially incorrect.[77]

Furthermore, there is general recognition that illegal activity online is a social norm, with no moral implications.[78] As early as 2003, surveys indicated that a substantial number of young people believed that sharing digital music was morally acceptable.[79] The Strategic Advisory Board for Intellectual Property Policy (SABIP) concluded in 2009 that: "There is also substantial evidence that many individuals do not perceive software piracy to be an ethical problem at all".[80]

This was supported by a study in 2010 that found students to have "relatively high levels of anti-copyright norms."[81] More recently, a study in 2012 continued to find that the younger population did not have moral or ethical concerns about the practice of online copyright infringement.[82] A further study concluded that the imposition of stricter penalties for copyright infringement would further erode respect for copyright law and may even prove counterproductive to the entertainment industries.[83] In this study, 404 non-law students were surveyed and the results suggested that students' evaluation of the music industry was negatively affected by the enforcement of copyright law.[84] The authors stated that: "The younger demographic are convinced that

75 *Ibid.*, p. 34.

76 Palfrey J., Gasse U., Simun M. and Barns R. F., Youth, Creativity and Copyright in the Digital Age (2009) 1(2) *International Journal of Learning and Media*, pp. 79–97.

77 *Ibid.*, p. 84.

78 Bowrey K., *Law and Internet Cultures* (Melbourne: Cambridge University Press, 2005); Lessig L., *Remix: Making Art and Commerce Thrive in the Hybrid Economy* (New York: Penguin Press, 2008); Schultz M. F., Copynorms: Copyright and Social Norms in Yu K. P. (ed.) *Intellectual Property and Information Wealth: Issues and Practices in the Digital Age, Vol 1 Copyright and Related Rights* (Connecticut: Praeger Publishers, 2006) p. 201.

79 Hanway S. and Lyons L., *Teens OK With Letting Music Downloads Play*, 30 September 2003, Gallup Poll: http://www.gallup.com/poll/9373/teens-letting-music-downloads-play.aspx. The poll reported 83% of people between the age of 13 and 17 found nothing wrong with file sharing.

80 SABIP, *Copycats? Digital Consumers in the Online Age* (London; CIBER, UCL, 2009) pp. 37–38.

81 Depoorter B., Van Hiel A., Vanneste S., Copyright Backlash (2010–11) 84 *Southern California Law Review*, pp. 1251–1292, p. 1278.

82 Bahanovich D. and Collopy D., *Music Experience and Behaviour in Young People: Winter 2012–2013 [2011 National Survey]*, International Association of Music Business Research: https://uhra.herts.ac.uk/bitstream/handle/2299/10867/681097.pdf?sequence=4&isAllowed=y, p. 19.

83 Depoorter B., Van Hiel A., Vanneste S., Copyright Backlash (2010–11) 84 *Southern California Law Review*, pp. 1251–1292, p. 1257.

84 *Ibid.*, p. 1272.

file sharing technology has many beneficial uses and that copyright law is out dated or biased towards music publishers".[85]

In the 2015 Kantar Media Online Copyright Infringement Tracker, awareness and understanding of copyright infringement remains confusing for users.[86] The study found that 40% of internet users claimed to be either "not particularly confident" or "not at all confident" in terms of what is and is not legal online.[87] In the most recent wave, the Online Copyright Infringement Tracker 2018 reported that 15% of UK internet users aged 12+ (equating to approximately 6,525,000 people) consumed at least one item of online content illegally in the "past three months", in line with the findings from 2017 and 2016.[88]

According to CISAC's Global Collections Report 2018, despite digital's rise for all repertoires to €1.27 billion, revenues from digital uses remain far below collections from broadcast, live and background uses, with 13.2% of creators' royalties coming from digital sources.[89] The report argues that this demonstrates the mismatch between the volume of creative work being made available via digital channels and the amounts being returned to creators, or the "value gap" as mentioned earlier.

These studies demonstrate that the development of new technology has had a significant impact on the way that copyright works are consumed and regulated. In recognising both the benefits and the challenges that online technological developments bring, Ben Bradshaw, the Secretary of State at the time stated that "the digital revolution has brought huge benefits and opportunities for a country such as Britain that is creative, innovative and flexible, but such rapid change also brings challenges. The overriding challenge … to address is that of keeping the legal framework that applies to our digital and creative sectors up to date in such a fast-moving world."[90]

The development of copyright law can be seen as a reaction to technological developments which create new types of works and new means of exploiting existing works.[91] Failing to adapt in these circumstances results in unintended consequences in the law: "New developments change the pitch of the playing field. Industries effected by copyright find that the application of old legal language to new contexts yields unanticipated results."[92] Thus, the law must

85 *Ibid.*, p. 1266.
86 Kantar Media, *Online Copyright Infringement Tracker Wave 5* (London: Intellectual Property Office, 2015).
87 *Ibid.*, p. 44.
88 Kantar Media, *Online Copyright Infringement Tracker Wave 8* (London, Intellectual Property Office, 2018) p. 5.
89 CISAC, Global Collections Report 2018, 8 November 2018: https://www.cisac.org/CISAC-University/Library/Global-Collections-Reports/Global-Collections-Report-2018
90 Hansard, Digital Economy Bill [Lords], Second Reading, 6 April 2010, Col 836, the Secretary of State for Culture, Media and Sport (Mr Ben Bradshaw).
91 Groves P., *Copyright and Designs Law: A Question of Balance* (London: Graham and Trotman Ltd, 1991) p. 7.
92 Litman J., *Digital Copyright*, 2nd edition (New York: Prometheus Books, 2006) p. 22.

adapt to new technologies in order to stay relevant[93] in balancing the interests of creators and rights-holders with the public interest of accessing and using creative material.[94]

This is ultimately the context of this book; the development of new online technologies and the effect on copyright regulation. In particular, the application of copyright law to online activities that are deemed to be infringement by copying or communication to the public.

Interpretation of online activity

The internet introduced a new dimension to the interpretation and application of the law to the facts of a case. In this regard, the nature of the internet presents challenges "of an entirely different order."[95]

The internal and external perspectives

As mentioned, the essential task of the judge is to interpret the law and apply the legal rules to facts of the case.[96] However, when applying this to the internet there can be more than one set of facts, depending on whether the physical (external) or virtual (internal) perspective is considered. The law is contingent on the facts, and the facts are contingent on the perspective.[97]

In his article *The Problem of Perspective in Internet Law*, Kerr set out the internal and external perspectives of the internet.[98] He explained that the internal perspective is where a user's understanding of their activity online derives from their understanding of real life. This is the virtual reality perspective that finds the internet as equivalent to the physical world. From this perspective, a person accepts the virtual world of cyberspace as a legitimate construct in order to cognitively process their

93 Hargreaves I., *Digital Opportunity; A Review of Intellectual Property and Growth*, May 2011, 8.5. More recently seen in the Communication from the Commission to the European Parliament, the Council, the European Economic and Social Committee and the Committee of the Regions, A Digital Single Market Strategy for Europe, COM (2015) 192 final, Brussels, 6 May 2015.

94 Drassinower A., From Distribution to Dialogue: Remarks on the Concept of Balance in Copyright Law (2009) 34(4) *The Journal of Corporation Law*, pp. 991–1007, p. 992: "Copyright discussion than the proposition that copyright is a balance between authors and users – a balance (as some like to say) between the incentive to create and the imperative to disseminate works of authorship. In spite of the pervasive, recurrent, and vigorous debate about copyright, there appears to be widespread agreement that copyright is structured as a balance."

95 Edward L., Rules and Standards for Cyberspace (2002) 77 *Notre Dame Law Review*, pp. 1275–1372, p. 1279.

96 Levi E., *An Introduction to Legal Reasoning* (Chicago: University of Chicago Press, 1949) pp. 1–3.

97 *Ibid.*, p. 362.

98 Kerr O. S., The Problem of Perspective in Internet Law (2003) 91 *Georgetown Law Journal*, pp. 357–405.

activity.[99] Kerr explained: "A computer connected to the Internet provides a window to a virtual world that is roughly analogous to the physical world of real space."[100]

In contrast, the external perspective focuses on the technical functioning of the computer or access device and the online network. This perspective considers the hardware and technicalities of how the information is presented to the user.[101] Kerr explained this as the external viewpoint whereby the internet is simply a network of computers located around the world and connected by wires and cables.[102] The hardware sends, stores and receives communications using a series of common protocols. Keyboards provide sources of input to the network and monitors provide destinations for output. The internet allows the transfer of trillions of 0s and 1s (binary digit, or bit), which computers connected to the network can translate into commands, text, sound and pictures.[103] The internet uses TCP to break the data into packets for transmission and recombines them in the receiving end, and the IP provides the addressing and routing of the data.[104] Kerr stated that: "the external perspective adopts the viewpoint of an outsider concerned with the functioning of the network in the physical world rather than the perceptions of a user. From this external viewpoint, the Internet is simply a network of computers located around the world and connected by wires and cables."[105]

For example, from an external perspective in order for an end-user to browse material online, the computer makes a copy of that material and temporarily stores it in the internet "cache" on the hard disk of the computer. Alternatively, from an internal perspective the end-user is simply viewing the material online. The user accepts the virtual world of cyberspace as a legitimate construct, and therefore perceives only that they are observing material online. The temporary copies retained in the cache are not relevant from this perspective. At most it is merely an incidental consequence of using a computer to view the material. In the case of *Meltwater*,[106] both Mrs Justice Proudman in the Chancery Division and Lord Justice Jackson and Lord Justice Elias in the Court of Appeal held that temporary copies in the end-user's computer were "generated by the user's voluntary decision to access the webpage."[107] Furthermore, the Supreme Court stated that "browsing by its very nature is an end-user function."[108] In these judgments, an external perspective on temporary

99 *Ibid.*, p. 359.
100 *Ibid.*, pp. 359–360.
101 *Ibid.*, p. 357.
102 *Reno v Am Civil Liberties Union* 521 US 844, 849 (1997) Syllabus, para 1.
103 Gralla, P., *How the Internet Works*, 8th edition (Indiana: Que Corporation, 2006).
104 Murray A., *Information Technology Law, The Law and Society*, 3rd edition (Oxford: Oxford University Press, 2016) p. 22.
105 Kerr O. S., The Problem of Perspective in Internet Law (2003) 91 *Georgetown Law Journal*, pp. 357–405, p. 360.
106 *Public Relations Consultants Association Ltd v The Newspaper Licensing Agency Ltd and Others* [2010] EWHC 3099 (Ch).
107 *Ibid.*, as per Proudman J at [109].
108 *Public Relations Consultants Association Ltd v The Newspaper Licensing Agency Ltd and Others* [2013] UKSC 18, on appeal from: [2011] EWCA Civ 1541, as per Lord Sumption at [27].

copying was taken[109] and copyright infringement based on the technical function of the computer process was established.[110]

In contrast, a more recent mention of perspective was made by Mr Justice Arnold. When considering online copyright infringement, he stated that: "Viewed from the perspective of the user, the websites do in a very real sense make the content available to the public."[111] This suggests an internal perspective as he considered the user's experience of the technology.

Kerr argued that the internet is a physical network, but that it can create a virtual world that can appear sufficiently realistic to its users to make a plausible claim for equal footing with the physical world.[112] Wu recognised the ability of code to submerge a user into virtual reality, particularly when sharing networks exploit ambiguity.[113] This is done through a design that is intended to look and *feel* more like non-commercial home copying than like breaking into a record shop.[114] In addition, Lior Jacob Strahilevitz suggested that charismatic code creates an illusion of reciprocity that can manipulate people into file sharing.[115]

Kerr suggested that the perspective of the law can be determined through analysis of the legal doctrine, the relevant case law or the perspective of the group of people the law seeks to regulate.[116] In the application of these concepts, Kerr suggested that a particular perspective can be established and should thereafter be applied. Kerr argued that "the fact that we can always present an internal and external version of the facts does not mean that those two versions are equally viable, any more than the fact that there are two sides to every argument means that we can never choose between them. Judgements can be made."[117]

Overall, it can be seen that taking either an internal or an external perspective on internet activity determines the facts of the case and therefore has a significant impact on the regulation of copyright online. This research therefore uses the internal and external perspectives as a catalyst for the analysis of the regulation of

109 Hugenholtz B. P., Caching and Copyright: The Right of Temporary Copying (2000) 22(10) *European Intellectual Property Review*, pp. 482–493.

110 *Public Relations Consultants Association Ltd v The Newspaper Licensing Agency Ltd and Others* [2013] UKSC 18.

111 *Paramount Home Entertainment Ltd, Sony Pictures Home Entertainment Ltd, Twentieth Century Fox Film Company Ltd, Universal Pictures (UK) Ltd, Warner Bros. Entertainment UK Ltd, Disney Enterprises Inc v British Sky Broadcasting Ltd, British Telecommunications Plc, Everything Everywhere Ltd, Talktalk Telecom Ltd, Telefónica UK Ltd, Virgin Media Ltd* [2013] EWHC 3479 (Ch), as per Arnold J at [34].

112 Kerr O. S., The Problem of Perspective in Internet Law (2003) 91 *Georgetown Law Journal*, pp. 357–405, p. 360; Nesson C. and Marglin D, The Day the Internet Met the First Amendment: Time and the Communications Decency Act (1996) 10 *Harvard Journal of Law and Technology*, pp. 113–136, p. 121.

113 Wu T., When Code Isn't Law (2003) 89 *Virginia Law Review*, pp. 101–170, p. 108.

114 *Ibid*., p. 109.

115 Strahilevitz J. L., Charismatic Code, Social Norms and the Emergence of Cooperation on the File Swapping Networks (2003) 89 *Virginia Law Review*, pp. 505–595.

116 Kerr O. S., The Problem of Perspective in Internet Law (2003) 91 *Georgetown Law Journal*, pp. 357–405.

117 *Ibid*., p. 390.

copyright infringement online. This is done by developing the internal and external perspectives into a framework for analysis in Chapter 2, which is then applied to the statutory law and case law in the remaining chapters.

The human element of legal drafting

When analysing statutory law, taking into account the context and circumstances of the drafting enables the understanding of its intended purpose and meaning. This book takes into account the context of the CDPA 1988 in two ways. The first is by considering the discussions and debates that occurred at the time of the drafting in order to reveal the intended meaning and policy purpose of the regulation. It is not possible to consider whether a regulation fulfils its intended purpose unless the purpose is first established. For example, in a House of Lords' debate on the interpretation of legislation Bill, Lord Chancellor Mr Quintin Hogg recalled a conversation with draftsman who stated: "It really is very difficult to understand what they mean sometimes. I always look at *Hansard*, I always look at the Blue Books, I always look at everything I can in order to see what is meant."[118]

Lord Denning also referred to *Hansard* in court on several occasions, for example in order to find out why cinematograph film exhibitions were excluded from the Obscene Publications Act 1959; Denning stated: "I propose to look at *Hansard* to find out. I know we are not supposed to do this. But the Law Commission looked at *Hansard* … So I have looked at *Hansard* to refresh my memory."[119] As a result he was able to ascertain the reasoning: "We have the reason why cinematograph films were omitted. It was because they could be left to the common law and the existing means of censorship."[120] Although the use of *Hansard* by the courts is controversial,[121] this research includes an analysis of the discussions, debates and development of the relevant law in order to understand the intended meaning of the statute. This is particularly reflected in the first part of Chapters 3 and 5.

The second factor to take into account is the nature of legal drafting. A key characteristic of legal drafting is the need to use wording that accurately reflects the intended policy decision.[122] However, in the context of copyright law, the challenge is two-fold, as the need for technologically accurate words has to be balanced with the need to be technologically neutral.[123] This is because if the

118 *Hansard*, Interpretation of Legislation Bill [H.L], Deb 26 March 1981 Vol 418 Cols 1341–1347, Cols 1341, 1344.
119 *Regina v Greater London Council, Ex Parte Blackburn and Another* [1976] 1 WLR 550, as per Lord Denning at 556.
120 *Ibid.*, as per Lord Denning at 556.
121 Discussed below in the following section.
122 Xanthaki H., *Drafting Legislation: Art and Technology of Rules for Regulation* (Oxford: Hart Publishing, 2014) Chapter 1.
123 Parliament, *The Preparation of Legislation, Report of a Committee appointed by the Lord President of the Council*, Cmnd 6053. Chairman: The Rt Hon Sir David Renton (London: Her Majesty's Stationery Office. 1975), para 11.5: "The draftsman must

wording is too specific to the technology, it becomes quickly out of date in the face of technological developments.

Technical reviews are required as part of the consultation process, which involves careful discussion on the specific choice of terminology used to define the intended meaning within the statute.[124] For example, in introducing the text and data mining exception,[125] the Government queried whether the term "electronic analysis" reflected the range of analytical techniques used in research.[126] Whilst some stakeholders felt that the term was appropriate to describe the range of activities normally meant by text and data mining, others argued that a more detailed definition was needed. Another response argued that the term was too technologically specific and suggested the word "computational" as an alternative.[127]

The Government stated its intention to draft legislation that is technologically neutral and, in this instance, to permit all activities that could reasonably be considered to be "text and data mining."[128] Therefore, the draft legislation was updated, and the wording of the exception can be seen to reflect this discussion. As such, the word "electronic" has been replaced by "computational": "The copy is made in order that a person who has lawful access to the work may carry out a computational analysis of anything recorded in the work for the sole purpose of research for a non-commercial purpose"[129]

Therefore, this book takes these nuances into account by considering the context of the drafting of the CDPA 1988 in order to ascertain the intended meaning of the law. As mentioned, the extent to which the courts are able to do this to inform their understanding is not straightforward. There are a number of controversies that arise within this area that should be noted. These revolve around the issue of the separation of powers between the judiciary and the courts. Namely, the judge's role in interpreting and applying the statutory law, whether or not there is an intended policy purpose, or meaning of the statutory law and whether or not that should be taken into account by the judge. These issues are

never be forced to sacrifice certainty for simplicity, since the result may be to frustrate the legislative intention."

124 Bosher H. and Mendis D., Swings and Roundabouts: The Impact of Legal Drafting on the Language and Understanding of Copyright Law and the Need for Educational Materials (2016) 30(3) *International Review of Law, Computers and Technology*, pp. 211–228, p. 215–216.

125 Copyright and Rights in Performances (Research, Education, Libraries and Archives) Regulations 2014 (SI 2014/1372), regulation 3(2), amending CDPA 1988, section 29A. See Lee Y. H., United Kingdom Copyright Decisions and Legislative Developments 2014 (2015) 46(2) *International Review of Intellectual Property and Competition Law*, pp. 226–237, pp. 231–232.

126 UK Intellectual Property Office, *Technical Review of Draft Legislation on Copyright Exceptions: Government Response* (Newport: UK Intellectual Property Office, 2014) p.12.

127 *Ibid.*

128 *Ibid.*

129 Copyright and Rights in Performances (Research, Education, Libraries and Archives) Regulations 2014 (SI 2014/1372), regulation 3(2), amending CDPA 1988, section 29A(1)(a).

considered in the discussion below and are relied upon throughout when analysing the judicial approach to the interpretation and application of the law.

The rules of judicial interpretation

There are three main approaches to statutory interpretation that are considered the cardinal rules in the way that judges should interpret the law:[130] the literal, golden and mischief rules. It is not clear whether these rules are descriptive of how statutes *are* interpreted or prescriptions of how they *should* be.[131] It is also not certain whether these rules should be considered together or whether one supersedes the other,[132] or indeed read together: "These are not totally distinct, much less mutually exclusive; they run together, and interpreters either choose between them or treat intention and mischief as techniques for establishing the 'true meaning' of the statutory text."[133]

The following section considers that when interpreting legislation, judges must take the ordinary meaning of the words in the statute under the literary rule. However, if those words in their ordinary meaning lead to absurdity then the court must consider the intent behind those words, and in particular what mischief the legislation attempting to solve. The golden rule allows the judges to consider the intended meaning behind the words where necessary. However, these rules create a tension with the "exclusionary rule", which traditionally prohibits the court from relying on parliamentary debates to separate the powers between the judiciary and Parliament, protecting the freedom of speech of members of the House. Thereafter, the *Pepper v Hart* rule introduced an exception to the exclusionary rule, which allows the courts to consider parliamentary debates in specific circumstances.

The literal, mischief and golden rules

Under the literal rule, judges take the plain meaning of the words in the statute. As explained by Lord Atkin: "the Legislature must be taken to have meant and intended what it has plainly expressed."[134] Some argue that the UK courts primarily take a literal approach to statutory interpretation.[135] However, using this approach alone has been considered limited.[136] The

130 Adams J. N. and Brownsword R., *Understanding Law* (London: Sweet & Maxwell 2006) p. 105.

131 *Ibid.*, p. 105.

132 *Ibid.*, p. 105.

133 Feldman D., Statutory Interpretation and Constitutional Legislation (2014) 130(Jul), *LQR*, pp. 473–497, p. 476.

134 *Vacher v London Society of Compositors* [1913] AC 107, LT 722, as per Lord Atkin at 121.

135 Stallworthy M., Construing Acts of Parliament in the United Kingdom: reference to Parliamentary debates – *Pepper v Hart* (1993) 4(4) *ICCLR*, pp. 159–162, p. 160.

136 Ekins R., The intention of Parliament (2010) *Public Law*, pp. 709–726, p. 720; Bach K., Context ex Machina, in Szabó Z. (ed.), *Semantics vs. Pragmatics* (Oxford: Oxford University Press, 2005), pp. 22–24.

reason for this is that it is not always straightforward to interpret literally the wording of a statute,[137] as the nature of language is such that it can be ambiguous and vague. As Lord Bingham stated: "The basic task of the court is to ascertain and give effect to the true meaning of what Parliament has said in the enactment to be construed. But that is not to say that attention should be confined and a literal interpretation given to the particular provisions which give rise to difficulty."[138]

This was illustrated in the case of *Smith v Hughes* (1960)[139] where Lord Parker found that the relevant legislation was vague and unclear. So instead of relying only on the literal reading of the words in the Act, he recalled the purpose of the legislation: "For my part, I approach the matter by considering what is the mischief aimed at by this Act. Everybody knows that this was an Act intended to clean up the streets … I am content to base my decision on that ground and that ground alone."[140] This is approach is called the mischief rule.

Taking a purely literal reading of the words in a statute may not enable the courts to remedy the mischief that Parliament intended to deal with.[141] The mischief rule is based on the principle that legislation is created to solve a problem, with the goal of suppressing the mischief and advancing the remedy.[142] As set out in *Heydon's case* (1584):[143] "By enquiring what was the mischief and defect against which the common law did not provide; what remedy the Parliament had appointed to cure the disease of the commonwealth; and what was the true reason of the remedy."[144]

The mischief rule can be understood in the context of Karl Llewellyn's "law-jobs" theory. This theory essentially argues that the purpose of law lies in the need to resolve conflicts that occur within a group of people.[145] The law then acts as a mechanism by which these conflicts or problems can be resolved. Accordingly, the mischief rule provides that regulation is drafted with the intention to address a problem that may occur in society, and remedy the issue to restore social order.[146] As Llewellyn stated the fundamental purpose of law is the "adjustment of people's behavior that the society (or the group) remains a society (or a group) and gets enough energy unleashed and coordinated to keep on with its job as a society (or a group)."[147]

137 Feldman D., Statutory Interpretation and Constitutional Legislation (2014) 130(Jul), *LQR*, pp. 473–497, p. 475.

138 *R (on the application of Quintaville) v Secretary of State for Health* [2003] 2 AC 687 as per Lord Bingham at [8].

139 *Smith v Hughes* [1960] 1 WLR 830.

140 *Ibid.*, as per Lord Parker at 832.

141 Bennion F., *Statutory Interpretation* (London: Longman, 1990) p. 88.

142 *Warburton v Loveland* (1832) 5 ER 499, as per Justice Burton at 22.

143 *Heydon's case* (1584) 3 Cop Rep 7a.

144 *Ibid.*

145 Llewellyn K. N., The Normative, The Legal and the Law-Jobs: The Problem of Juristic Method (1940) 49(8) *Yale Law Journal*, pp. 1355–1400

146 Adams J. N and Brownsword R., *Understanding Law* (London: Sweet & Maxwell, 2006) p. 9.

147 Llewellyn K. N., The Normative, The Legal and the Law-Jobs: The Problem of Juristic Method (1940) 49(8) *Yale Law Journal*, pp. 1355–1400, p. 1373.

In order to understand what the mischief was that Parliament intended to remedy, the judge may need to know the previous law, the history and context that led the legislator to pass the new regulation.[148] Therefore, as Lord Hailsham stated, the courts may look at committee reports "for the purpose of defining the mischief of the Act but not to construe it."[149]

However, Bennion noted that the courts have been seen to go beyond simply ascertaining the mischief and also consider the legal effect of an Act. For example, in the case of *British Leyland Motor v Armstrong Patents* [1986][150] the House of Lords considered detailed argument in relation to the Gregory Committee Report which, as discussed in Chapter 3, was the basis for the Copyright Act 1956. In this case, Lord Templeman stated: "S9(8) of the Copyright Act 1956 was defective to achieve the intended purpose."[151] Lord Edmund-Davies added: "My Lords, I have to say respectfully that I do not know what Parliament intended to do. Assume, as one reasonably may, that the Gregory Report was available to the legislators in 1956, and one will l still have no knowledge of how far they intended to implement any of its recommendations when legislating as expansively as they did. We may think that they could, and should, have done better, but that is by the way."[152]

These remarks appear to go beyond simply recognising the mischief that the legislation intended to remedy, to commenting on the effectiveness of the legislation itself in achieving the mischief identified by the committee. However, the court must not question the sufficiency of the parliamentary debate.[153] Bennion argued that this was beyond the role of the judge and as such "transcended mere statutory interpretation and struck a blow for justice."[154] As Lord Nicholls stated in a later case: "The court is called upon to evaluate the proportionality of the legislation, not the adequacy of the minister's exploration of the policy options or of his explanations to Parliament."[155]

The literal rule and mischief rule are supplemented[156] by the golden rule, which is understood to mean that legislation should be construed according to the intention expressed in the language used. When the language is not clear, or would produce an absurd outcome, the judges may assume that this was not the intention and instead consider the words to mean something other than their ordinary meaning.[157]

148 Bennion F., *Statutory Interpretation* (London: Longman, 1990) p. 108.
149 *R v Allen (Christopher)* [1985] AC 1029, as per Lord Hailsham of St Marylebone LC at 1035.
150 *British Leyland Motor Corporation Ltd v Armstrong Patents Co Ltd* [1986] AC 577.
151 *Ibid.*, as per Lord Templeman at 871.
152 *Ibid.*, as per Lord Edmund-Davies at 853.
153 *Recovery of Medical Costs for Asbestos Diseases (Wales) Bill, Re* [2015] UKSC 3, as per Lord Mance at [55].
154 Bennion F., Executive Estoppel: Pepper v Hart Revisited (2007) *Public Law*, pp. 1–12, p. 8.
155 *Wilson and Others v Secretary of State for Trade and Industry* [2003] UKHL 40, [2004] 1 AC 816 as per Lord Nicholls of Birkenhead at [67].
156 Tay Y., Reading law as literature: a forced relation (1996) 3 *UCL Juris Rev*, pp. 58–83, p. 76.
157 *River Wear Commissioners v Adamson* (1877) 2 App Cas 743, as per Lord Blackburn at 764–765.

As such, the function of the court is to interpret legislation according to the intent of the legislator, understood through the language. As Lord Wensley dale stated in *Grey v Pearson* (1857):[158] "I have been long and deeply impressed with the wisdom of the rule, now, I believe, universally adopted-at least in the courts of law in Westminster Hall that in construing wills, and indeed statutes and all written instruments, the grammatical and ordinary sense of the words is to be adhered to, unless that would lead to some absurdity, or some repugnance or inconsistency with the rest of the instrument, in which case the grammatical and ordinary sense of the words may be modified so as to avoid the absurdity and inconsistency, but no farther."[159]

Thus, according to the golden rule, the courts seek the intention of the legislation, taking a purposive approach,[160] rather than a literal one as described above in the literal rule. However, Stephan argued[161] that the Bennion quote mentioned at the beginning of this section[162] rejects the distinction between literal and golden rules.

A principal point of disagreement has been how far the courts can do in presuming from the context, the underlying policy intention for the purposes of drawing from it inferences, in cases of doubt as to their literal application. As Lord Loreburn stated: "[the courts] are not entitled to read words into an Act of Parliament unless clear reason for it is to be found within the four corners of the Act itself."[163]

As such, there are three rules which have been discussed above, the literal, mischief and golden rule. As mentioned, the relationship between these rules is not clear. For example, in his seminal article on statutory interpretation, Willis argued that the judge uses "whichever of the rules produces a result which satisfies its sense of justice in the case before it."[164]

However, Bennion argued that Willis was wrong, stating that "the court takes (or should take) an overall view, weighs all the relevant factors, and arrives at a balanced conclusion."[165] This is how Mr Justice Charleton described[166] the decision of Mr Justice Arnold in the *Golden Eye* case:[167] " …

158 *Grey v Pearson* (1857) 10 ER 1216.
159 *Ibid.*, as per Lord Wilkinson at 1234.
160 Stephan A., The UK Cartel Offence: A Purposive Interpretation? (2014) 12 *Criminal Law Review*, pp. 879–892, p. 884.
161 *Ibid.*, p. 885.
162 "Legal meaning corresponds to the legislative intention": Bennion F., *Bennion on Statutory Interpretation*, 5th edition (London: LexisNexis, 2008) p. 469.
163 *Vickers, Sons and Maxim Ltd v Evans* (1910) AC 444, at 445.
164 Willis J., Statutory Interpretation in a Nutshell (1938) 16(1) *Can Bar Rev*, pp. 1–27, p. 16.
165 Bennion F., *Statutory Interpretation* (London: Longman, 1990) p. 105.
166 *EMI Records (Ireland) Ltd and Others v Data Protection Commissioner and Another* [2012] IEHC 264, as per Charleton J at 8.9.
167 *Golden Eye (International) Ltd, Ben Dover Productions, Celtic Broadcasting Ltd, Easy on the Eye, DMS Telecoms Ltd, Gary Baker, Harmony Films Ltd, Justin Ribeiro Dos Santos t/a Joybear Pictures, Orchid MG Ltd, Kudetta BVBA, RP Films Ltd, Sweetmeats Productions t/a SMP, Sll Films Ltd, Terence Stephens t/a One Eyed Jack Productions v Telefónica UK Ltd, and Consumer Focus* [2012] EWHC 723 (Ch).

balancing the proportionality of the order sought judged in the context of the mischief at issue and the competing rights and the burdens and benefits to the parties was taken."

These rules appear to suggest that the courts must first consider the literal meaning of the wording of the legislation. The golden rule allows the judges to consider the intended meaning behind the words where necessary. In addition, where the wording is ambiguous or unclear, the courts may consider the intended mischief that the legislation was created to deal with.

The exclusionary rule and the **Pepper v Hart** *rule*

However, these rules create a tension with the exclusionary rule, which traditionally prohibits the court from relying on parliamentary debates as an aid to statutory construction.[168] The exclusionary rule is rooted in the doctrine of the separation of powers,[169] whereby the roles of Parliament and the court are distinct.[170] The exclusionary rule[171] meant that the use of *Hansard* in statutory interpretation was considered contrary to the Bill of Rights 1688.[172]

Article 9 of the Bill of Rights protects freedom of speech of Members of Parliament[173] and is a fundamental part of the structure ensuring the separation of powers between the judiciary and the legislator. As Mr Justice Lewison stated in the case of *Baron Mereworth v Ministry of Justice* [2011]: "The separation of powers ... part of the demarcation line between the province of the Courts and the province of Parliament is written down, notably in art.9 of the Bill of Rights 1688 which provides that freedom of speech and debates or proceedings in Parliament ought not to be impeached or questioned in any Court or place out of Parliament. Article 9 protects not only freedom of speech in Parliament but also proceedings in Parliament."[174]

This was acknowledged by Lord Browne-Wilkinson in the *Pepper v Hart* case: "Article 9 is a provision of the highest constitutional importance and should not

168 First stated by Willes J in *Millar v Taylor* (1769) 4 Burr 2303 at 2332.

169 See Marshall G., *Hansard* and the Interpretation of Statutes, in Oliver D. and Drewry G. (eds) *The Law and Parliament* (London: Butterworths, 1998) pp. 139–140.

170 *Wilson and Others v Secretary of State for Trade and Industry* [2003] UKHL 40, [2004] 1 AC 816, as per Lord Nicholls at [55].

171 *Davis v Johnson* [1979] AC 264 and *Hadmor Productions Ltd v Hamilton* [1982] ICR 114.

172 The Bill of Rights 1689, Article 9 states: "That the Freedome of Speech and Debates or Proceedings in Parlyament ought not to be impeached or questioned in any Court or Place out of Parlyament."

173 "The Bill of Rights 1689 reflected the attitude of Parliament, after the Restoration, to events in the reign of Charles I, and in particular the acceptance by the Court of King's Bench that parliamentary privilege did not protect against seditious comments in the Chamber *R v Eliot, Holles and Valentine* (1629) 3 St Tr 293–336. The primary object of the article was unquestionably to protect freedom of speech in the House of Commons.": *R v Chaytor* [2010] UKSC 52, as per Lord Phillips at [28].

174 *Baron Mereworth v Ministry of Justice* [2011] EWHC 1589 (Ch), as per Lewison J at [8].

be narrowly construed. It ensures the ability of democratically elected Members of Parliament to discuss what they will (freedom of debate) and to say what they will (freedom of speech) … the plain meaning of art.9, viewed against the historical background in which it was enacted, was to ensure that Members of Parliament were not subjected to any penalty, civil or criminal for what they said and were able, contrary to the previous assertions of the Stuart monarchy, to discuss what they, as opposed to the monarch, chose to have discussed."[175]

Moreover, the purpose of the exclusionary rule was to ensure that the courts applied the legislation as passed, and not by eliciting the intentions of the Government in their proposals and debates. This approach lends itself to the literary rule, discussed above, as Lord Lester of Herne Hill QC described the exclusionary rule as "part and parcel of … austere judicial literalism."[176]

However, the exclusionary rule is not absolute and, as explained, taking a purely literal reading is not always adequate, as was seen in the matter of *Pepper v Hart* [1992][177] where an issue arose about the interpretation of section 63(1) and (2) of the Finance Act 1976 in relation to the interpretation of the words "cash equivalent of the benefit."[178] In order to understand the intended meaning behind the wording of the Act, the House of Lords relaxed the exclusionary rule, which prohibited the court from referencing parliamentary material to aid the construction of legislation, where the wording was ambiguous, obscure or would lead to absurdity.[179]

This was a narrow exception to the exclusionary rule which, as explained, had previously stated that the use of *Hansard* was prohibited. However, as Lord Browne-Wilkinson recognised, relaxing the rule in these circumstances was not in order to question the independence of Parliament and its debates, but so that the courts could give effect to what was said and done by it.[180]

As a result, the *Pepper v Hart* rule gave the courts permission to consider parliamentary papers, and in particular *Hansard*, as an aid to interpretation, in certain circumstances. As Lord Browne-Wilkinson stated: "the exclusionary rule should be relaxed so as to permit reference to parliamentary materials where: (a) legislation is ambiguous or obscure, or leads to an absurdity; (b) the material relied on consists of one or more statements by a minister or other promoter of the Bill together if

175 *Pepper (Inspector of Taxes) v Hart* [1992] 3 WLR 1032, House of Lords, 26 November 1992 as per Lord Browne-Wilkinson.

176 Lester of Herne Hill, QC Lord, *Pepper v Hart* Revisited (1994) 15(1) *Statute LR*, pp. 10–22, p. 20.

177 *Pepper (Inspector of Taxes) v Hart* [1992] 3 WLR 1032, House of Lords, 26 November 1992; on appeal from: *Pepper (Inspector of Taxes) v Hart and Others* [1990] 1 WLR 204, Chancery Division, 24 November 1989; and *Pepper, Derek John (HM Inspector of Taxes) v Hart, John Thornton (and nine related appeals)* 1990 WL 754668, 13 November 1990, Court of Appeal.

178 The facts of the case related to taxpayer teachers who appealed against a decision concerning the basis for the tax treatment of benefits (the education of their children on payment of concessionary school fees).

179 *Pepper (Inspector of Taxes) v Hart* [1993] ICR 291, at 303, 317 and 323.

180 *Ibid.*, at 316.

necessary with such other parliamentary material as is necessary to understand such statements and their effect; (c) the statements relied on are clear."[181]

However, the judgment has been subject to much criticism. For example, Bennion argued "that the majority opinions were seriously flawed" and that on the whole it "amounted to a failure of law-text analysis."[182] Kavanagh argued that the *Pepper v Hart* rule undermines the rationale and integrity of the legislative process and the doctrine of the separation of powers, as well as wrongly attributing the intention of an individual Minister to Parliament as a whole.[183] Kavanagh goes on to explain that considering one Minister's statement to define the law gives law-making powers which goes against the constitutional principle which vests law-making power in Parliament.[184] Concerns were also raised about the potential for the rule to permit other types of materials into the judge's consideration: "One could go so far as to say that since *Pepper v Hart*, any hearsay; any blog, social network, lobbying, or other forceful act can change the meaning of a statute, making a mockery of the law."[185]

Another issue with the *Pepper v Hart* rule is that it could introduce more sources of law for citizens and lawyers to understand. For example, as Lord Simon recognised: "in a society living under the rule of law citizens are entitled to regulate their conduct according to what the statute said, rather than by what it was meant to say or by what it would otherwise have said if the newly considered situation had been envisaged."[186] This was confirmed by Lord Diplock, who regarded it a matter of elementary justice for citizens to be bound by law that they have access to by way of identifiable sources.[187] As a result, judges have been cautious about their utility of the rule. As Greenberg warned: "But the courts will certainly wish to be mindful of the fact that Hansard is not, and has never purported to be, a transcript or verbatim record, and that its usefulness depends on an understanding of the nature of and constraints upon its reliability and accuracy."[188] In addition, the reasoning in *Pepper v Hart* was criticised and rejected by the Irish Supreme Court in the case of *Crilly v Farrington Ltd* [2002].[189]

On the other hand, the *Pepper v Hart* rule has been seen to provide helpful support. For example, the rule was utilised in the case of *Innes v Information Commissioner* [2014][190] where Longmore LJ stated: "I can hardly say, in the light

181 *Ibid.*, at 323.
182 Bennion F., Executive Estoppel: *Pepper v Hart* Revisited (2007) (Spring) *Public Law*, pp. 1–12, p.1.
183 Kavanagh A., *Pepper v Hart* and Matters of Constitutional Principle (2005) 121(Jan) *LQR*, pp. 98–122, p. 98–99.
184 *Ibid.*, p. 102.
185 Ramage S., Statutory Interpretation in English Law Today (2011) *202 Crim Law*, pp. 1–7, p. 2.
186 *Stock v Frank Jones (Tipton) Ltd* [1978] ICR 347, as per Lord Simon at 354.
187 *Fothergill v Monarch Airlines Ltd* [1981] AC 251.
188 Greenberg D., *Hansard*, the Whole *Hansard* and Nothing But the *Hansard* (2008) 124(Apr) *LQR*, pp. 181–185, p. 185.
189 *Crilly v Farrington Ltd* [2002] 1 ILRM 161.
190 *Innes v Information Commissioner* [2014] EWCA Civ 1086.

of the views referred to above, that my own preferred reading of section 11(1) is unambiguously correct, and this seems to me one of the rare cases in which the *Pepper v Hart* criteria are satisfied."[191]

The use of official committee reports can be used to identify the intention of the legislation, or the mischief it intended to remedy.[192] Parliamentary material can be insightful for establishing the background and context of the legislation in order for the courts to determine a purposive construction. This was stated in a more recent case: "domestic courts may … examine background material, including a white paper, explanatory departmental notes, ministerial statements and statements by members of parliament in debate."[193]

Nevertheless, it continues to be the case that the courts are fairly reluctant to consider *Hansard* where there is any doubt as to the application of the *Pepper v Hart* criteria. As Lord Nicholls of Birkenhead has stated: "Experience has shown that the occasions on which reference to parliamentary proceedings is of assistance are rare."[194]

In a seminal case on the issue, *Wilson* [2003],[195] Lord Nicholls reverted to the golden rule explained above. He stated that "it is a cardinal constitutional principle that the will of Parliament is expressed in the language used by it in its enactments."[196] He also reported that use of additional committee materials should only be for background information and should not control the meaning of an Act of Parliament.[197]

The court has recently referred to the *Pepper v Hart* rule in a copyright infringement case, namely *Phonographic Performance Ltd v Hagan* [2016].[198] This case involved the application of section 97(2) of the CDPA 1988, which concerns additional damages for copyright infringement to be dissuasive. The court considered that there were two ways to read the word "dissuasive": to dissuade the defendant or to dissuade other infringers or potential infringers. This was considered a legitimate case for use of the *Pepper v Hart* rule.[199]

Overall, there are several different rules in the interpretation of legislation. The literal, mischief and golden rule explain different ways in which judges can interpret statutory law. The literal rule emphasises a literal approach, whereas the mischief and golden rule lean towards a more purposive approach. The exclusionary

191 *Ibid.*, as per Longmore LJ at [36].

192 *Fothergill v Monarch Airlines Ltd* [1981] AC 251 as per Lord Diplock at 281.

193 *Recovery of Medical Costs for Asbestos Diseases (Wales) Bill, Re* [2015] UKSC 3, as per Lord Mance at [55].

194 *R (on the application of Spath Holme Ltd) v Secretary of State for the Environment, Transport and the Regions* [2001] 2 AC 349, at 399.

195 *Wilson and Others v Secretary of State for Trade and Industry* [2003] UKHL 40, [2004] 1 AC 816.

196 *Ibid.*, at [67].

197 *Ibid.*, at [58].

198 *Phonographic Performance Ltd v Hagan (t/a Lower Ground Bar and Brent Tavern)* [2016] EWHC 3076 (IPEC), 30 November 2016.

199 Referring to *Broadhurst v Tan* [2016] EWCA Civ 94, [2016] 1 WLR 1928, as per Lord Dyson at [28]. The court determined that the intended meaning was to dissuade the defendant and the general public.

rule prohibits the use of parliamentary material; however, the *Pepper v Hart* rule has provided an exception. Whilst this exception has received much criticism, it continues to be utilised by the courts where appropriate.

The following section considers in more detail the wider issues underlying the tension between the rules discussed above. The controversy behind the use of the mischief, golden and *Pepper v Hart* rules stems from their purposive nature.

Judge's interpretation and application of copyright law

As mentioned, the compromises made in the drafting of a statute can create an imperfect text and deem it necessary for legislation to be interpreted and applied by the courts.[200] The essential task of the judge is to apply legal rules to facts.[201] In approaching this task, there are different opinions on whether or not judges should take policy into consideration. As discussed above, there is no clear agreement between the use of the literal, mischief and golden rules, for example. However, it seems that judges are able to introduce a more purposive approach through the golden rule and the mischief rule, when the literal rule does not suffice. Furthermore, the use of the *Pepper v Hart* rule allows the courts to consider the policy intentions behind an Act of Parliament in certain circumstances.

Posner suggested that judges should interpret and apply the law whilst taking into consideration the stakeholder's interest considered in the legislation.[202] Lord Denning also argued that a court must be free to decide a novel case on policy grounds.[203] Furthermore, it would be inconvenient to have to send all cases of unsettled law back to the legislature for democratic resolution.[204]

On the other hand, Dworkin contended that judges do not have the discretion to make policy-based decisions as they are not elected, and that policy-based law-making would render the law retrospective instead of upholding rights and duties that already exist.[205]

In relation to how judges might interpret the law, the approach that judges should take is equally non-consensus. For example, Posner stressed that interpretation is a matter of reading carefully and letting the plain meaning of the words dictate the interpretation of the text.[206] Holmes, however, argued that when interpreting legal

200 Penner J. E., *McCoubrey & White's Textbook on Jurisprudence* (New York: Oxford University Press, 2008) p. 216.
201 Levi E., *An Introduction to Legal Reasoning* (Chicago: University of Chicago Press, 1949) pp. 1–3.
202 Posner R., *The Problems of Jurisprudence* (Cambridge, MA: Harvard University Press, 1990) p. 335: Judges have "a dual role: to interpret the interest group deals embodied in legislation and to provide the basic public service of authoritative dispute resolution."
203 *Spartan Steel & Alley Ltd v Martin & Co* [1973] 1 QB 27.
204 Penner J. E., *McCoubrey & White's Textbook on Jurisprudence* (New York: Oxford University Press, 2008) p. 125.
205 Dworkin R., *Taking Rights Seriously* (Cambridge, MA: Harvard University Press, 1978) p. 84.
206 Posner R., *The Problems of Jurisprudence* (Cambridge, MA: Harvard University Press, 1990) p. 262.

text, the judge should consider the ordinary meaning of the word in the circumstances: "We ask not what the author meant, but what those words would mean in the mouth of a normal speaker of English, using them in the circumstances in which they are used."[207]

The difficulty with this approach is that words often have more than one meaning in the normal use of the language. For this reason, the judge must take the context of the statute and the circumstances of the case into consideration in order to determine the meaning: "Any document purporting to be serious and to have some legal effect has one meaning and no other, because the known object is to achieve some definite result."[208]

Holmes argued that as words have more than one dictionary meaning, when interpreting legal evidence or statutory law, the method requires not an understanding of what the author intended, but taking the general meaning of the word within the context.[209]

As noted above, in practice, draftsman and judges have been known to refer back to *Hansard* in order to determine the intended meaning behind the words in the statute.[210] Furthermore, Denning noted that European judges in particular adopt a schematic and teleological method, which means taking a purposive approach. He explained: "The judges do not go by the literal meaning of the words … They go by the design or purpose … behind it. When they come upon a situation which is to their minds within the spirit – but not the letter – of the legislation, they solve the problem by looking at the design and purpose of the legislature – at the effect it was sought to achieve. They then interpret the legislation so as to produce the desired effect. This means they fill in gaps, quite unashamedly, without hesitation. They ask simply: what is the sensible way of dealing with this situation so as to give effect to the presumed purpose of the legislation? They lay down the law accordingly."[211] It is established that when interpreting European Union (EU) law, it is necessary to consider the wording as well as the context and objectives of the rules.[212]

Denning's approach contrasted with T. S. Eliot's sardonic version of the English lawyer's motto: "The spirit killeth, the letter giveth life."[213] Denning was initially met with opposition, for example, Viscount Simonds responded that it "appears to

207 Holmes O. M., The Theory of Legal Interpretation (1899) 12(6) *Harvard Law Review*, pp. 417–420, pp. 419–420.

208 *Ibid*., p. 417.

209 *Ibid*., p. 418.

210 *Regina v Greater London Council, Ex Parte Blackburn and Another* [1976] 1 WLR 550, as per Lord Denning at 556.

211 *James Buchanan & Co Ltd v Babco Forwarding & Shipping (UK) Ltd* [1977] 2 WLR 107, as per Lord Denning at 112.

212 Rosati E., *Copyright and the Court of Justice of the European Union* (Croydon: Oxford University Press, 2019) p. 56 referring to *SGAE* (Case C-306/05), EU:C:2006:764 para 34 and others.

213 Cited by Lord Hailsham LC in *Hamlyn Revisited, The British Legal System Today*, The Hamlyn Lectures, Thirty-fifth Series (Published under the auspices of the Hamlyn Trust by Stevens & Sons, 1983) p. 49.

me to be a naked usurpation of the legislative function under a thin disguise of interpretation."[214]

Nevertheless, Denning continued to argue for the European approach.[215] Bennion suggested that British lawyers tended only to use this approach in relation to EU law, however, Denning's view of the creative function of the judiciary in relation to statutes has grown in influence: "Lord Denning may in the end have his way."[216]

Patterson disagreed, arguing that copyright is a statutory concept which leaves little room for judges to define functions and formulate guiding principles: "Copyright statutes provided rules not principles."[217] However, the ability for the CDPA 1988 to adapt to technologies never possibly envisaged at the time of drafting could only come from the judge's interpretation and application of the law in a way that goes beyond the literary meaning of the original terms. Furthermore, in certain circumstances the legislature has stated that defining law is better left to courts.[218] The judge's role, therefore, is to understand the purpose of law in society and to enable the law to achieve its purpose in the present day.[219] In doing so, the judge may give the statute a new meaning that seeks to bridge the gap between the law and life's changing reality without changing the statute itself.[220]

Therefore, the analysis in this book tackles legal drafting and statutory law, including a consideration of the historical context and the meaning of the words chosen by the drafters to reflect the policy. The analysis then looks closely at the judge's understanding and application of the wording of the law to the facts of the case in order to determine the meaning given to the statute through its interpretation and application by the courts. The analysis of both statutory law and case law is viewed through the lens of the internal and external perspectives.

Although it is likely that due to the internal and external perspectives providing alternative meanings, the criteria for the *Pepper v Hart* rule would be met,[221] this book does not take a view as to whether judges should or should not consider *Hansard* in their judgments. This book considers *Hansard* in its research

214 *Magor and St Mellons RDC v Newport Corpn* [1952] AC 189, as per Simonds at 190.

215 Bennion F., Judges as Legislators (2000) 9 *JSB Journal*, p. 3; see also Bennion F., *Bennion on Statute Law* (London: Longman, 1990).

216 *Ibid.*, Bennion, Judges as Legislators, p. 3.

217 Patterson R., *Copyright in Historical Perspective* (Nashville: Vanderbilt University Press, 1968) p. 229.

218 Hansard, HL, Copyright, Designs and Patents Bill [HL], 5th Ser, Col 268 2 November 1988.

219 Barak A., *Judge in a Democracy* (Princeton, NJ: Princeton University Press: 2008) p. 3.

220 *Ibid.*, pp. 4–5.

221 As Lord Mackay argued in his dissent, the criteria would easily be fulfilled: "I believe that practically every question of *statutory* construction that comes before the courts will involve an argument that the case falls under one or more of these three heads." (original emphasis) *Pepper (Inspector of Taxes) v Hart* [1993] ICR 291, as per Lord Mackay at 297.

methodology in order to analyse legal drafting and case law application, in light of the internal and external perspectives, to highlight the tensions in the regulation of copyright infringement online.

The analysis should be considered in light of the discussion above, which demonstrates that whilst the courts aim to abide by the literal and exclusionary rules, at times it is appropriate to consider a more purposive approach by way of the mischief, golden and *Pepper v Hart* rules.

In resolving the tensions that the Framework for Constructing Digital Perspectives illuminates, this book does, however, suggest that in applying copyright law to the internet, judges should take copyright, as a doctrine, in the context of its intended purpose, in line with the mischief rule[222] and the *Wilson* [2003][223] case, both discussed above.

Bibliography

Books

Adams J. N. and Brownsword R., *Understanding Law* (London: Sweet & Maxwell, 2006).
Aiken M., *The Cyber Effect* (London: John Murray Publishers, 2016).
Bach K., Context ex Machina, in Szabó Z. (ed.) *Semantics vs. Pragmatics* (Oxford: Oxford University Press, 2005).
Barak A., *Judge in a Democracy* (Princeton, NJ: Princeton University Press: 2008).
BCS The Chartered Institute for IT, *Leaders in Computing: Changing the Digital World* (Swindon: British Informatics Society, 2011).
Bennion F., *Bennion on Statute Law* (London: Longman, 1990).
Bennion F., *Bennion on Statutory Interpretation*, 5th edition (London: LexisNexis, 2008).
Bennion F., *Statutory Interpretation* (London: Longman, 1990).
Bowrey K., *Law and Internet Cultures* (Melbourne: Cambridge University Press, 2005).
Davis G., *Copyright and the Public Interest*, 2nd edition (London: Sweet & Maxwell, 2002).
Dworkin G. and Taylor R. D., *Blackstone's Guide to the Copyright, Designs and Patents Act 1988* (London: Blackstone Press Ltd, 1989).
Dworkin R., *Taking Rights Seriously* (Cambridge, MA: Harvard University Press, 1978).
Feather J., *Publishing, Piracy and Politics: An Historical Study of Copyright in Britain* (London: Mansell Publishing, 1994).
Gralla P., *How the Internet Works*, 8th edition (Indiana: Que Corporation, 2006).
Groves P., *Copyright and Designs Law: A Question of Balance* (London: Graham and Trotman Ltd, 1991).
Kivistö M., The DSM Directive: A Package (Too) Full of Policies in Pihlajarinne T., Vesala J. and Honkkila O., *Online Distribution of Content in the EU* (Cheltenham: Edward Elgar, 2019).
Larsson S., *Metaphors and Norms: Understanding Copyright Law in a Digital Society* (Sweden: Lund University, 2011).
Lessig L., *Code and Other Laws of Cyberspace* (New York: Basic Books, 1999).
Lessig L., *Code Version 2.0* (New York: Basic Books, 2006).

222 *Heydon's case* (1584) 3 Cop Rep 7a.
223 *Wilson and Others v Secretary of State for Trade and Industry* [2003] UKHL 40, [2004] 1 AC 816.

Lessig L., *Free Culture* (New York: Penguin Book Press, 2004).
Lessig L., *Remix: Making Art and Commerce Thrive in the Hybrid Economy* (New York: Penguin Press, 2008).
Levi E., *An Introduction to Legal Reasoning* (Chicago: University of Chicago Press, 1949).
Levine R., *Free Ride, How the Internet is Destroying the Culture Business and How it Can Fight Back* (London: Vintage, 2012).
Litman J., *Digital Copyright*, 2nd edition (New York: Prometheus Books, 2006).
Marshall G., *Hansard* and the Interpretation of Statutes in Oliver D. and Drewry G. (eds) *The Law and Parliament* (London: Butterworths, 1998).
Murray A., *Information Technology Law, The Law and Society*, 2nd edition (Oxford: Oxford University Press, 2013).
Murray A., *Information Technology Law: The Law and Society*, 3rd edition (Oxford: Oxford University Press, 2016).
Murray A., *The Regulation of Cyberspace: Control in the Online Environment* (Oxford: Routledge Cavendish, 2007).
Patterson L. R., *Copyright in Historical Perspective* (Nashville: Vanderbilt University Press, 1968).
Penner J. E., *McCoubrey & White's Textbook on Jurisprudence* (New York: Oxford University Press, 2008).
Peitz M. and Waldfogel J., *The Oxford Handbook of The Digital Economy* (Oxford: Oxford University Press, 2012).
Ploman E. W. and Hamilton L. C., *Copyright: Intellectual Property in the Information Age* (London: Routledge and Kegan Paul, 1980).
Posner R., *The Problems of Jurisprudence* (Cambridge, MA: Harvard University Press, 1990).
Reed C., *Making Laws for Cyberspace* (Oxford: Oxford University Press, 2013).
Reed T. V., *Understanding Our Digitized World: Culture, Power, and Social Change in the Internet Era* (Oxford: Routledge, 2014).
Rosati E., *Copyright and the Court of Justice of the European Union* (London: Oxford University Press, 2019).
Schultz M. F., Copynorms: Copyright and Social Norms in Yu K. P. (ed.) *Intellectual Property and Information Wealth: Issues and Practices in the Digital Age, Vol 1 Copyright and Related Rights* (Connecticut: Praeger Publishers, 2006).
Sherman B. and Bently L., *The Making of Modern Intellectual Property* (Cambridge: Cambridge University Press, 1999).
Tapscott D. and Williams A. D., *Wikinomics How Mass Collaboration Changes Everything* (London: Atlantic Books, 2008).
Van Santen R., Khoe D. and Vermeer B., *2030 Technology That Will Change the World* (Oxford: Oxford University Press, 2010).
Vitoria M., et al (eds), *Laddie, Prescott and Vitoria: The Modern Law of Copyright and Designs*, 4th edition (London: Butterworths Law, 2011).
Xanthaki H., *Drafting Legislation: Art and Technology of Rules for Regulation* (Oxford: Hart Publishing, 2014).

Case law

Baron Mereworth v Ministry of Justice [2011] EWHC 1589 (Ch).
British Leyland Motor Corporation Ltd v Armstrong Patents Co Ltd [1986] AC 577.
Broadhurst v Tan [2016] EWCA Civ 94, [2016] 1 WLR 1928.

*Chamber R v Eliot, Holles and Valentine (*1629*) 3 St Tr 293–336.*

Crilly v Farrington Ltd [2002] 1 ILRM 161.

Davis v Johnson [1979] AC 264.

EMI Records (Ireland) Ltd and Others v Data Protection Commissioner and Another [2012] IEHC 264.

Fothergill v Monarch Airlines Ltd [1981] AC 251.

Golden Eye (International) Ltd, Ben Dover Productions, Celtic Broadcasting Ltd, Easy on the Eye, DMS Telecoms Ltd, Gary Baker, Harmony Films Ltd, Justin Ribeiro Dos Santos t/a Joybear Pictures, Orchid MG Ltd, Kudetta BVBA, RP Films Ltd, Sweetmeats Productions t/a SMP, Sll Films Ltd, Terence Stephens t/a One Eyed Jack Productions v Telefónica UK Ltd, and Consumer Focus [2012] EWHC 723 (Ch).

Grey v Pearson (1857) 10 ER 1216.

Hadmor Productions Ltd v Hamilton [1982] ICR 114.

Heydon's case (1584) 3 Cop Rep 7a.

Innes v Information Commissioner [2014] EWCA Civ 1086.

James Buchanan & Co Ltd v Babco Forwarding & Shipping (UK) Ltd [1977] 2 WLR 107.

Magor and St Mellons RDC v Newport Corpn [1952] AC 189.

Millar v Taylor (1769) 4 Burr 2303.

Paramount Home Entertainment Ltd, Sony Pictures Home Entertainment Ltd, Twentieth Century Fox Film Company Ltd, Universal Pictures (UK) Ltd, Warner Bros. Entertainment UK Ltd, Disney Enterprises Inc v British Sky Broadcasting Ltd, British Telecommunications Plc, Everything Everywhere Ltd, Talktalk Telecom Ltd, Telefónica UK Ltd, Virgin Media Ltd [2013] EWHC 3479 (Ch).

Pepper (Inspector of Taxes) v Hart [1992] 3 WLR 1032, [1993] ICR 291.

Pepper (Inspector of Taxes) v Hart and Others [1990] 1 WLR 204.

*Pepper, Derek John (HM Inspector of Taxes) v Hart, John Thornton (and nine related appeals)*1990 WL 754668.

Phonographic Performance Ltd v Hagan (t/a Lower Ground Bar and Brent Tavern) [2016] EWHC 3076 (IPEC).

Public Relations Consultants Association Ltd v The Newspaper Licensing Agency Ltd and Others [2010] EWHC 3099 (Ch).

Public Relations Consultants Association Ltd v The Newspaper Licensing Agency Ltd and Others [2013] UKSC 18.

R v Allen (Christopher) [1985] AC 1029.

R v Chaytor [2010] UKSC 52.

R (on the application of Quintaville) v Secretary of State for Health [2003] 2 AC 687.

R (on the application of Spath Holme Ltd) v Secretary of State for the Environment, Transport and the Regions [2001] 2 AC 349.

Recovery of Medical Costs for Asbestos Diseases (Wales) Bill, Re [2015] UKSC 3.

Regina v Greater London Council, Ex Parte Blackburn and Another [1976] 1 WLR 550.

Reno v Am Civil Liberties Union, 521 US 844, 849 (1997) Syllabus.

River Wear Commissioners v Adamson (1877) 2 App Cas 743.

Smith v Hughes [1960] 1 WLR 830.

Spartan Steel & Alley Ltd v Martin & Co [1973] 1 QB 27.

Stock v Frank Jones (Tipton) Ltd [1978] ICR 347.

Vacher v London Society of Compositors [1913] AC 107, LT 722.

Vickers, Sons and Maxim Ltd v Evans (1910) AC 444.

Warburton v Loveland (1832) 5 ER 499.

Wilson and Others v Secretary of State for Trade and Industry [2003] UKHL 40, [2004] 1 AC 816, [2003] 3 WLR 568.

Journals

Bennion F., Executive Estoppel: *Pepper v Hart* Revisited (2007) (Spring) *Public Law*, pp. 1–12.

Bennion F., Judges as Legislators (2000) 9 *JSB Journal*, p. 3.

Bosher H. and Mendis D., Swings and Roundabouts: The Impact of Legal Drafting on the Language and Understanding of Copyright Law and the Need for Educational Materials (2016) 30(3) *International Review of Law, Computers and Technology*, pp. 211–228.

Bracha O., Copyright History as History of Technology (2013) 5(1) *The World Intellectual Property Journal*, pp. 45–53.

Burk D. L., Copyright and the Architecture of Digital Delivery (2014) *University of California Irvine School of Law, Research Paper No 2014–2057.*

Depoorter B., Van Hiel A. and Vanneste S., Copyright Backlash (2010–11) 84 *California Law Review*, pp. 1251–1292.

Drassinower A., From Distribution to Dialogue: Remarks on the Concept of Balance in Copyright Law (2009) 34(4) *The Journal of Corporation Law*, pp. 991–1007.

Dworkin G., Reports of Committees, the Whitford Committee Report on Copyright and Designs Law (1977) 40 *Modern Law Review*, pp. 685–700.

Edward L., Rules and Standards for Cyberspace (2002) 77 *Notre Dame Law Review*, pp. 1275–1372.

Ekins R., The intention of Parliament (2010) *Public Law*, pp. 709–726.

Epstein R. A., Privacy, Publication, and the First Amendment: The Dangers of First Amendment Exceptionalism (2000) 52 *Stanford Law Review*, pp. 1003–1048.

Feldman D., Statutory Interpretation and Constitutional Legislation (2014) 130(Jul), *LQR*, pp. 473–497.

Filby M., Code is Law? Assessing Architectural File Sharing Regulation in the Online Environment (2013) 8(1) *Journal of International Commercial Law and Technology*, pp. 81–103.

Giancarlo F., From Horizontal to Vertical: An Intermediary Liability Earthquake in Europe (2017) 12(7) *JIPLP*, pp. 565–575.

Giancarlo F., To Filter, Or Not To Filter? That Is The Question In EU Copyright Reform (2018) 36(2) *Cardozo Arts & Entertainment Law Journal*, pp. 331–368.

Goldsmith J. L., Against Cyberanarchy (1998) 65 *University of Chicago Law Review*, pp. 1199–1250.

Greenberg D., *Hansard*, the Whole *Hansard* and Nothing But the *Hansard* (2008) 124 (Apr) *LQR*, pp. 181–185.

Hardy T., Computer RAM Copies: A Hit or a Myth? Historical Perspectives on Caching as a Microcosm of Current Copyright Concerns (1997) 22 *University of Dayton Law Review*, pp. 423–621.

Holmes O. M., The Theory of Legal Interpretation (1899) 12(6) *Harvard Law Review*, pp. 417–420.

Hugenholtz B. P., Caching and Copyright: The Right of Temporary Copying (2000) 22 (10) *European Intellectual Property Review*, pp. 482–493.

Jones R., Intellectual Property Reform for the Internet Generation: An Accident Waiting to Happen (2010) 1(2) *European Journal of Law and Technology*, pp. 1–17.

Kavanagh A., *Pepper v Hart* and Matters of Constitutional Principle (2005) 121(Jan) *LQR*, pp. 98–122.

Kerr O. S., The Problem of Perspective in Internet Law (2003) 91 *Georgetown Law Journal*, pp. 357–405.

Landes W. and Posner R., An Economic Analysis of Copyright Law (1989) 18 *Journal of Legal Studies*, pp. 325–364.

Lee Y. H., United Kingdom Copyright Decisions and Legislative Developments 2014 (2015) 46(2) *International Review of Intellectual Property and Competition Law*, pp. 226–237.

Lemley M., Place and Cyberspace (2003) 91(2) *California Law Review*, pp. 521–542.

Lesterof Herne Hill, QCLord, *Pepper v Hart* Revisited (1994) 15(1) *Statute LR*, pp. 10–22.

Llewellyn K. N., The Normative, The Legal and the Law-Jobs: The Problem of Juristic Method (1940) 49(8) *Yale Law Journal*, pp. 1355–1400.

Mollick E., Establishing Moore's Law (2006) 28(3) *IEEE Annals of the History of Computing*, pp. 62–75.

Nesson C. and Marglin D., The Day the Internet Met the First Amendment: Time and the Communications Decency Act (1996) 10 *Harvard Journal of Law and Technology*, pp. 113–136.

Ola K., Fundamentals of Open Access (2014) 36(2) *European Intellectual Property Review*, pp. 112–123.

Palfrey J., Gasse U., Simun M. and Barns R. F., Youth, Creativity and Copyright in the Digital Age (2009) 1(2) *International Journal of Learning and Media*, pp. 79–97.

Ramage S., Statutory Interpretation in English Law Today (2011) *202 Crim Law*, pp. 1–7.

Shaw J. A., From Homo Economicus to Homo Roboticus: An Exploration of the Transformative Impact of the Technological Imaginary (2015) 11(3) *International Journal of Law in Context*, pp. 245–264.

Sommer J. H., Against Cyberlaw (2000) 15 *Berkeley Technology Law Journal*, pp. 1145–1232.

Stallworthy M., Construing Acts of Parliament in the United Kingdom: reference to Parliamentary debates – Pepper v Hart (1993) 4(4) *ICCLR*, pp. 159–162.

Stephan A., The UK Cartel Offence: A Purposive Interpretation? (2014) 12 *Criminal Law Review*, pp. 879–892.

Strahilevitz J. L., Charismatic Code, Social Norms and the Emergence of Cooperation on the File Swapping Networks (2003) 89 *Virginia Law Review*, pp. 505–595.

Tay Y., Reading law as literature: a forced relation (1996) 3 *UCL Juris Rev*, pp. 58–83.

Watson S., Zizzo D. and Fleming P., Determinants and Welfare Implications of Unlawful File Sharing: A Scoping Review (2014) *CREATe Working Paper 2014/05.*

Willis J., Statutory Interpretation in a Nutshell (1938) 16(1) *Can Bar Rev*, pp. 1–27.

Wu T., When Code Isn't Law (2003) 89 *Virginia Law Review*, pp. 101–170.

Yan M., The Law Surrounding the Facilitation of Online Copyright Infringement (2012) 34(2) *European Intellectual Property Review*, pp. 122–126.

Legislation

An Act for the Encouragement of Learning, by vesting the Copies of Printed Books in the Authors or Purchasers 1709, commonly referred to as the Statute of Anne.

Bill of Rights 1689.

Copyright and Rights in Performances (Research, Education, Libraries and Archives) Regulations 2014 (SI 2014/1372).
Copyright, Designs and Patents Act 1988.
Directive 2001/29/EC of the European Parliament and of the Council of 22 May 2001 on the harmonisation of certain aspects of copyright and related rights in the information society [2001] *OJ* L 167/10.
Directive (EU) 2019/790 of the European Parliament and of the Council of 17 April 2019 on Copyright and Related Rights in the Digital Single Market and Amending Directives 96/9/EC and 2001/29/EC [2019] *OJ* L 130/92.

Official documents and reports

Bahanovich D. and Collopy D., *Music Experience and Behaviour in Young People: Winter 2012–2013* [*2011 National Survey*], International Association of Music Business Research: https://uhra.herts.ac.uk/bitstream/handle/2299/10867/681097.pdf?sequence=4&isAllowed=y
Communication from the Commission to the European Parliament, the Council, the European Economic and Social Committee and the Committee of the Regions, A Digital Single Market Strategy for Europe, COM (2015) 192 final, Brussels, 6 May 2015.
Gregory Committee, *The Board of Trade Report of the Copyright Committee*, Cmnd 8662 (London: Her Majesty's Stationery Office, 1952).
Hailshamof St Marylebone, Lord, *Hamlyn Revisited, The British Legal System Today*, The Hamlyn Lectures, Thirty-fifth Series (Published under the auspices of the Hamlyn Trust by Stevens & Sons, 1983).
Hansard, HL, Copyright, Designs and Patents Bill [HL], 5th Ser, Col 268 2 November 1988.
Hansard, Interpretation of Legislation Bill [HL], Deb 26 March 1981 Vol 418 Cols 1341–1347.
Hansard, Interpretation of Legislation Bill [HL], Deb 26 March 1981 Vol 418 Cols 1341–1347.
Hansard, Digital Economy Bill [Lords], Second Reading, 6 April 2010, Col 836, the Secretary of State for Culture, Media and Sport (Mr Ben Bradshaw).
Hargreaves I., *Digital Opportunity, A Review of Intellectual Property and Growth*, May 2011.
Kantar Media, *Online Copyright Infringement Tracker Wave 5* (London: Intellectual Property Office, 2015).
Kantar Media, *Online Copyright Infringement Tracker Wave 8* (London: Intellectual Property Office, 2018).
Parliament, *The Preparation of Legislation, Report of a Committee appointed by the Lord President of the Council*, Cmnd 6053. Chairman: The Rt Hon Sir David Renton (London: Her Majesty's Stationery Office. 1975).
SABIP, *Copycats? Digital Consumers in the Online Age* (London: CIBER, UCL, 2009).
UK Intellectual Property Office, *Technical Review of Draft Legislation on Copyright Exceptions: Government Response* (Newport: UK Intellectual Property Office, 2014).
Whitford Committee, *Copyright and Designs Law, Report of the Committee to Consider the Law on Copyright and Designs*, Cmnd 6732 (London: Her Majesty's Stationery Office, 1977).

Web sources

Barlow J. P., The Next Economy of Ideas, After the Copyright Revolution, 1 October 2000: http://www.wired.com/2000/10/download/.

Berners-Lee T., Speech at the Newseum in Washington at the announcement of the World Wide Web Foundation, 14 September 2008, Washington, DC: http://webfoundation.org/about/community/transcript-of-tim-berners-lee- video/.

Berners-Lee T., Information Management: A Proposal, March 1989, May 1990: https://www.w3.org/History/1989/proposal.html.

CISAC, Global Collections Report 2018, 8 November 2018: https://www.cisac.org/CISAC-University/Library/Global-Collections-Reports/Global-Collections-Report-2018.

Facebook, Newsroom: http://newsroom.fb.com/company-info.

Hanway S. and Lyons L., Teens OK With Letting Music Downloads Play, 30 September 2003, Gallup Poll: http://www.gallup.com/poll/9373/teens-letting-music-downloads-play.aspx.

Instagram: https://business.instagram.com/getting-started/#why-instagram.

Internet World Stats: http://www.internetworldstats.com/stats.htm

Leiner B. M., Cerf V. G., Clark D. D., Kahn R. E., Kleinrock L., Lynch D. C., Postel J., Roberts L. G. and Wolff S., Brief History of the Internet, 1997: http://www.internetsociety.org/internet/what-internet/history-internet/brief-history-internet.

Omnicore: https://www.omnicoreagency.com/instagram-statistics/

2 The internal and external perspectives of the internet

Introduction

This chapter goes into deeper critical analysis of Kerr's external and internal perspectives[1] and thereafter develops them into a framework which is utilised as the lens through which the research questions are addressed in the subsequent chapter. As such, the first part of this chapter recognises that the internet has introduced a new phenomenon for the application of copyright law, in that there are two sets of facts available for the judges to take: the internal and external perspectives. After undertaking an analysis of the internal and external perspectives, the concepts are modified and grounded in the theoretical basis of purposivism and literalism.

Secondly, the chapter establishes the methodology and method for the application of the Framework for Constructing Digital Perspectives. Thereafter, the Framework is applied in the subsequent chapters to the statutory law and case law relating to copying[2] and communication to the public[3] to determine the current state of digital copyright infringement and highlight the tensions of applying copyright regulation to online activity.

Applying copyright law online: the two perspectives of the internet

When applying copyright law to the internet, there is more than one set of facts to which the law can be applied.[4] As introduced in Chapter 1, two perspectives can be taken when considering online activity. As a result, the problem of perspective occurred for the first time.[5]

This new problem of interpretation of the internet and the application of digital copyright infringement was captured by Kerr who explained that the facts of the

1 Kerr O. S., The Problem of Perspective in Internet Law (2003) 91 *Georgetown Law Journal*, pp. 357–405, p. 360.
2 See Chapter 3 and Chapter 4.
3 See Chapter 5 and Chapter 6.
4 Wu T., Application Centred Internet Analysis (1999) *Virginia Law Review*, pp. 1163–1204, p. 1193.
5 Kerr O. S., The Problem of Perspective in Internet Law (2003) 91 *Georgetown Law Journal*, pp. 357–405, p. 358.

internet depend entirely on taking either the internal or the external perspective: "the law is contingent on the facts, and the facts are contingent on the perspective."[6] Accordingly, there are two possible perspectives that can determine the meaning of online behaviour.

On the one hand, there is the internal perspective; the understanding of the internet as equivalent to the physical world. From this perspective, a person understands the virtual world of cyberspace as a legitimate construct.[7] On the other hand, the external perspective considers only the physical reality, which is the technical functioning of the network[8] whereby the internet is simply a network of computers located around the world and connected by wires and cables.[9]

To demonstrate the effect of taking either the internal or the external perspective, Kerr referred to four examples,[10] one of which was MP3.com.[11] This case involved a website providing a service whereby users, who had legitimately purchased a compact disc (CD), could register their purchase and then access an MP3 version of the music online, by running a copy from MP3.com's servers which users had uploaded from their own CD collection. Kerr explained that in this case the record companies relied on an external perspective,[12] arguing that MP3.com made unauthorised copies of copyright protected works when digitalising music files from CD to MP3, and then distributed these copies on its website.[13] However, MP3.com argued, from an internal perspective, that no copyright infringement had taken place[14] as it was simply allowing legitimate owners of music to access their CD collections without physically having to carry them around; effectively acting as the functional equivalent of storing its subscribers' CDs.[15] The difficulty is that both perspectives are descriptively valid.[16] In addition, judges and

6 *Ibid.*, p. 362.
7 *Ibid.*, p. 1.
8 *Ibid.*, p. 357.
9 *Reno v Am Civil Liberties Union* 521 US 844, 849 (1997) Syllabus para 1; describing the internet as "an international network of interconnected computers that enables millions of people to communicate with one another in 'cyberspace' and to access vast amounts of information from around the world." The term "cyberspace" is actually a metaphorical construct that allows the human mind to understand the internet as if it is a physical space, which is technically incorrect.
10 Kerr O. S., The Problem of Perspective in Internet Law (2003) 91 *Georgetown Law Journal*, pp. 357–405.
11 *UMG Recordings Inc v MP3.com Inc*, 92 F Supp 2D 349, 350 (SDNY 2000).
12 Kerr O. S., The Problem of Perspective in Internet Law (2003) 91 *Georgetown Law Journal*, pp. 357–405, p. 379.
13 *UMG Recordings Inc v MP3.com Inc*, 92 F Supp 2D 349, 350 (SDNY 2000) as per Rakoff J.
14 Except by way of "space-shift" from real space to cyber space which is permitted under the fair use doctrine; *ibid.*, as per Rakoff J at 351.
15 *Ibid.*, as per Rakoff J at 350.
16 Frischmann B. M., The Prospect of Reconciling Internet and Cyberspace (2004) 35 *Loyola University Chicago Law Journal*, pp. 205–234, p. 206.

commentators often switch between the two perspectives frequently without any awareness.[17]

Kerr's perspectives can be aligned with a literal or purposive approach to legal interpretation. Literalists focus exclusively on the text of the law, whilst purposivism places emphasis on the purpose behind the rule.[18] Building on this, the following section analyses the internal and external perspectives in more detail.

The external perspective: taking a literal approach

As explained, one way in which the facts of the internet can be interpreted is by taking the external perspective. This involves taking the point of view of the physical world, rather than the virtual one. It is concerned with the technical functioning of the network in the physical world, focusing on the physical network and the technical details of how it works.[19] Therefore, in applying copyright law to the internet, the judge would consider the electronic transactions underlying the network's operation.[20]

Hutchison explains that "a technical understanding might consider the internet to be a series of electronic impulses that transfer packets of data between a network of computers by means of a common protocol."[21] He elaborated that this means considering the internet from the outside, real-space point of view: "The external perspective focuses on the Internet from the outside. From this external perspective, one perceives the Internet in terms of its technical real-space operations – the Internet is a global meta-network that serves as an open platform for the transmission of information among end users that connect computers to the network."[22]

Frischmann supported Kerr's analysis and stated that he agreed "wholeheartedly with Kerr that we need to be aware of the problem of perspective. Both perspectives are descriptively valid and real, and both perspectives yield important insights about the facts of the internet and the interests at stake in a legal decision."[23]

Kerr's internal and external perspectives of the internet can serve to illuminate the challenges of legal regulation online, particularly considering digital copyright infringement provisions which are regarded as especially ill-adapted to the internet.[24] It can be argued that this is because copyright law is a regulatory tool for protecting and balancing the interests of the copyright owners and the public interest, within a

17 Kerr O. S., The Problem of Perspective in Internet Law (2003) 91 *Georgetown Law Journal*, pp. 357–405, p. 358.
18 Hutchison C. J., Interpretation and the Internet (2010) 28 *John Marshall Journal of Computer and Information Law*, pp. 251–272, p. 257.
19 Kerr O. S., The Problem of Perspective in Internet Law (2003) 91 *Georgetown Law Journal*, pp. 357–405, p. 360.
20 *Ibid.*, pp. 361–362.
21 Hutchison C. J., Interpretation and the Internet (2010) 28 *John Marshall Journal of Computer and Information Law*, pp. 251–272, p. 255.
22 Frischmann B. M., The Prospect of Reconciling Internet and Cyberspace (2004) 35 *Loyola University Chicago Law Journal*, pp. 205–234, p. 206.
23 *Ibid.*, p. 207.
24 Reed C., *Making Laws for Cyberspace* (Oxford: Oxford University Press, 2013) p. 237.

factual context. However, the evolution of technological has fundamentally changed the factual context of copyright and thereby disturbed previously struck balances.[25] Furthermore, these insights are critical to the outcome of copyright infringement cases. As Burk stated: "Judicial adoption of an internal or external approach to digital content delivery relates directly to the structure of statutory requirements governing such cases."[26]

When consideration how these concepts can be utilised in practice, Kerr suggests that a particular perspective can be established and should thereafter be applied.[27] However, Hutchison pointed out that taking a purely literal interpretation can lead to the law falling short of serving its purpose.[28] He illustrated this point by considering substantial-taking of digital copyright material via BitTorrent software, from a purely literal perspective BitTorrent software communicates copyright material from multiple computers, and therefore, from an external perspective may not constitute substantial-taking.[29] However, judges have determined substantial-part from an internal perspective, as it is a matter of quality and not quantity.[30] Therefore, it could be argued that whilst the file is in many parts, the quality of the file is intact. Nevertheless, Hutchinson's example illustrates the impact of taking the external perspective.

This is also the case across many different types of online activity. For example, from an external perspective, the CDPA 1988 provides that it is an infringement to copy a copyright work.[31] It is also an infringement of copyright for a person to authorise such an activity.[32] However, it is a feature of the internet that communications pass through the memories of a series of computers, from which it follows that each computer makes a copy of the material and does so, not at the instigation of the server's owner, but of the client whose owner wanted the material in the first place.[33]

When the courts apply the external perspective, the specific workings of the technology form an important component of the legal analysis.[34] This means that

25 Frischmann B. M., The Prospect of Reconciling Internet and Cyberspace (2004) 35 *Loyola University Chicago Law Journal*, pp. 205–234, p. 210.

26 Burk D. L., Copyright and the Architecture of Digital Delivery (2014) University of California Irvine School of Law, *Research Paper No. 2014–2057*, p. 12.

27 Kerr O. S., The Problem of Perspective in Internet Law (2003) 91 *Georgetown Law Journal*, pp. 357–405, p. 390.

28 Hutchison C. J., Interpretation and the Internet (2010) 28 *John Marshall Journal of Computer and Information Law*, pp. 251–272, pp. 259–260.

29 *Ibid.*, pp. 259–260. *Warwick Film Productions Ltd v Eisinger* [1969] 1 Ch 508: in relation to the work as a whole or any substantial part of it: section 16(3)(a) Copyright Designs and Patents Act 1988. Therefore, taking an insubstantial part does not constitute infringement.

30 *Ladbroke (Football) Ltd v William Hill (Football) Ltd* [1964] 1 WLR 273, as per Lord Reid at 276: substantial part "depends much more on the quality than on the quantity of what he has taken."

31 CDPA 1988, section 16(1)(a); without a licence or the benefit of an exception.

32 CDPA 1988, section 16.

33 Vitoria M., et al (eds), *Laddie, Prescott and Vitoria: The Modern Law of Copyright and Designs*, 4th edition (London: Butterworths Law, 2011) 37.6.

34 Burk D. L., Copyright and the Architecture of Digital Delivery (2014) University of California Irvine School of Law, *Research Paper No. 2014–2057*, p. 11.

the law can become very specific, technologically accurate and, from an external perspective, provides clarity on the legality of technological function. However, drafting copyright regulation in such a way can also create difficulties. These drawbacks are discussed below, such as incentivising avoidance creations,[35] as well as being too specific and therefore quickly becoming obsolete.

The disadvantages of taking a purely external perspective

The first challenge of taking the external perspective is that taking a literal reading of the wording of copyright regulation can influence the shape of technological development. Karjala identified this as an unintended consequence of the way in which copyright regulation is drafted: "Instead of the law adapting itself to meet the needs of society under conditions of new technology, these judicial interpretations push technology in odd directions as systems engineers seek to avoid falling on the wrong side of what is essentially an arbitrary line."[36]

The development of peer-to-peer file sharing technology exemplifies this point. After Napster was held liable for secondary copyright infringement based on its centralised file-sharing system,[37] the reaction from the next generation of services with the same aim was to deliberately decentralise their systems, in order to avoid secondary liability under the legal definition[38] set out in the *Napster* case.

Regulators responded, and the law was developed to encompass the decentralised systems, finding websites such as Grokster[39] liable for secondary copyright infringement. However, as before, the designers of services adapted the architecture of their systems and, now, currently the most popular format is BitTorrent.[40] This online technology differs significantly from the previous generation of online activity as the website software is disassociated with the indexing and searching functions.[41] As the law works to adapt and encompass this activity, more advanced software is already being developed. For example, The Pirate Bay[42] was subject to a High Court ban due to being found liable for copyright infringement via BitTorrent technology. However, the site has now begun phasing out the

35 Such as the Aereo software which was "designed solely to avoid the letter of the copyright statute": *American Broadcasting Cos, Inc, Et Al v Aereo, Inc, Fka Bamboom Labs, Inc*, 2nd Circ 13–461 (2013) Judge Chin Dissent Aereo at 29.

36 Karjala D. S, Copying and Piracy in the Digital Age (2013) 52 *Washburn Law Journal*, pp. 245–266, p. 263.

37 *AandM Records, Inc v Napster, Inc*, 114 F Supp. 2d 896 (2000).

38 David M., *Peer to Peer and the Music Industry: The Criminalization of Sharing* (London: Sage Publications, 2010) p. 35.

39 *MGM Studios, Inc v Grokster, Ltd*, 545 US 913 (2005).

40 Johns A., *Piracy: The Intellectual Property Wars from Gutenberg to Gates* (Chicago: The University of Chicago Press, 2009) p. 454.

41 Filby M., Code is Law? Assessing Architectural File Sharing Regulation in the Online Environment (2013) 8(1) *Journal of International Commercial Law and Technology*, pp. 81–103, p. 89.

42 *Dramatico Entertainment Ltd and Others v British Sky Broadcasting Ltd and Others* [2012] EWHC 268 (Ch) (20 February 2012).

majority of the torrent files it hosts and replacing them with magnet links.[43] As a result, the current law fails in its aim to encompass this type of online activity.[44]

In the case of *Aereo*, [45] the technology was noted to be explicitly designed to conform to definitions of permissible activity articulated in previous copyright cases.[46] Judge Chin commented that the Aereo software was "over-engineered ... designed solely to avoid the letter of the copyright statute."[47] Burk commented that "every step of the Aereo transmission was designed to permit only 'private' performances, not public performances as defined by the Courts."[48]

As the cases of *Napster*, [49] *Grokster*, [50] *Pirate Bay* [51] and *Aereo* [52] demonstrate, the wording of copyright law can encourage designers to adopt a formalistic view of technological architecture.[53] The designers take the external perspective as a springboard to avoid architectural liability.

From this perspective, the law can be criticised as simply creating parameters of rights around which digital designers can create architecture, specifically to avoid the formal definition of infringement. By defining copyright infringement from an external perspective, according to particular technological determinants, it is simultaneously sign-posting the direction of future technology. Developers will simply take direction as to what, technically, is not infringement, and create accordingly. Therefore, the law shapes technology, although not necessary as desired, as an unintended outcome of taking an external perspective.

The second challenge for the external perspective is that if the law is drafted and interpreted specifically in relation to technical function, it will quickly become obsolete in the face of developing technology.[54] Regulating and interpreting from a technologically specific and accurate perspective suggests that the law will be clear and increases legal certainty, a goal repeatedly stated in the EU Directive's

43 Filby M., Code is Law? Assessing Architectural File Sharing Regulation in the Online Environment (2013) 8(1) *Journal of International Commercial Law and Technology*, pp. 81–103, p. 89.
44 Litman J., *Digital Copyright* (New York: Prometheus Books, 2001) p. 22.
45 *American Broadcasting Cos, Inc, Et Al v Aereo, Inc, Fka Bamboom Labs, Inc*, 2nd Circ 13–461 (2013).
46 Burk D. L., Copyright and the Architecture of Digital Delivery (2014) University of California Irvine School of Law, *Research Paper No. 2014–2057*, p. 8.
47 *American Broadcasting Cos, Inc, Et Al v Aereo, Inc, Fka Bamboom Labs, Inc*, 2nd Circ 13–461 (2013) Judge Chin Dissent Aereo at 29.
48 Burk D. L., Copyright and the Architecture of Digital Delivery (2014) University of California Irvine School of Law, *Research Paper No. 2014–2057*, p. 8.
49 *AandM Records, Inc v Napster, Inc*, 114 F Supp 2d 896 (2000).
50 *MGM Studios, Inc v Grokster, Ltd*, 545 US 913 (2005).
51 *Dramatico Entertainment Ltd and Others v British Sky Broadcasting Ltd and Others* [2012] EWHC 268 (Ch) (20 February 2012).
52 *American Broadcasting Cos, Inc, Et Al v Aereo, Inc, Fka Bamboom Labs, Inc*, 2nd Circ 13–461 (2013).
53 Burk D. L., Copyright and the Architecture of Digital Delivery (2014) University of California Irvine School of Law, *Research Paper No. 2014–2057*, p. 13.
54 Litman J., *Digital Copyright* (New York: Prometheus Books, 2001) p. 22.

Recitals.[55] In addition, when developing new copyright legislation, the Government has stated its intention to draft legislation that is technologically neutral.[56]

However, Hugenholtz remarked that due to the way in which the law is drafted, this actually creates new uncertainties by the use of unintelligible language.[57] He stated that: "The last thing the information industry needs in these dynamic times are rigid rules that are cast in concrete for the years to come. How can a legislature in his right mind even contemplate drafting … inflexible, technology-specific language, when the Internet produces new business models and novel uses almost each day?"[58]

The challenge is that if the law relates to specific technology it becomes obsolete at the introduction of new and unforeseen technological developments. As internet technologies are subject to continual change, if the law is drafted with specific technology in mind, new developments may not fall within the meaning of the law intending to encompass it.[59]

Furthermore, in the meantime, it would not be clear how the law would address the new technology and therefore the law would be uncertain until such a time that it is updated.[60] In addition, this creates a ripe environment for another wave of lobbying and infighting at the national level, followed by the court having fill the gaps left by the legislator.[61]

Moreover, this approach contradicts the European Commission's intention that "the general legal frameworks should be applied online as they are offline. In view of the speed at which new technologies are developing, they will strive to frame regulations which are technology-neutral, whilst bearing in mind the need to avoid unnecessary regulation."[62]

Overall, taking the external perspective involves considering the technical function of the internet. The benefits of taking this perspective are that the law is specific, can be technologically accurate for a time and, from an external perspective, provides clarity on the legality of technological function. However, difficulties include incentivising avoidance creations, the risk of becoming quickly obsolete and uncertainty for the legality of new technologies.

55 Directive 2000/31/EC of the European Parliament and of the Council of 8 June 2000 on certain legal aspects of information society services, in particular electronic commerce, in the Internal Market [2000] OJ L 178/1, Recitals 4, 6, 7 and 21.

56 UK Intellectual Property Office, *Technical Review of Draft Legislation on Copyright Exceptions: Government Response* (Newport: UK Intellectual Property Office, 2014) p. 12: https://www.gov.uk/government/uploads/system/uploads/attachment_data/file/308732/response-copyright-techreview.pdf

57 Hugenholtz B., Why the Copyright Directive is Unimportant and Possibly Invalid (2000) 22(11) *European Intellectual Property Review*, pp. 499–502, p. 499.

58 *Ibid.*, p. 499.

59 Reed C., *Making Laws for Cyberspace* (Oxford: Oxford University Press, 2013) p. 134.

60 Hugenholtz B., Why the Copyright Directive is Unimportant and Possibly Invalid (2000) 22(11) *European Intellectual Property Review*, pp. 499–502.

61 *Ibid.*

62 European Ministerial Conference, Global Information Networks: Realising the Potential, 6–8 July 1997, Bonn, Ministerial declaration, Two Important Roles for Governments: Providing the Framework and Stimulating New Services at 22: http://ec.europa.eu/archives/ISPO/bonn/Min_declaration/i_finalen.html

The internal perspective: taking a metaphorical approach

The other way in which the facts of the internet can be determined is from the internal perspective. This involves a consideration of the virtual reality, as opposed to the physical reality discussed above. From the internal perspective, the virtual world is accepted as a legitimate construct. Kerr described this as "trying to map the physical world of 'realspace' onto the virtual world of cyberspace. We look for analogies between cyberspace and realspace, and try to match the rules between them."[63] He explained that although we may know that virtual reality is not reality, in order to comprehend what we experience online, we might treat the virtual world as if it were real: "The virtual perspective is like the perspective inside the Matrix: it accepts the virtual world of cyberspace as akin to a reality. Of course, unlike Neo, we know all along that the virtual world that the computer generates is only virtual. But as we try to make sense of what the Internet is, to understand what we experience online, we might decide to treat that virtual world as if it were real."[64]

What is important about this perspective is not knowledge, but cognition. From the internal perspective, the technical function of the internet is not relevant because it is essentially a cognitive tool for people to process their online experience. As Kerr explained, from an internal perspective: "A computer connected to the Internet provides a window to a virtual world that is roughly analogous to the physical world of real space. The technical details of what the computers attached to the Internet actually do 'behind the scenes' don't particularly matter. What matters is the virtual world of cyberspace that the user encounters and interacts with … online."[65]

Frischmann interpreted Kerr's internal perspective as an experiential explanation of the workings of the internet: "From this internal perspective, one perceives the Internet in terms of the applications it enables and the ways in which those applications affect end users; the technical operation of the network infrastructure may be largely irrelevant in terms of one's experience. It is this internal perspective that leads to the conception of cyberspace as a sort of virtual reality."[66] He suggested that Kerr's definition of the internal perspective could be improved by leaving open the empirical question of whether end-users employ the virtual reality construct in a particular circumstance.[67] Instead, Frischmann suggested that the internal perspective could be simply based on users' perceptions of their experience.[68]

However, Kerr's internal perspective need not be interpreted to require knowledge of the personal or empirical perspective of the end-user at all. In fact, it could be argued that in his article Kerr explained what this would mean to the end-user simply just to *illustrate* his definitions of the internal and external perspectives.

63 Kerr O. S., The Problem of Perspective in Internet Law (2003) 91 *Georgetown Law Journal*, pp. 357–405, p. 361.
64 *Ibid.*, p. 359.
65 *Ibid.*, p. 360.
66 Frischmann B. M., The Prospect of Reconciling Internet and Cyberspace (2004) 35 *Loyola University Chicago Law Journal*, pp. 205–234, p. 206.
67 *Ibid.*, p. 211.
68 *Ibid.*, p. 211.

The definition of the internal perspective is based on a choice of interpretation of the facts of the internet, not a user's personal perception. Kerr says that the user chooses to see cyberspace as realspace. However, it is argued that this is a subconscious choice made automatically in normal cognitive functioning of the human brain. Hunter also argued that this tendency is an inevitable by-product of human cognition.[69] Therefore, considerations of the user's perspectives or opinions should be avoided.

Furthermore, Kerr clearly stated that the problem of perspective is an issue due to the legitimacy of taking either approach. Therefore, the question that needs to be addressed is not: what perspective do end-users take? Rather it is: based on the principles of the particular regulation, which perspective *should* we take?

This is why the internal and external perspectives are perspectives, and not perceptions. A perspective is a point of view, an angle from which the internet is observed. Conversely, a perception is an understanding that a person gains through awareness. Considering users' personal perceptions on copyright and the internet is not the objective. This affirms that actual knowledge of the technical function of the network, or social attitudes towards copyright industries does not validate or influence a choice of perspective. Kerr stated that both perspectives are valid and legitimate on the basis of fact finding.[70]

Therefore, from an internal perspective, activity online is understood by analogies with the physical world. Thus, we try to "map the physical world of real space onto the virtual world of cyberspace."[71] The process of understanding the internet from an internal perspective therefore involves a consideration of past technologies; adopting a metaphorical projection onto new technologies.

As with the external perspective, there are challenges faced by taking a purely internal perspective in applying copyright law online, in particular due to the nature of metaphorical cognition. The following sections consider the difference between metaphors and skeumorphs and the impact that these devices have on copyright regulation.

The challenges of applying the internal perspective

This internal approach tends to merge the viewpoint of the decision maker into the technology, pushing technical processes into the unnoticed background.[72] Consequently, under this approach, the legal decision maker treats the results of a given technological process as epiphenomenal, largely divorced from the actual structure and function of the technology. The mechanics or workings of the technology are of little interest, rather it is the result that matters, regardless of

69 Hunter D., Cyberspace as Place and the Tragedy of the Digital Anticommons (2003) 91 *California Law Review*, pp. 439–519, p. 443.

70 Kerr O. S., The Problem of Perspective in Internet Law (2003) 91 *Georgetown Law Journal*, pp. 357–405, p.357.

71 Hutchison C. J., Interpretation and the Internet (2010) 28 *John Marshall Journal of Computer and Information Law*, pp. 251–272, p. 255.

72 Burk D. L., Copyright and the Architecture of Digital Delivery (2014) University of California Irvine School of Law, *Research Paper No. 2014–2057*, p. 10.

how it was produced.[73] Therefore, the internal approach can be understood as purposive and outcome driven.

However, the internal perspective can lead judges to treat new media as old media that had similar characteristics. For example, in the case of *Aereo*, [74] which allowed subscribers to view live and time-shifted streams of over-the-air television on internet-connected devices, the court chose to treat Aereo as if it were a cable transmission because ultimately it *acted* as a cable transmission and the outcome was the same.

Lemley warned that the internal approach could be taken too far if judges were to literally take cyberspace as if it were real space: "should the law assume that I am, in fact, hitting someone in this game because it looks to the outside world like I'm hitting someone, even though on some level we all know that we are merely sending electrical impulses back and forth across copper wires?"[75] Cohen also argued that there is a danger, at any rate, in over-physicalizing the virtual.[76]

The courts tends to apply the internal perspective through the use of metaphor. An appropriate metaphor can be used to understand the activities that take place online and apply the legal rule to an analogical representation of the facts that best fit. Calo maintained that "case law more commonly turns on finding the proper metaphor or analogy … Courts look to whether a given digital activity is 'like' an activity for which there are already rules. Legal, policy, and academic debates become battles over the proper analogy or metaphor."[77] For example, a court might consider whether email is a postcard or a sealed letter.

Taking the internal perspective therefore invites the use of a metaphorical approach to the internet and the law. Thinking metaphorically is the ordinary processing of information in human cognition.[78] Lakoff and Johnson, leading scholars in cognitive theory of conceptual metaphors, explain that metaphors are not only language-based, but "form an important part of our conceptual system and how we understand reality … to bring order to abstract phenomena."[79] Lakoff elaborated that "a metaphor is not just a figure of speech it is a figure of thought."[80] Modell agreed that: "Metaphor is not merely a figure of speech but is a fundamental form of cognition."[81]

73 *Ibid.*, p. 10.
74 *American Broadcasting Cos, Inc, Et Al v Aereo, Inc, Fka Bamboom Labs, Inc*, 2nd Circ 13-461 (2013).
75 Lemley M. A., The Dubious Autonomy of Virtual Worlds (2012) 2 *University of California Irvine Law Review*, pp. 575–583, p. 580.
76 Cohen J. E., Cyberspace As/And Space (2007) 107 *Columbia Law Review*, pp. 210–256.
77 Calo R., Robotics and the New Cyberlaw (2014) 103 *California Law Review*, pp. 101–146, p. 143.
78 Larsson S., Metaphors, Law and Digital Phenomena: The Swedish Pirate Bay Court Case (2013) 21(4) *International Journal of Law, Information and Technology*, pp. 354–380, p. 358.
79 Lakoff G. and Johnson M., *Philosophy in the Flesh: The Embodied Mind and its Challenge to Western Thought* (New York: Basic Books, 1999) p. 3.
80 Lakoff G., A Figure of Thought (1986) 1(3) *Metaphor and Symbol*, pp. 215–225.
81 Modell A., Emotional Memory, Metaphor and Meaning (2005) *Psychoanalytic Inquiry*, pp. 555–568, p. 562.

It has been argued that people not only talk in metaphor, but also think, reason and make sense of their world through metaphor, acting in ways that are consistent with their metaphors.[82] Therefore, changes in a metaphorical landscape reflect changes in cognition which, in turn, generate new thoughts, feelings and behaviour.[83] Metaphors "make use of everyday concrete things to illustrate intangible, complex and relational aspects of life, they are vivid and memorable ... Metaphors carry a great deal of information in a compact and memorable package."[84]

A key feature of a metaphor is one concept being projected onto other concepts, from the source domain to the target domain, in order to create an effect of meaning.[85] Richards proposed that a metaphor is the interaction between the "vehicle" and the "tenor" which results in a meaning.[86] The vehicle describes the concept that is being transferred and the tenor is the concept that is to be understood through the vehicle. The intention of the metaphor is that "the vehicle is not merely an embellishment of a tenor which is otherwise unchanged by it but that the vehicle and the tenor in cooperation give a meaning of more varied powers than can be ascribed to either."[87]

Therefore, metaphorical understanding is an omnipresent principle of both language and cognitive understanding. Metaphorical understanding is particularly relevant in the interpretation of new technologies because the more abstract a concept is, the more heavily we rely on metaphors to support our understanding.[88]

Copyright law is grounded in the use of conceptual metaphors.[89] For example, in the seminal case of *Designers Guild*, Lord Bingham relied on the metaphor "no one else may for a season reap what the copyright owner has sown."[90] This metaphorical reference to ploughing has a long-standing history in copyright discourse. Rose explained that "the writing implement being a kind of plow which one makes furrows on the field of a wax tabled ... [and] the conceit of a mind as a field is as old as pastoral poetry, and in the Middle Ages, under the influence of the evangelic trope of the word of God as a seed, the author was often represented as a sower of seeds."[91]

This explanation shows that from the use of a short metaphor, Bingham was able to conjure up a range of imagery and meaning to support his argument.

82 Lawley J. and Tompkins P., *Metaphors in Mind: Transformation Through Symbolic Modelling* (London: The Developing Company, 2003) p. 18.
83 *Ibid.*, p. 19.
84 *Ibid.*, p. 9.
85 Larsson S., Metaphors, Law and Digital Phenomena: The Swedish Pirate Bay Court Case (2013) 21(4) *International Journal of Law, Information and Technology*, pp. 354–380, p. 357.
86 Richards L. A, *The Philosophy of Rhetoric* (Oxford: Oxford University Press, 1936).
87 *Ibid.*, p. 96.
88 *Ibid.*, p. 94.
89 Patry W., *Moral Panics and the Copyright Wars* (New York: Oxford University Press, 2009) p. 59.
90 *Designers Guild Ltd v Russell Williams (Textiles) Ltd* [2001] All ER 700, as per Lord Bingham at para 2.
91 Rose M., Copyright and Its Metaphors (2002) 50(1) *California Law Review*, pp. 1–15, p. 6.

Advancing on our basic understanding of agriculture, he gains the cultural emotive connotations of farmers hard at work sowing seeds, which grow into the fruits of their labour, for which they are able to reap the benefits.

The contemporary copyright debate also attracts metaphorical rhetoric devices, for example the "pirates", "thieves" and "trespassers" against the "Luddites" and "monopolists" squelching freedom of expression and forcing corporate culture.[92] The tension between copyright industries and users who illegally download copyright material is often referred to as a "battle"[93] or the "copyright wars".[94] These are loaded metaphors that transport meaning to influence and frame the discourse.

The use of metaphorical thinking enables the cognitive digestion of new technology, as a normal function of human cognition and in particular in assisting in the interpretation and application of copyright law. Although Patry warned that the use of an inappropriate metaphor can have adverse consequences: "The acceptance of inapposite metaphors have led to an unjustified expansion of our copyright law."[95]In relation to new technology, the metaphor usually stems from the understanding of the ancestral technology. The internet technology is novel and therefore concepts of previous copyright delivery are metaphorically transferred because they share some similar elements or associations. The transition from analogue to digital requires a learning process that involves the deployment of metaphors from the physical representations in order to orient the novelty of the new media. The development of internet technologies has created a considerable need for labels and concepts that can describe the multitude of phenomena that follow.[96]

92 Patry W., *Moral Panics and the Copyright Wars* (New York: Oxford University Press, 2009) p. xviii.

93 *Ibid.*: Patry noted that there have been a number of copyright wars, and as Lawrence Lessig pointed out, the internet is merely a new "battleground for an old war": Lessig L., The Law of the Horse: What Cyberlaw Might Teach (1999) 113 *Harvard Law Review*, pp. 501–549, p. 501.

94 In 2002, the head of Motion Picture Association of America (MPAA) Jack Valenti submitted testimony to Congress entitled "A Clear Present and Future Danger", invoking the wartime metaphor "clear and present danger" coined by Justice Oliver Wendell Holmes Jr in his 1919 opinion for the US Supreme Court in *Schenck v United States* 249 US 47 (1919), creating the impression of the copyright industries under siege from hostile forces. The metaphor continues to be used, as shown by a recent publication by Peter Baldwin titled *The Copyright Wars: Three Centuries of Trans-Atlantic Battle* (Princeton, NJ: Princeton University Press, 2014). Edgar Bronfman Jr, CEO of Warner Music Group acknowledged the aptness of the phrase in a 2007 speech, agreeing that the recording industry had "gone to war with consumers": Edgar Bronfman Jr, Speech to GSMA Mobile Asia Congress in Macau, 28 November 2007: https://technicalconclusions.wordpress.com/2007/11/28/war-with-consumers/.

95 Patry W., *Moral Panics and the Copyright Wars* (New York: Oxford University Press, 2009) pp. xv–xvi.

96 Larsson S., *Metaphors and Norms: Understanding Copyright Law in a Digital Society* (Sweden: Lund University, 2011), p. 62

Metaphors and a skeumorphs

When a new phenomenon arises, it is processed by the mind and cognitively understood through the terms already known by currently accepted concepts of the mind. Therefore, this explains why new technology is often addressed in a similar way to its ancestor, for example email has been likened to postal mail.[97]

This particular type of metaphorical device is known as a skeumorph: this is the reuse of old concepts for new phenomena.[98] Whilst this theory of skeumorphs as a way to cognitively digest new technologies is relevant to all areas of online activity, it is particularly compelling for copyright law and digital copyright infringement. There are two key reasons for this.

The first reason is that copyright is a legal concept that is constantly changing over time in response to technology and is therefore strongly path-dependent.[99] This is as a result of the nature of copyright invoking competing stakeholder interests. In particular, it is beneficial for those who have historically exercised control over dissemination of copyright works to rely heavily upon tradition.

The second reason is that the application of copyright law online is a portrait of the obvious challenges to regulating in the digital context. As such, copyright illuminates the tension between new technological phenomena, regulation and cognitive understanding through both skeumorphs and metaphors.[100] This is because copyright attempts to control the creation and dissemination of copyright works using traditional understanding in a new environment that has fundamentally revolutionised the concepts of both reproduction and distribution, based on the assumption that digitally mediated behaviour online surrounding the consumption of music, movies and games follows the same pattern as more traditional consumption of physical artefacts.[101]

Cass and Lauer argued that the use of skeumorphs has implications for social norms and collective understanding. By borrowing an understanding of a phenomenon from an older concept, the norms connected to that older concept will likely transfer to the new phenomenon.[102] This means that the metaphorical bridge between the old and the new is important not just for cognitive understanding of the new reality, but also for how the process sustains normative behaviour. Metaphor shapes our thinking in a subtle but significant way.[103]

97 Cass K. and Lauer T. W., Media Transitions: The Cases of Digital Imagery and E-mail (2004) 17 *Information Technology and People*, pp. 252–262.

98 Larsson S., *Metaphors and Norms: Understanding Copyright Law in a Digital Society* (Sweden: Lund University, 2011) p. 63.

99 *Ibid.*, p.128.

100 Larsson S., Metaphors, Law and Digital Phenomena: The Swedish Pirate Bay Court Case (2013) 21(4) *International Journal of Law Information and Technology*, pp. 354–380, p. 378.

101 *Ibid.*, p. 378.

102 Cass K. and Lauer T. W., Media Transitions: The Cases of Digital Imagery and E-mail (2004) 17 *Information Technology and People*, pp. 252–262, p. 255.

103 Bellia P., Berman P, Frischmann B. and Post D., *Cyberlaw: Problems of Policy and Jurisprudence in the Information Age* (St Paul: West Academic, 2010) p. 49

This could be explained by considering the divide between the approach of the entertainment industries and the social norms relating to the use of digital copyright material. The illegal use of digital copyright material has been recognised as a social norm,[104] particularly among young people.[105] The entertainment industries attempted to project their historical understanding of physical copyright control onto digital material,[106] by turning to the legislator to enforce draconian measures,[107] much to the confusion and hostility of the users.[108] As the Depoorter, Van Hiel and Vanneste study suggested: "the younger demographic are convinced that file sharing technology has many beneficial uses and that copyright law is outdated or biased towards music publishers."[109] This demonstrates a clear divide between the user's understanding and that of the entertainment industries.[110] The distance between the entertainment industry, the law and the internet users continues to expand.[111] The moral arguments litigated by the entertainment industry, that there will be no more creation if artists do not get paid, appear to have had little impact.[112]

Perhaps this could be better understood by using the theory of skeumorphs. The entertainment industries' understanding is based on their previous normative experience with control over copyright material connected to tangible products such as CDs. However, for young people growing up in the digital

104 McAdams R. H., The Origin, Development, and Regulation of Norms (1997) 96 *Michigan Law Review*, pp. 338–433: A social norm is a behaviour that is widely adopted in society, not only because it is what people do, but also because it corresponds with a normative conception within society, of what people should do.

105 Hanway S. and Lyons L., Teens OK With Letting Music Downloads Play, 30 September 2003, Gallup Poll: http://www.gallup.com/poll/9373/teens-letting-music-downloads-play.aspx. This survey indicated that a substantial number of young people believe that sharing digital music is morally acceptable, reporting that 83% of people between the age of thirteen and seventeen found nothing wrong with file sharing. In addition, the Strategic Advisory Board for Intellectual Property Policy (SABIP) concluded in 2009 that there is also substantial evidence that many individuals do not perceive software piracy to be an ethical problem at all: SABIP, *Copycats? Digital Consumers in the Online Age* (London: CIBER UCL, 2009) pp. 37–38.

106 Horten M., *The Copyright Masquerade, How Corporate Lobbying Threatens Online Freedoms* (London: Zen Books, 2013).

107 Vitoria M., et al (eds), *Laddie, Prescott and Vitoria: The Modern Law of Copyright and Designs*, 4th edition (London: Butterworths Law, 2011) 63.78.

108 Depoorter B., Van Hiel A., Vanneste S., Copyright Backlash (2010–11) 84 *California Law Review*, pp. 1251–1292, p. 1257: this study concluded that stricter penalties for copyright infringement will further erode respect for copyright law and may even prove counterproductive to the entertainment industries.

109 *Ibid.*, p. 1266.

110 Levine R., *Free Ride How The Internet Is Destroying The Culture Business And How It Can Fight Back* (London: Vintage, 2012) p. 246: "The longer the current online chaos lasts, the more bitter the fight between creators and copyright infringers gets."

111 Schultz M. F., Fear and Norms and Rock and Roll: What Jambands Can Teach Us About Persuading People to Obey Copyright Law (2006) 21 *Berkeley Technology Law Journal*, pp. 651–728, p. 651.

112 Wu T., When Code Isn't Law (2003) 89 *Virginia Law Review*, pp. 101–170, p. 162.

age with access to, and sophisticated skills in, technology,[113] their normative behaviour is based on a largely digital experience. Larsson recognised that the difficulties of conceptual metaphorical developments are particularly evident when new types of phenomena emerge more frequently, and when society is changing more rapidly than normal.[114] This is relevant as the pace of technological development is clearly moving very fast, requiring adjustment from all humans acquainted with previous processes.

The use of skeumorphs enables the new to become more easily acceptable when it refers back an earlier iteration that it is displacing.[115] However, a skeumorph simultaneously focuses on the past and the future, while reinforcing and undermining both.[116] Therefore the use of skeumorph projection within legal regulation should be taken with caution. As Justice Cardozo famously observed: "Metaphors in law are to be narrowly watched, for through starting as devices to liberate thought, they end often by enslaving it."[117]

Litman argued that the development of metaphors in relation to copyright infringement online, such as the use of the term "pirate" has allowed copyright to expand without real consideration, as: "this evolution in metaphors conceals immense sleight of hand … into believing that copyright had always been intended to offer content owners extensive control."[118] The issue appears prevalent when metaphors are used without awareness that a metaphorical approach is being taken. This is because the use of metaphorical devices is subconscious, thereby carrying potentially unintended meaning. As Patry explained: "When we say that man is a wolf, we are aware we are pretending. But when it is said that internet service providers are pirates, there is no pretence: The statement is meant to be taken as true."[119]

The benefits of a metaphorical perspective are evident: it allows the quick understanding of modern concepts and can help to provide a smooth transition into the new. It also means that new legal regulation does not need to be created every time a new technological concept arises, overcoming the challenges of taking a purely external perspective.

However, the metaphor must be recognised as a metaphor. Bellia *et al* explained that this can be difficult, but that awareness of this perspective is essential: "Metaphor and analogy play a central role in legal reasoning, and

113 Palfrey J., Gasser, U., Simun, M. and Barns, R. F, Youth, Creativity and Copyright in the Digital Age (2009) 1(2) *International Journal of Learning and Media*, pp. 79–97, p. 82.

114 Larsson S., Metaphors, Law and Digital Phenomena: The Swedish Pirate Bay Court Case (2013) 21(4) *International Journal of Law, Information and Technology*, pp. 354–380, p. 365.

115 *Ibid.*, p. 365.

116 Hayles N. K., *How We Became Posthuman: Virtual Bodies in Cybernetics, Literature and Information* (Chicago: University Chicago Press, 1999) p.17.

117 *Berkey v Third Avenue Railway*, 244 NY 84, 94, 155 NE 58, 61 (1926) at 9.

118 Litman J., *Digital Copyright* (New York: Prometheus Books, 2001) p. 89.

119 Patry W., *Moral Panics and the Copyright Wars* (New York: Oxford University Press, 2009) pp. 46–47.

understanding their use (and misuse) is a critical skill for lawyers to develop … Metaphor is a two-edged sword."[120] The difficulty is that we do not always recognise that we are thinking metaphorically, as it is an automatic cognitive response,[121] since "human thought processes are largely metaphorical."[122] When metaphors are not perceived as metaphors, the original conceptions could unknowingly transfer the meaning of the previous concept and be perceived as the only purpose of a given regulation.[123]

Secondly, caution must be taken when using skeumorphs because of the connotations that carry when using past concepts for understanding new technology. Due to the pace of technological development, trying to map the old understanding of copyright material is incompatible with the divide in social norms. Furthermore, the choice or appropriateness of the particular skeumorph as a bridge from the old to the new must be questioned.[124]

However, this concern could be overcome when considering Kerr's internal perspective within a purposive approach. The chosen metaphorical understanding should reflect the purpose of copyright in the digital age, and not attempt to mimic the nature of control previously understood by the entertainment industry. An opportunity is presented here to determine the way that copyright is applied online. As Lemley highlighted: "One of the things that the novelty of technological space does is open up the possibility of novelty in legal space. Because we don't have a clear and direct analogy, we have an opportunity to rethink certain legal rules not only as they apply to that technology, but in ways that might feed back into other spaces as well."[125]

The final section of this chapter sets out how the Framework will be utilised in this research.

The framework for analysis

The internal and external perspectives are the critical vantage points outside the law that nourish the doctrinal analysis of digital copyright law with a wider understanding of the relevant social phenomena: the human interaction with the internet. This approach views the operation of law through a critical lens that adopts a particular theoretical perspective.[126] The inside out approach[127] facilitates

120 Bellia P., Berman P, Frischmann B. and Post D., *Cyberlaw: Problems of Policy and Jurisprudence in the Information Age* (St Paul: West Academic, 2010) pp. 27 and 39.
121 Glucksberg S., How Metaphors Create Categories – Quickly in Gibbs W., *The Cambridge Handbook of Metaphor and Thought* (Cambridge: Cambridge University Press, 2008) pp. 67–83.
122 Lakoff G. and Johnson M., *Metaphors We Live By* (Chicago: University of Chicago Press, 1987) p. 6.
123 Larsson S., Metaphors, Law and Digital Phenomena: The Swedish Pirate Bay Court Case (2013) 21(4) *International Journal of Law, Information and Technology*, pp. 354–380, p. 367.
124 Litman J., *Digital Copyright* (New York: Prometheus Books, 2001) p. 86.
125 Lemley M. A., The Dubious Autonomy of Virtual Worlds (2012) 2 *University of California Irvine Law Review*, pp. 575–583.
126 Brownsword R., An Introduction to Legal Research (2008) *Scribd*, pp. 1–24, p. 15.
127 Dworkin R. M., *Life's Dominion* (London: Harper Collins, 1993) p. 29.

the address of the research question concerning the effectiveness of the law and allows for the assessment of whether the law is fit for purpose.[128]

This approach enables the exploration of questions concerning regulatory legitimacy. Taking either the internal or the external perspective determines the outcome of a legal decision. Therefore, it is necessary to investigate whether judges apply either an internal or an external perspective when defining digital copyright infringement. Furthermore, how does this impact the scope of the law in relation to communication to the public and copying online? And, lastly, is this approach consistent with the intended purpose of the law?

Ultimately, this leads to the consideration of whether the application of copyright law online is consistent with the values of the doctrine and the intended purpose of the regulation when taking either an internal or an external perspective of the internet. As Kerr stated: "Once we agree on our goals, we can then use them to develop a framework for choosing between perspectives."[129]

The Framework for Constructing Digital Perspectives

The method of application will now be addressed to identify how the internal and external concepts will be applied to the law. As mentioned, Kerr set out the internal and external concepts as practical ways of interpreting activity online.[130] He demonstrated that there are two distinct, yet both viable, ways of interpreting the facts of the internet. Therefore, the choice of virtual reality or technical basis is available to judges and legislators.[131]

For this framework of analysis, Kerr's definitions have been interpreted, defined and grounded in the theoretical basis of purposivism and literalism. The result is a theoretically grounded framework for the analysis of the construction of digital facts: to determine whether the application of legal regulation online is being interpreted from either an internal or an external perspective.

This Framework for Constructing Digital Perspectives can be extracted and applied to any number of online circumstances that are regulated by law. In order to measure the impact and legitimacy of taking either the internal or the external perspective (as developed), or the type of fact constructed, the framework needs to be tailored to that particular circumstance. This would involve taking into consideration the purpose or justification of the relevant legislation, thereby looking at the historical developments, to consider whether these are achieved by either perspective.

Kerr suggested a normative framework for resolving the problem of perspective: firstly, looking at the importance of the doctrine, rooted in

128 Hutchinson T., Doctrinal Research; Researching the Jury in Watkins D. and Burton M. (eds) *Research Methods in Law* (Abingdon: Routledge, 2013) p. 7: "The first step is to check that the doctrine, properly interpreted, is being complied with."

129 Kerr O. S., The Problem of Perspective in Internet Law (2003) 91 *Georgetown Law Journal*, pp. 357–405, p. 390.

130 *Ibid.*, p. 361: "This is a very practical problem."

131 *Ibid.*, p. 358.

faithfulness to text; and then, secondly, considering the perspective of the people the law seeks to regulate.[132] However, Kerr acknowledged that this approach was simply "a guidepost [that] can help resolve the problem of perspective, they are not self-executing."[133] Therefore this requires some consideration.

Kerr's suggestion to determine perspective through the examination of the language used in statutory and case law[134] is useful for this research. He suggested that the language of statutory law will often signal the adoption of an internal or an external approach.[135] Legislation is a literary manifestation of law[136] and is therefore one of the ways in which law exposes its intentions.[137]

It is unlikely that the legislator explicitly considered whether it wanted courts to follow either an internal or an external perspective when the CDPA 1988 was enacted. However, Kerr suggested that the language used may nevertheless point to a particular perspective today.[138] As Holmes argued: "We do not inquire what the legislature meant; we ask only what the statute means."[139]

In contrast, Hicks argued that: "Legislation is the ideas of legislators, symbolized by combinations of words ... Whenever we deal with written or spoken words we are one remove from the idea which they represent."[140] And as Mr Justice Holmes stated "a word is not a crystal, transparent and unchanged; it is the skin of a living thought and may vary greatly in colour or content according to the circumstances and the time in which it is used."[141]

Thus, the words used in legislation are symbols of the legislator's ideas and may become symbols for other ideas in the mind of the reader.[142] Therefore, it is also necessary to consider the case law, where the statutory provisions are interpreted by the judges.

132 *Ibid.*, p. 396.
133 *Ibid.*, p.400.
134 *Ibid.*, p. 391.
135 Kerr O. S., The Problem of Perspective in Internet Law (2003) 91 *Georgetown Law Journal*, pp. 357–405, p. 391.
136 Hicks F. C., *Materials and Methods of Legal Research* (New York: The Lawyers Co-operative Publishing Company, 1942) p. 38.
137 *Ibid.*, p. 39.
138 Kerr O. S., The Problem of Perspective in Internet Law (2003) 91 *Georgetown Law Journal*, pp. 357–405, p. 393.
139 Holmes O. W., The Theory of Legal Interpretation (1899) 12 *Harvard Law Review*, pp. 417–420, p. 419.
140 Hicks F. C., *Materials and Methods of Legal Research* (New York: The Lawyers Co-operative Publishing Company, 1942) p. 38.
141 *Towne v Eisner* 245 US 418, as per Mr Justice Holmes at p. 245. Also referring to the case of *Lamar v United States*, 240 US 60 (1916) p. 240: "The same words may have different meanings in different parts of the same act, and, of course, words may be used in a statute in a different sense from that in which they are used in the Constitution."
142 Hicks F. C., *Materials and Methods of Legal Research* (New York: The Lawyers Co-operative Publishing Company, 1942) p. 39.

Furthermore, it is a basic principle of justice that like cases ought to be decided alike; the doctrine of precedent.[143] Therefore, the perspective taken by judges when making their decisions may influence the scope of digital copyright infringement.

Kerr also suggested that when considering a doctrine that has a complex heritage[144] or was derived from common law, the viewpoint must also be assessed from a body of case law.[145] This requires a close reading of the cases interpreting the statutory provisions.[146]

Conclusion

This chapter has discussed the intersection between internet technology, interpretation and cognitive perceptions within the context of digital copyright infringement. This chapter first discussed Professor Orin Kerr's internal and external perspectives of the internet.[147] It was explained that the external perspective offers a technical perspective of the internet and can be aligned with the literal reading of the law. This allows precision, accuracy and clarity in determining the facts of the case. However, this perspective encounters challenges such as attaching law to specific technological function which could result in a quick expiry date when a new technology is developed.

Thereafter, the internal perspective was explored, aligning with a more purposive approach which looks beyond the literal meaning of the words and leads to the use of metaphorical interpretations of the law of copyright online. This perspective can overcome the limitations of the external perspective as it is not based on a technicality and therefore would be more sustainable. However, the use of skeumorphs – old concepts projected onto new phenomena – limits the usefulness of this approach.

Ultimately, it is important to recognise that there are two ways in which the facts of the internet can be interpreted; particularly as choosing a perspective can determine the outcome of a decision, and as Frischmann concluded "it would be better if such choices were made consciously and explicitly."[148]

Both perspectives are equally valid and legitimate and each perspective has a particular effect on the regulation of copyright material online. Kerr stated that

143 Campbell E., Glasson E. J., York L. P. and Sharpe J. M., *Legal Research Methods and Materials* (Sydney: The Law Book Company, 1988) p. 8.

144 As is the case for copyright law; see Deazley R., *On the Origin of the Right to Copy: Charting the Movement of Copyright Law in Eighteenth Century Britain (1695–1775)* (Portland: Hart Publishing, 2004).

145 Kerr O. S., The Problem of Perspective in Internet Law (2003) 91 *Georgetown Law Journal*, pp. 357–405, p. 394.

146 *Ibid.*, p. 401.

147 Kerr O. S., The Problem of Perspective in Internet Law (2003) 91 *Georgetown Law Journal*, pp. 357–405.

148 Frischmann B. M., The Prospect of Reconciling Internet and Cyberspace (2004) 35 *Loyola University Chicago Law Journal*, pp. 205–234, p. 206.

courts and commentators switch frequently between perspectives without even recognising the change.[149]

The application of the Framework was then considered, whereby the most appropriate and effective method takes on three phases of analysis. Firstly, a historical consideration of the development of the regulation is required in order to understand the intended purpose of the law. Secondly, the wording of statutory law is considered as to whether it takes on either an internal or an external perspective. Thirdly, the relevant case law then needs to be analysed, in order to determine the meaning of the law as interpreted and applied by the courts.

This book therefore follows these steps, applying them first to digital copyright infringement by way of copying and thereafter applying the same method to investigate digital copyright infringement by way of communication to the public.

Bibliography

Books

Baldwin P., *The Copyright Wars: Three Centuries of Trans-Atlantic Battle* (Princeton, NJ: Princeton University Press, 2014).

Bellia P., Berman P., Frischmann B. and Post D., *Cyberlaw: Problems of Policy and Jurisprudence in the Information Age* (St Paul: West Academic, 2010).

Bowrey K., *Law and Internet Cultures* (Melbourne: Cambridge University Press, 2005).

Campbell E., Glasson E. J., York L. P. and Sharpe J. M., *Legal Research Methods and Materials* (Sydney: The Law Book Company, 1988).

Cross R., *Precedent in English Law* (Oxford: Clarendon Press, 1968).

David M., *Peer to Peer and the Music Industry: The Criminalization of Sharing* (London: Sage Publications, 2010).

Deazley R., *On the Origin of the Right to Copy: Charting the Movement of Copyright Law in Eighteenth Century Britain (1695–1775)* (Portland: Hart Publishing, 2004).

Dworkin R. M., *Life's Dominion* (London: Harper Collins, 1993).

Glucksberg S., How Metaphors Create Categories – Quickly in Gibbs W. (ed), *The Cambridge Handbook of Metaphor and Thought* (Cambridge: Cambridge University Press, 2008).

Gralla P., *How the Internet Works* (Indiana: Que Corporation, 1999).

Hayles N. K., *How We Became Posthuman: Virtual Bodies in Cybernetics, Literature and Information* (Chicago: University Chicago Press, 1999).

Hicks F. C., *Materials and Methods of Legal Research* (New York: The Lawyers Co-operative Publishing Company, 1942).

Horten M., *The Copyright Masquerade, How Corporate Lobbying Threatens Online Freedoms* (London: Zen Books, 2013).

Hutchinson T., Doctrinal Research, Researching the Jury in Watkins D. and Burton M. (eds) *Research Methods in Law* (Abingdon: Routledge, 2013).

Johns A., *Piracy: The Intellectual Property Wars from Gutenberg to Gates* (Chicago: The University of Chicago Press, 2009).

149 Kerr O. S., The Problem of Perspective in Internet Law (2003) 91 *Georgetown Law Journal*, pp. 357–405, p. 358.

Lakoff G. and Johnson M., *Metaphors We Live By* (Chicago: University of Chicago Press, 1987).

Lakoff G. and Johnson M., *Philosophy in the Flesh: The Embodied Mind and its Challenge to Western Thought* (New York: Basic Books, 1999).

Larsson S., *Metaphors and Norms: Understanding Copyright Law in a Digital Society* (Sweden: Lund University, 2011).

Lawley J. and Tompkins P., *Metaphors in Mind: Transformation Through Symbolic Modelling* (London: The Developing Company, 2003).

Lessig L., *Remix: Making Art and Commerce Thrive in the Hybrid Economy* (New York: Penguin Press, 2008).

Levine R., *Free Ride, How the Internet is Destroying the Culture Business and How it Can Fight Back* (London: Vintage, 2012).

Litman J., *Digital Copyright* (New York: Prometheus Books, 2001).

Patry W., *Moral Panics and the Copyright Wars* (New York: Oxford University Press, 2009).

Reed C., *Making Laws for Cyberspace* (Oxford: Oxford University Press, 2013).

Richards L. A., *The Philosophy of Rhetoric* (Oxford: Oxford University Press, 1936).

Schultz M. F., Copynorms: Copyright and Social Norms in Yu K. P. (ed) *Intellectual Property and Information Wealth: Issues and Practices in the Digital Age, Vol 1 Copyright and Related Rights* (Connecticut: Praeger Publishers, 2006).

Vitoria M., et al (eds), *Laddie, Prescott and Vitoria: The Modern Law of Copyright and Designs*, 4th edition (London: Butterworths Law, 2011).

Case law

AandM Records, Inc v Napster, Inc, 114 F Supp 2d 896 (2000).

American Broadcasting Cos, Inc, Et Al v Aereo, Inc, Fka Bamboom Labs, Inc, 2nd Circ 13–461 (2013).

Berkey v Third Avenue Railway, 244 NY 84, 94, 155 NE 58, 61(1926).

Designers Guild Ltd v Russell Williams (Textiles) Ltd [2001] All ER 700.

Dramatico Entertainment Ltd and Others v British Sky Broadcasting Ltd and Others [2012] EWHC 268 (Ch).

Ladbroke (Football) Ltd v William Hill (Football) Ltd [1964] 1 WLR 273.

Lamar v United States, 240 US 60 (1916).

MGM Studios, Inc v Grokster, Ltd, 545 US 913 (2005).

Public Relations Consultants Association Ltd v The Newspaper Licensing Agency Ltd and Others [2010] EWHC 3099 (Ch).

Public Relations Consultants Association Ltd v The Newspaper Licensing Agency Ltd and Others [2011] EWCA Civ 890.

Public Relations Consultants Association Ltd v The Newspaper Licensing Agency Ltd and Others [2013] UKSC 18.

Reno v Am Civil Liberties Union, 521 US 844, 849 (1997) Syllabus.

Schenck v United States, 249 US 47 (1919).

Towne v Eisner 245 US 418 (1918).

UMG Recordings Inc v MP3.com Inc, 92 F Supp 2D 349, 350 (SDNY 2000).

Warwick Film Productions Ltd v Eisinger [1969] 1 Ch 508.

Journals

Brownsword R., An Introduction to Legal Research (2008) *Scribd*, pp. 1–24.

Burk D. L., Copyright and the Architecture of Digital Delivery (2014) University of California Irvine School of Law, *Research Paper No 2014–2057.*

Calo R., Robotics and the New Cyberlaw (2014) 103 *California Law Review*, pp. 101–146.

Cass K. and Lauer T. W., Media Transitions: The Cases of Digital Imagery and E-mail (2004) 17 *Information Technology and People*, pp. 252–262.

Cohen J. E., Cyberspace As/And Space (2007) 107 *Columbia Law Review*, pp. 210–256.

Depoorter B., Van Hiel A. and Vanneste S., Copyright Backlash (2010–11) 84 *California Law Review*, pp. 1251–1292.

Filby M., Code is Law? Assessing Architectural File Sharing Regulation in the Online Environment (2013) 8(1) *Journal of International Commercial Law and Technology*, pp. 81–103.

Frischmann B. M., The Prospect of Reconciling Internet and Cyberspace (2004) 35 *Loyola University Chicago Law Journal*, pp. 205–234.

Froomkin M. A., The Metaphor is the Key: Cryptography, the Clipper Chip, and the Constitution (1995) 143 *University of Pennsylvania Law Review*, pp. 709–897.

Holmes O. M., The Theory of Legal Interpretation (1899) 12(6) *Harvard Law Review*, pp. 417–420.

Hugenholtz B., Why the Copyright Directive is Unimportant and Possibly Invalid (2000) 22(11) *European Intellectual Property Review*, pp. 499–502.

Hunter D., Cyberspace as Place and the Tragedy of the Digital Anticommons (2003) 91 *California Law Review*, pp. 439–519.

Hutchison C. J., Interpretation and the Internet (2010) 28 *John Marshall Journal of Computer and Information Law*, pp. 251–272.

Karjala D. S., Copying and Piracy in the Digital Age (2013) 52 *Washburn Law Journal*, pp. 245–266.

Kerr O. S., The Problem of Perspective in Internet Law (2003) 91 *Georgetown Law Journal*, pp. 357–405.

Lakoff G., A Figure of Thought (1986) 1(3) *Metaphor and Symbol*, pp. 215–225.

Larsson S., Metaphors, Law and Digital Phenomena: The Swedish Pirate Bay Court Case (2013) 21(4) *International Journal of Law, Information and Technology*, pp. 354–380.

Lemley M., Place and Cyberspace (2003) 91(2) *California Law Review*, pp. 521–542.

Lemley M. A., The Dubious Autonomy of Virtual Worlds (2012) 2 *University of California Irvine Law Review*, pp. 575–583.

Lessig L., The Law of the Horse: What Cyberlaw Might Teach (1999) 113 *Harvard Law Review*, pp. 501–549.

McAdams R. H., The Origin, Development, and Regulation of Norms (1997) 96 *Michigan Law Review*, pp. 338–433.

Modell A., Emotional Memory, Metaphor and Meaning (2005) *Psychoanalytic Inquiry*, pp. 555–568.

Palfrey J., Gasser U., Simun M. and Barns R. F., Youth, Creativity and Copyright in the Digital Age (2009) 1(2) *International Journal of Learning and Media*, pp. 79–97.

Rose M., Copyright and Its Metaphors (2002) 50(1) *California Law Review*, pp. 1–15.

Schultz M. F., Fear and Norms and Rock and Roll: What Jambands Can Teach Us About Persuading People to Obey Copyright Law (2006) 21 *Berkeley Technology Law Journal*, pp. 651–728.

Wu T., Application Centred Internet Analysis (1999) 85 *Virginia Law Review*, pp. 1163–1204.
Wu T., When Code Isn't Law (2003) 89 *Virginia Law Review*, pp. 101–170.

Legislation

Copyright, Designs and Patents Act 1988.
Directive 2000/31/EC of the European Parliament and of the Council of 8 June 2000 on certain legal aspects of information society services, in particular electronic commerce, in the Internal Market [2000] *OJ* L 178/1.

Official documents and reports

European Ministerial Conference, Global Information Networks: Realising the Potential, 6–8 July 1997, Bonn, Ministerial declaration, Two Important Roles for Governments: Providing the Framework and Stimulating New Services: http://ec.europa.eu/archives/ISPO/bonn/Min_declaration/i_finalen.html.
SABIP, *Copycats? Digital Consumers in the Online Age* (London: CIBER, UCL, 2009).
UK Intellectual Property Office, *Technical Review of Draft Legislation on Copyright Exceptions: Government Response* (Newport: UK Intellectual Property Office, 2014): https://www.gov.uk/government/uploads/system/uploads/attachment_data/file/308732/response-copyright-techreview.pdf.

Web sources

BronfmanJrEdgar, Speech to GSMA Mobile Asia Congress in Macau, 28 November 2007: https://technicalconclusions.wordpress.com/2007/11/28/war-with-consumers/.
Hanway S. and Lyons L., Teens OK With Letting Music Downloads Play, 30 September 2003, Gallup Poll: http://www.gallup.com/poll/9373/teens-letting-music-downloads-play.aspx.

3 Drafting the reproduction right

Introduction

Copyright law is a product of its time and a beast of substantial historical ancestry.[1] This is a challenge for copyright, as it must also keep up to date with new technological developments that create new types of works and new means of exploiting existing works.[2] Failing to adapt in these circumstances results in unintended consequences in the law: "Industries effected by copyright find that the application of old legal language to new contexts yields unanticipated results."[3] Thus, the law must adapt to new technologies in order to stay relevant in balancing the interests of creators and rights-holders with the public interest of accessing and using creative material.[4]

The development of the CDPA 1988 required a lengthy consultation process; spanning over 15 years of consideration.[5] The challenge of trying to make policy decisions that reflected the many different stakeholder interests were demonstrated by the number of consultations, proposals and amendments that led up to the Bill, including last-minute changes made whilst the Bill proceeded to Royal Assent.[6]

In order to understand why and how the development of the CDPA 1988 occurred, as explained in Chapter 2, the method of applying the Framework for Constructing Digital Perspectives will be applied first by considering the historical development of the law. As such, this chapter first looks at the historical

1 Light S. N., Parody, Burlesque and the Economic Rationale for Copyright (1979) 11 (4) *Connecticut Law Review*, pp. 615–636, p. 615.

2 Groves P., *Copyright and Designs Law: A Question of Balance* (London: Graham and Trotman Ltd, 1991) p. 7.

3 Litman J., *Digital Copyright* (New York: Prometheus Books, 2006) p. 22.

4 Directive 2001/29/EC of the European Parliament and of the Council of 22 May 2001 on the harmonisation of certain aspects of copyright and related rights in the information society [2001] OJ L 167/10 (hereafter the Information Society Directive), Recital 31: "The existing exceptions and limitations to the rights as set out by the Member States have to be reassessed in the light of the new electronic environment."

5 The Whitford Committee was set up in 1973 and the CDPA 1988 came into force in 1989.

6 Merkin R., *Richards Butler on Copyright, Designs and Patents: The New Law* (London: Longman, 1989) p. 1.

development of the CDPA 1988, considering the context and development of the current statutory law in order to understand the intended meaning and purpose behind it. The narrative moves through the long and complex journey from Committee to Green Papers, White Papers and the Bill, to the law as it stands today.

The second part of this chapter then applies the second phase of the Framework by focusing specifically on section 17 of the CDPA 1988; the most fundamental restricted act of copying. The language of the law is analysed in detail in order to determine the meaning and purpose of the law, in light of the analysis undertaken in the first part of this chapter. The drafting of section 17 was determined long before the modern technologies used to access, use, create and copy copyright material, and the discussion considers the impact of the wording on the meaning of the law in light of the internet. In particular, analysing the wording to determine whether either the internal or the external perspective has been taken and what impact that has on the meaning of the law.

The historical development of the CDPA 1988

This section will set out the context within which the CDPA 1988 was developed, to understand the reasons why the new regulation was needed and the effect that the previous laws had on the development of it, in order to establish the intended meaning behind the regulation. This can then be analysed in relation to the Framework for Constructing Digital Perspectives to discover how the meaning and perspective of the law has developed in its application to the internet.

The Gregory Committee

In 1951, Harold Wilson MP, president of the then Board of Trade, appointed a Committee, chaired by H. S. Gregory to consider and report on whether and what changes were desirable in the law relating to copyright in literary, dramatic, musical and artistic works with particular regard to technical developments and to the revised International Convention for the Protection of Literary and Artist Works signed at Brussels in June 1948.[7]

The Committee held 57 meetings,[8] receiving representations in writing from 34 organisations and nine individuals.[9] The Committee also heard oral evidence from 29 organisations and five individuals.[10] Of this evidence, which was published and available from the Patent Office Library, it transpired that one of the main criticisms of the previous Copyright Act of 1911 was its complexity in presentation.

7 Gregory Committee, *The Board of Trade Report of the Copyright Committee* (London: Her Majesty's Stationery Office, 1952) Cmnd 8662 (hereafter, the Gregory Committee Report), preliminary to the Report; p. 1

8 *Ibid.*, p. 1.

9 *Ibid.*, p. 128.

10 *Ibid.*, Appendix A Part I, pp. 126–127.

The Committee reported that it heard from many witnesses that the Act required clarification and that there was doubt as to the precise effect of the Act.[11]

In light of this, the Gregory Committee recommended that the form of any future Act be drafted so as to reduce complexities.[12] In order to achieve this, the Committee suggested that the provisions be organised thematically: "Complexities which have been introduced by the compression of a number of different subjects into a single section ... would be more clearly expressed if the appropriate provisions were expanded and dealt with separately. It appears to us that drafting the Act by reference to the subject matter of the particular right – its scope, and whatever special conditions attach to the right – together with a re-arrangement of its various provisions, would make the position clearer for the public generally."[13]

The technological developments that the Gregory Committee specifically considered included broadcasting, television and technical developments used in libraries by micro-film processes and in book production by photo-lithography.[14] Photocopying was considered to be a cheap, quick and simple way to copy and therefore "the real threat."[15] The Gregory Committee considered the issuing of photocopying to be one of its most important considerations;[16] it was an issue of real contention and conflict between stakeholders.[17] The Committee reported on the competing interests, that the "publishers objected to a law which would allow large scale copying ... scholars wanted to be able to make copies for their own use ... librarians needed a clear law which would give them unequivocal guidelines."[18]

In order to resolve this conflict, the Gregory Committee recommended a compromise in the form of an extension of fair dealing.[19] It was suggested that photocopying a work would be an infringement, but that an exception would allow the reproduction by mechanical or photographic means of extracts up to a certain length for private study, either by the person or a librarian.[20] This solution was considered to be an important conceptual innovation. Feather described it as "an ingenious compromise, which the publishers eventually accepted."[21]

However, the Gregory Committee was considered to have taken a conservative and minimalist approach in its recommendations.[22] The Bill was brought to Parliament in June 1956, it was supported from all sides of the House and passed all

11 *Ibid.*, para 11.
12 *Ibid.*, para 328, Summary of Principal Recommendations p. 3, and Arrangement of the Act p. 116.
13 *Ibid.*, para 11.
14 *Ibid.*, para 12.
15 Feather J., *Publishing, Piracy and Politics, An Historical Study of Copyright in Britain* (London: Mansell Publishing, 1994) p. 205.
16 Gregory Committee Report, para 43.
17 *Ibid.*, para 52.
18 *Ibid.*, para 4.
19 *Ibid.*, para 52.
20 *Ibid.*, para 52.
21 Feather J., *Publishing, Piracy and Politics, An Historical Study of Copyright in Britain* (London: Mansell Publishing, 1994) p. 206.
22 *Ibid.*, p. 207.

stages without difficulty.[23] This quick and smooth adoption demonstrates that the Bill was not considered particularly controversial.

Nevertheless, legal language is difficult to understand for those who are not legally trained, largely due to the syntax characteristics.[24] This is particularly the case for copyright legislation, as it reflects the debates and compromises made between the different stakeholders at the time of drafting.[25] This leads to law that may appear to be archaic and obscure to a layperson.[26] Thus, despite good intentions to simplify the law, the Copyright Act 1956 was met with much criticism. Sir William Dale heavily criticised the draftsmanship of the Act, using it as an example of how *not* to draft legislation, and castigated the 1956 Act and suggested that statute law should be understood by the people that it intends to regulate.[27]

Bennion, one of the draftsmen of the Copyright Act 1956, responded to Dale's criticism with a review, arguing that Dale's suggestions were impractical.[28] In response to Dale's argument, Bennion highlighted the Swedish copyright statute as an example of legislation drafted in layman's language, which stated that: "The performance of a work at a place of business for a comparatively large closed group of people shall be considered a public performance." Bennion argued that this language created ambiguity in the law: "it would be interesting to hear laymen discussing whether a public hall hired by a firm for a staff party is a place of business, or 43 persons consisting of the firm's staff with a few relatives and friends is a comparatively large closed group."[29]

Nevertheless, the Copyright Act 1956 was considered complicated, badly constructed[30] and inflexible legislation: "The Gregory Committee's apparent determination to avoid enunciating general principles, left the United Kingdom with a very specific law which was applicable to the technological, economic and political situation of 1956."[31]

23 *Hansard*, HC Deb 4 June 1956 Vol 553 Cols 715–811 (Second Reading); Hansard, HC Deb 24 October 1956 Vol 558, Cols 665–685 (Report Stage).

24 Cucchi C., Vague Expressions in the European Parliament: A Marker of Cultural Identity? in Garzone G. and Archibald J., *Discourse, Identities and Roles in Specialized Communication* (Switzerland: Peter Lang, 2010) p. 85.

25 Dworkin G. and Taylor R. D., *Blackstone's Guide to the Copyright, Designs and Patents Act 1988* (London: Blackstone Press Ltd, 1989) p. 15; see also Whitford Committee, *Copyright and Designs Law, Report of the Committee to Consider the Law on Copyright and Designs* (London: Her Majesty's Stationery Office, 1977) Cmnd 6732 (hereafter, the Whitford Committee Report); Leopold P. M., Reports of Committees; the Whitford Committee Report on Copyright and Designs Law (1977) 40(6) *Modern Law Review*, pp. 685–700.

26 Litman J., *Digital Copyright*, 2nd edition (New York: Prometheus Books, 2006) p. 29.

27 Dale W., *Legislative Drafting: A New Approach a Comparative Study of Methods in France, Germany, Sweden and the United Kingdom* (London: Butterworths, 1977).

28 Bennion F., Review of Legislative Drafting: A New Approach by Sir William Dale KCMG – Reviewing the Reviewers (1980) *Statute Law Review*, pp. 61–76, p. 61.

29 *Ibid.*, p. 61.

30 Groves P., *Copyright and Designs Law: A Question of Balance* (London: Graham and Trotman Ltd, 1991) p. 2.

31 Feather J., *Publishing, Piracy and Politics, An Historical Study of Copyright in Britain* (London: Mansell Publishing, 1994) p. 207.

The Whitford Committee

The CDPA 1988 was introduced following the Whitford Committee Report.[32] The development of new technologies and the continuing evolution of the Berne Convention[33] prompted the setting up of a new departmental Committee in 1973. The Committee was set up under the Chairmanship of Mr Justice Whitford[34] to consider the impact of the Universal Copyright Convention 1971 and the Rome Convention for the Protection of Performers, Producers of Phonograms and Broadcasting Organisations 1961.[35]

Twenty years after the Copyright Act 1956, the Department of Trade established a Committee under Mr Justice Whitford to consider and report on what changes were desirable in the law under the 1956 Act and the Design Copyright Act 1968.[36]

The Whitford Committee's consultation process was considerably more in depth than that of the Gregory Committee;[37] it held over twice the number meetings (106), as well as smaller working group meetings and four outside visits, and received written and oral evidence from a considerable number of organisations, companies and individuals.[38] However, unlike its predecessors, the Whitford Committee did not publish any of this evidence.[39]

In the introduction to the Report, the Whitford Committee re-stated the continuing theme that the law needed to be simplified: "The Act of 1956 is a remarkable feat of draftsmanship but … has proved a nightmare to those who have to try to understand it whether as laymen for their own purposes or as lawyers seeking to guide their clients. It is for this reason no doubt that one of the most constant themes in the submissions received by the [Whitford] Committee has been the request that something must be done to simplify the law. A principal objective in any future legislation must be that copyright law should be 'placed on a plain and uniform basis' to adopt the words of the 1952 [Gregory] Committee echoing the words of the 1909 Committee."[40]

32 Whitford Committee Report.
33 The Berne Convention for the Protection of Literary and Artistic Works 1886, revised in Stockholm in 1967 and again in Paris in 1973 requiring the UK Copyright Act 1956 to be updated.
34 Members of the Committee: The Hon Mr Justice Whitford (Chairman), Professor W. H. Barber, Mr G. V. K. Burton CBE, Mr G. H. Doughty, Miss Rosina Harris, Mr E. P. Skone James, Mrs Jacqueline A. Thwaites, Mr W. Wallace CMG (Vice Chairman) and Mr W. Weston: the Whitford Committee Report, p. iii.
35 Arnold R., The Need for a New Copyright Act: A Case Study in Law Reform, The Herchel Smith Intellectual Property Lecture (2014) 5(2) *Queen Mary Journal of Intellectual Property*, pp. 110–131, p. 118.
36 Whitford Committee Report, para 1.
37 Gregory Committee Report, p. 1.
38 The Whitford Committee took oral evidence from 56 organisations and companies and 11 individuals.
39 Arnold R., The Need for a New Copyright Act: A Case Study in Law Reform, The Herchel Smith Intellectual Property Lecture (2014) 5(2) *Queen Mary Journal of Intellectual Property*, pp. 110–131, p. 118.
40 Whitford Committee Report, para 16.

The Whitford Committee Report submitted that no re-examination of the concepts of copyright can throw off the shackles of history,[41] recommending that the law simply be re-stated rather than reformed: "This is simply a restatement of the existing law and further support for the status quo is provided by the generally held view that the balance between the rights of the copyright owner on the one hand and the exceptions in favour of copyright users on the other is about right and that no abrupt change in the balance is called for."[42]

However, the Whitford Committee also considered specific technological developments such as the photocopier, audio and video recording and computer programs.[43] The copyright regulation was considered inadequate to cope with photocopying and recording machines.[44] The Report also acknowledged the desire to find a *modus vivendi* between, on the one hand, the legitimate copyright interests of authors and publishers to control or at least receive remuneration in respect of reproduction of their works and, on the other hand, the equally legitimate interest of those engaged in research and education who were mainly interested in the dissemination of information.[45]

The Whitford Committee Report was four years in the making and was presented to Parliament in March 1977. It was considered at the time to be the most thorough investigation of British copyright law and practice for over half a century;[46] however, whilst it was acclaimed to be a highly valuable contribution to the copyright debate, legislation did not follow for over a decade.[47]

Attempting to update copyright regulation

The anticipated early implementation of the recommendations made by the Whitford Committee Report did not occur.[48] The Government stated that whilst it was prepared to accept many of the recommendations, the Committee was not unanimous in its view on a number of important matters, and a further consultative document was issued in 1981.[49]

41 Leopold P. M, Reports of Committees: The Whitford Committee Report on Copyright and Designs Law (1977) 40(6) *The Modern Law Review*, pp. 685–705, p. 685.
42 *Ibid.*, p. 696.
43 Whitford Committee Report.
44 Leopold P. M, Reports of Committees; the Whitford Committee Report on Copyright and Designs Law (1977) 40(6) *Modern Law Review*, pp. 685–705, p. 696.
45 Whitford Committee Report, para 22.
46 Feather J., *Publishing, Piracy and Politics, An Historical Study of Copyright in Britain* (London: Mansell Publishing, 1994) p. 208.
47 Davis G., *Copyright and the Public Interest*, 2nd edition (London: Sweet & Maxwell, 2009) p. 43.
48 Merkin R., *Richards Butler on Copyright, Designs and Patents: The New Law* (London: Longman, 1989) p. 1.
49 Green Paper 1: Department of Trade and Industry, *Reform of the Law Relating to Copyright, Designs and Performers' Protection* (London: Her Majesty's Stationery Office, 1981) Cmnd 8302.

The subsequent Green Paper, titled *Reform of the Law Relating to Copyright, Designs and Performers' Protection*, invited further comment on proposals made for the revision of the law.[50] In particular, the Green Paper recognised that the Copyright Act 1956 needed to be updated in light of changing economic conditions, social requirements and technical developments. The Green Paper also made use of statistics provided by the British Phonographic Industry that supported the argument that private recording resulted in lost sales to the recording industry.[51]

Among other matters, the Government was debating the idea of introducing a levy system on audio, video or blank tape equipment, but stated that it had not received enough convincing evidence that the introduction of a levy would provide an acceptable solution. It welcomed further evidence but admitted a short-sighted view, stating that "at the end of the day it may have to be accepted that there is in fact no acceptable solution."[52]

Several hundred responses to the 1981 Green Paper were considered but there were still issues left unresolved and further consultation was required. As a result, a further Green Paper conducted in 1983 considered exceptional measures, and was published in 1985.[53] Although this Green Paper had limited effect on the law, it was noteworthy for the fact that it contradicted some of the first Green Paper's recommendations.[54] It had three primary concerns: to heighten awareness of the system inside and outside Government, to make the system more effective and accessible, and to ensure that the interests of British industry were fully reflected in international negotiations.[55] The second Green Paper contained a number of thoughts on the proper balance between, on the one hand, the protection of authorship and initiative, and on the other hand, the need to free industry from restrictions imposed by intellectual property rights.[56] The Government received about 1,000 comments and submissions in response to the 1985 Green Paper,[57] showing increased engagement and concern.

Taking on board the Whitford Committee Report, the responses to the 1981 Green Paper and the responses to the 1985 Green Paper; the Government finally produced the White Paper *Intellectual Property and Innovation* in 1986.[58] At this stage the Government conceded that there was no realistic alternative to a

50 *Ibid.*, para 1.

51 *Ibid.*, para 4.

52 *Ibid.*, para 23.

53 Second Green Paper: Department of Trade and Industry, *The Recording and Rental of Audio and Video Copyright Material* (London: Her Majesty's Stationery Office, 1985) Cmnd 9445 (hereafter the Second Green Paper).

54 Groves P., *Copyright and Designs Law: A Question of Balance* (London: Graham and Trotman Ltd, 1991) p. 3.

55 Second Green Paper.

56 Merkin R., *Richards Butler on Copyright, Designs and Patents: The New Law* (London: Longman, 1989) p. 2.

57 White Paper: Department of Trade and Industry, *Intellectual Property and Innovation* (London: Her Majesty's Stationery Office, 1986) Cmnd 9712, p. 35 – reporting on the statistics of the Second Green Paper.

58 *Ibid.*

compulsory levy on blank recording tape as a means of providing remuneration to copyright owners and performers.[59] In relation to reproduction by computers, the White Paper stated that the new law would be clear in providing that the rights given to copyright owners over reproduction extended to copying by fixing a work on any medium from which the work could principally be reproduced.[60]

The subsequent CDPA Bill was finally brought to the House of Commons in the spring of 1988 after a great deal of research and consultation between lawyers, civil servants, publishers, authors, librarians, broadcasters, designers, industrialists and many others who would be affected by it.[61]

Despite a plea from Sir Geoffrey Pattie MP to interest groups to refrain from trying to get too many amendments made to the Bill,[62] over 1,500 amendments were made.[63] The Bill also received detailed scrutiny from Parliament, and many changes were made.[64] The Bill was announced in the Queen's Speech on 25 June 1987. Exceptionally, the then Department of Trade and Industry was permitted to retain the services of Parliamentary Counsel on the Bill.[65] Furthermore, 46 draft clauses on copyright were circulated even at the late stage of July 1987.[66]

The numerous and competing interests of different stakeholder representatives continued to be reflected in the complex and lengthy Bill.[67] At the introduction of the second reading of the Bill, the Chancellor of the Duchy of Lancaster and Minister of Trade and Industry, Mr Kenneth Clarke acknowledged: "This Bill comes here from another place, is, as every hon. Member can see, lengthy and complex. It has 285 clauses and eight schedules."[68]

Nevertheless, the Government sought to produce policy that balanced these competing interests. As the Secretary of State for Trade and Industry, Lord Young demonstrated: "Those with ideas deserve a fair reward for their labours but they cannot expect to be completely sheltered from the real world. This would stifle

59 *Ibid.*, p. 38.

60 *Ibid.*, p. 50.

61 *Hansard*, Copyright, Designs and Patents Bill [HL], HL Deb 12 November 1987 Vol 489 Cols 1476–540, The Secretary of State for Trade and Industry, Lord Young of Graffham at 1476.

62 The then Minister for Information Technology, speaking at a seminar on the White Paper, organised by the Common Law Institute of Intellectual Property (CLIP) July 1986.

63 Groves P., *Copyright and Designs Law: A Question of Balance* (London: Graham and Trotman Ltd, 1991) p. 4.

64 Dworkin G. and Taylor R. D., *Blackstone's Guide to the Copyright, Designs and Patents Act 1988* (London: Blackstone Press Ltd, 1989).

65 Groves P., *Copyright and Designs Law: A Question of Balance* (London: Graham and Trotman Ltd, 1991) p. 3.

66 *Ibid.*, p. 3: Noting that the exercise could have been better timed as "many people were on holiday. The draft circulated on 31 July and comments were requested by 4 September."

67 *Hansard*, Legislative Drafting, HL Deb 11 November 1987 Vol 489 Cols 1417–1449, Lord Elwyn-Jones at 1437.

68 *Hansard*, Copyright, Designs and Patents Bill [Lords] HC Deb 28 April 1988 Vol 132 Cols 525–599, Order for Second Reading read, Mr Kenneth Clarke at 252.

rather than stimulate creativity. In drawing up the Bill we have sought to provide a fair return for creative talent and those who develop and use their work, while ensuring that ideas are not locked away but are accessible to society as a whole."[69] But the process of reaching such a consensus between the stakeholders was evidently challenging; as has been demonstrated by the long and complicated consultation process.

The drafting of the Bill was praised by representatives of some of the stakeholders who took part in the consultation process.[70] The Government claimed that the Bill restricted the law on a more logical and consistent basis and took into account the technological advances made in the 30 years since the last Act, and even strived to anticipate further developments.[71]

However, academic discourse acknowledged that the need to achieve agreement between stakeholders imposed constraints on the legislation. For example, Cornish described the debate as "a ferment of proposition and counter-proposition",[72] recognising the distortion effect of drafting legislation in this way. As Litman highlighted, the question of "is this a Bill that current stakeholders agree on?" is not the same as asking "is this a good Bill?"[73] Thus highlighting the challenges faced by the legislator and the drafters of the CDPA 1988 and offering insight into why the regulation later appeared as it did, which is discussed in more detail below.

Fifteen years later: the CDPA 1988

The CDPA 1988 eventually received Royal Assent on 15 November 1988 and came into force on 1 August 1989. As demonstrated, this was not a hastily-conceived measure, but perhaps no amount of consultation and deliberation could avoid the multiple difficulties in reforming copyright law.[74] In fact, it appeared that the more consultation that took place, the more irreconcilable viewpoints became apparent.[75] As a result of such negotiation, the law became very long and specific.[76]

Litman explained that one of the difficulties with developing copyright law is that stakeholders will not support changes that would leave them worse off: "no effected party is going to agree to support a bill that leaves it worse off than it is under current law."[77] Therefore, the outcome of new regulation, subject to the

69 *Hansard*, Copyright, Designs and Patents Bill [HL], HL Deb 12 November 1987 Vol 489 Cols 1476–540, The Secretary of State for Trade and Industry, Lord Young of Graffham at 1476.

70 *Hansard*, Legislative Drafting, HL Deb 11 November 1987 Vol 489 Cols 1417–1449, Lord Cameron of Lochbroom at 1442.

71 *Ibid.*

72 Cornish W. R., *Intellectual Property: Patents, Copyright, Trade Marks and Allied Rights* (London: Sweet & Maxwell, 1999) para 9–17.

73 Litman J., *Digital Copyright* (New York: Prometheus Books, 2006) p. 63.

74 Groves P., *Copyright and Designs Law: A Question of Balance* (London: Graham and Trotman Ltd, 1991) p. 3.

75 *Ibid.*, p. 3–4.

76 Litman J., *Digital Copyright* (New York: Prometheus Books, 2006) p. 25.

77 *Ibid.*, p. 23.

debates of current stakeholders, would likely fall in their favour, or at least retain their current position. Laddie argued that some of the drafting of the new law was clearly advantageous towards the copyright owner.[78] He determined that an examination of the parliamentary debates showed areas of drafting specifically intended as a form of *quid pro quo* to copyright owners who were unhappy at the amendment of other areas.[79]

Lord Preston was also of the view that the consultation process, the debate and, consequently, the law were heavily represented by the copyright owners and, in contrast, hardly a word was said on the consumers' side:[80] "I find that lack of balance less than satisfying."[81]

Groves, on the other hand, suggested that the CDPA 1988 appeared to have moved away from exclusivity and towards a right to remuneration for the use of one's work.[82] Others praised the new law, for example Feather named it "the great consolidated law which some have been seeking for over a century."[83]

However, doubts on its meaning arose quickly.[84] One reason for such doubt was that, on recommendation of the Whitford Committee, many of the provisions in the CDPA 1988 were simply a re-statement of the previous law, but using different words.[85] A key aim of the law reform was to simplify the law and therefore it was not actually updated. In fact, section 172(2) of the CDPA 1988 stated, in setting out how the Act should be interpreted, that: "A provision of this Part which corresponds to a provision of the previous law shall not be construed as departing from the previous law merely because of a change of expression."[86] Lord Lloyd of Kilgerran recognised the illogicality in a new law that should be read in line with its predecessor; pointing out that this was "one of the most curious clauses that any Bill could possible contain … The previous law is to apply although we have changed the words of the Act. That sounds very curious from a

78 Laddie J., Copyright: Over-Strength, Over-Regulated, Over-Rated? (1996) 18(5) *European Intellectual Property Review*, pp. 253–260, p. 256: For example, it is was made easier to qualify for damages and it is clear that they are designed to give the copyright owner financial relief over and above what is necessary merely to compensate for damage done.

79 *Ibid.*, p. 256.

80 He stated: "I am an author. However, I assure your Lordships that I should starve if I had to live on the royalties which I have earned from my writing." *Hansard*, Copyright, Designs and Patents Bill [HL], HL Deb 12 November 1987 Vol 489 Cols 1476–540, Lord Preston at 1525.

81 *Hansard*, Copyright, Designs and Patents Bill [HL], HL Deb 12 November 1987 Vol 489 Cols 1476–540, Lord Preston at 1525.

82 Groves P., *Copyright and Designs Law: A Question of Balance* (London: Graham and Trotman Ltd, 1991) p. 8.

83 Feather J., *Publishing, Piracy and Politics, An Historical Study of Copyright in Britain* (London: Mansell Publishing, 1994) p. 209.

84 Lester D. and Mitchell P., *Joynson-Hicks on UK Copyright Law* (London: Sweet & Maxwell, 1989).

85 Groves P., *Copyright and Designs Law: A Question of Balance* (London: Graham and Trotman Ltd, 1991) p. 4.

86 CDPA 1988, section 172(2).

lawyer's point of view."[87] Lord Lloyd also noted that much of the law had been recited as it was in the 1911 and 1956 Copyright Acts, leading it to be named the "Humpty Dumpty Bill".[88]

Some acknowledged the CDPA 1988 as an improvement on the 1956 law[89] in terms of logic and clarity.[90] However, others disagreed, recognising the ambiguity in certain terms, for example: "With a word like reasonable in a statute, lawyers can make fortunes. They can argue about it for days. They may not be able to make so much out of 'substantial'. They can still make a great deal."[91]

So far this chapter has considered: firstly, the contextual basis for the development of the CDPA 1988; and, secondly, the legislative process by which the law was reformed. It has been shown that the reform of the law which led to the enactment of the CDPA 1988 was no hasty measure;[92] the consultation process was extremely long and far more thorough than had previously been undertaken.[93] The Whitford Committee considered competing stakeholder interests in light of the development of new technologies such as the photocopier, and attempted to make recommendations that held these factors into account.[94] However, the result of this was that the law became very long and complex.[95] Furthermore, a key aim was to simplify the law and this led to much of the new legislation being a re-statement of the old legislation,[96] leaving copyright law in the 21st century dating back to 1956.

The subsequent sections look closely at the wording of the restricted acts set out section 17 of the CDPA 1988. This is done by taking each subsection in turn to consider the way in which it was drafted, what it means in light of the development of online technology, and whether an internal or an external perspective was taken.

87 *Hansard*, Copyright, Designs and Patents Bill [HL], HL Deb 30 November 1987 Vol 490 Cols 813–874, Lord Lloyd of Kilgerran at 816.

88 *Ibid.*, 816: Lord Lloyd noting the name in a recent *Financial Times* publication.

89 Arnold R., The Need for a New Copyright Act: A Case Study in Law Reform, The Herchel Smith Intellectual Property Lecture (2014) 5(2) *Queen Mary Journal of Intellectual Property*, pp. 110–131.

90 Davis G., *Copyright and the Public Interest*, 2nd edition (London: Sweet & Maxwell, 2009) p. 49.

91 *Hansard*, Copyright, Designs and Patents Bill [HL], HL Deb 3 December 1987 Vol 490 Cols 1149–1227, Viscount Massereene and Ferrard at 1196.

92 Groves P., *Copyright and Designs Law: A Question of Balance* (London: Graham and Trotman Ltd, 1991) p. 3.

93 Whitford Committee Report, para 1.

94 *Ibid.*

95 Merkin R., *Richards Butler on Copyright, Designs and Patents: The New Law* (London: Longman, 1989) pp. 1–2; Litman J., *Digital Copyright* (New York: Prometheus Books, 2006) p. 25.

96 Groves P., *Copyright and Designs Law: A Question of Balance* (London: Graham and Trotman Ltd, 1991) p. 4.

The reproduction right

This part of the chapter now applies the second phase of the Framework by focusing specifically on section 17 of the CDPA 1988. The language of the law is analysed in detail in order to determine the meaning and purpose of the law through a holistic understanding, in light of the analysis above, before considering if it is drafted from either an internal or an external perspective.

The restricted act of copying is arguably the most fundamental in copyright legislation. As Mr Clarke stated in the second reading of the copyright Bill: "the rights which the copyright owner is to enjoy, of which the most fundamental is contained in clause 17: the right to prevent copying."[97] Furthermore, Drassinower argued that "copyright law is not a prohibition on copying but rather an institutionalized distinction between lawful and wrongful copying."[98]

Section 17 of the CDPA 1988 specifies that it is an infringement to reproduce a copyright work in any material form, including storing the work in any medium by electronic means.[99] The specific language of legislation that is so closely tied to technology is evidently crucial.[100] However, terms are often used interchangeably, for example the CDPA 1988 refers to section 17 as the creator's "exclusive right to copy."[101] As a general controversy, the term "copying" has been criticised on the basis that it combines and confuses two separate concepts: the mental act of derivation and the act of making a copy.[102]

However, the CDPA 1988 refers to a "reproduction right" in relation to the performer's right,[103] following amendment by the Copyright and Related Rights Regulations 1996 (SI 1996/2967). The Information Society Directive[104] also used the term

97 *Hansard*, Copyright, Designs and Patents Bill [Lords] HC Deb 28 April 1988 Vol 132 Cols 525–599, Order for Second Reading read, Mr Kenneth Clarke at 256–257.

98 Drassinower A., *What's Wrong With Copying?* (Cambridge, MA: Harvard University Press, 2015) p. 2.

99 CDPA 1988, section 17, implementing Article 2(1) of the copyright and related rights in the Information Society Directive.

100 Reinbothe J., Martin-Prat M. and Lewinski S., The New WIPO Treaties: A First Resume (1977) *European Intellectual Property Review*, pp. 171–184, p. 172: "Questions such as these taxed the collective mind of the Diplomatic Conference which concluded the World Intellectual Property Organisation Copyright Treaty in 1996; unable to agree on treaty language to cope with electronic copying, they resorted to a mere statement that the right to restrict copying applies in the digital environment."

101 Groves P., *Copyright and Designs Law: A Question of Balance* (London: Graham and Trotman Ltd, 1991) p. 55.

102 Vitoria M., et al (eds), *Laddie, Prescott and Vitoria: The Modern Law of Copyright and Designs*, 4th edition (London: Butterworths Law, 2011) (hereafter *Laddie, Prescott and Vitoria*) 14.1.

103 CDPA 1988, Chapter 2, sections 182(3), 190(1), 190(2), 190(6), 205B(b). Defined in the Copyright and Related Rights Regulations 1996 (SI 1996/2967), regulation 20(2)(3) as: "The right of a performer under this section to authorise or prohibit the making of such copies is referred to in this Part as reproduction right."

104 The Information Society Directive is based on principles and rules already laid down in the Directives currently in force in this area – in particular, Directives 91/250/EEC, 92/100/EEC, 93/83/EEC, 93/98/EEC and 96/9/EC – and aimed to

"reproduction right" and defined it as "the exclusive right to authorise or prohibit direct or indirect, temporary or permanent reproduction by any means and in any form, in whole or in part"[105] of the work. Nevertheless, section 17(2) defined the meaning of copying as "reproducing the work in any material form".[106]

Section 17 of the CDPA 1988 has six subsections. The first subsection is section 17(1) which stated that: "The copying of the work is an act restricted by the copyright in every description of copyright work; and references in this Part to copying and copies shall be construed as follows."[107]

The opening paragraph to the section sets the scene of restricted act of copying; as is to protect the copyright owner.[108] During the consultation process the words "and copies" were added to replace the words "in that context",[109] presumably to be more specific although there is no explanation provided.

At this stage there appears to be no indication of either an internal or an external perspective, although terms such as "very description of the work" suggest an attitude of broad and encompassing rights.[110] Subsections 2–6 are considered below.

Reproducing in any medium by electronic means

Section 17(2) of the CDPA 1988 stated that it is an infringement to reproduce a work: "Copying in relation to a literary, dramatic, musical or artistic work means reproducing the work in any material form. This includes storing the work in any medium by electronic means."

The words "this includes storing the work in any medium by electronic means" are prevailing, and controversially, were added into the CDPA 1988 at the very late stages of the consultation.[111] To dive deeper into the meaning, this analysis will first consider the meaning of storage, and then electronic means.

To uncover the meaning of storing a work it is necessary to first consider its conception. This subsection reflected the provisions that were set out in the Copyright (Computer Software) Amendment Act 1985. The clause to restrict the

develop those principles and rules and place them in the context of the information society. It aimed to further implement the WIPO Copyright Treaty and the WIPO Performances and Phonograms Treaty, which the EU became party to in 1996.

105 The Information Society Directive, Article 2

106 CDPA 1988, section 17(2).

107 CDPA 1988, section 17(1).

108 *Hansard*, Copyright, Designs and Patents Bill [Lords] HC Deb 28 April 1988 Vol 132 Cols 525–599, Order for Second Reading read, Mr Kenneth Clarke at 256–257 stated that this section was "for the copyright owner."

109 *Hansard*, Copyright, Designs and Patents Bill [HL], HL Deb 29 March 1988 Vol 495 Cols 607–696, Lord Mottistone at 618: "Clause 17 [Infringement of copyright by copying]: §Lord Beaverbrook moved Amendment No. 8: Page 8, line 24, leave out ('in that context') and insert ('and copies')."

110 *Laddie, Prescott and Vitoria*, 14.13.

111 *Hansard*, Infringement of Copyright by Copying, HC Deb 25 July 1988 Vol 138, Col 129, Mr Butcher at 129: "Amendment made: No. 38, in page 8, line 41, at end insert 'This includes storing the work in any medium by electronic means.'"

storing of a work was supported by Lord Coville, who admitted to having limited computer knowledge.[112] He gave an example of the circumstances for which the clause was designed: "If you switch off the machine at any time the electronic memory is erased and you have nothing left. The matter may not be complete at the time when such a disaster occurs ... It is not written down, it is not recorded anywhere else, it is not palpable in any shape or form ... Thus, in the amendment we are referring to the storage of the work in the electronic memory of the computer so that when you put in something which you consider constitutes a work which deserves to be protected by copyright the Bill will, in fact, protect it; that is, the creation of the work."[113] He stated that his intention was to make sure that where a work had "not yet been written down it is still protected."[114] This statement appears to suggest that the requirement for copyright to subsist in a literary, dramatic or musical work being recorded or written down[115] would be met by the storage of a work. Protection had not previously extended this far before the introduction of section 17(2).[116]

Lord McIntosh accepted the suggestion on behalf of the Whitford Committee, who applauded Lord Coville's expertise and also admitted to having "no particular knowledge of copyright law."[117] Lord McIntosh did suggest that the concept of storage on a computer should only be relevant when it related to "the concept of access to that work and the use of that work."[118] Meaning that storage of a work on a computer would only invoke copyright when that work is accessed or used, not simply by the fact that it is stored.

Subsequently, Lord Brabazon supported the amendment on behalf of the Government.[119] He affirmed that the main motivation for the clause was to protect a new copyright work created and stored on a computer "it will also apply, for example, to a novel or to any other sort of work being written directly into computer storage. In so far as there is any doubt now that such a work is 'fixed in material form', and therefore qualifies for copyright protection at the instant of its creation within the machine, the amendment will remove that doubt."[120]

Curiously, the clause was originally neglected from the CDPA Bill. However, the Government was held to account on maintaining the policy that storing a

112 *Hansard*, Copyright (Computer Software) Amendment Bill, HL Deb 5 June 1985 Vol 464 Cols 823–829, Viscount Colville of Culross at 824.

113 *Ibid.*, Viscount Colville at 824.

114 *Ibid.*, Viscount Colville at 828.

115 CDPA 1988, section 3(2).

116 For example, in the US case of *Data Cash Systems Inc v JS and A Group*, 480 F Supp 1063 (ND) III (1979), it was held that as information stored on a chip could not be seen or read by a person, it could not be protected under copyright. Additionally, in the Australian case of *Apple Computer Inc v Computer Edge Pty Ltd* [1984] FSR 487, the court stated that adaptations of literary works must be capable of being seen or heard.

117 *Hansard*, Copyright (Computer Software) Amendment Bill, HL Deb 5 June 1985 Vol 464 Cols 823–829, Lord McIntosh at 825.

118 *Ibid.*, Lord McIntosh at 825.

119 *Ibid.*, Lord Brabazon at 826.

120 *Ibid.*, Lord Brabazon at 826.

work in a computer was a form of reproduction which required the copyright owner's consent:[121] "We have the excellent Copyright (Computer Software) Amendment Act 1985. One of the provisions in that Act was important. It made it clear that storing a work in a computer is a form of reproduction which requires the copyright owner's consent. The Bill does not make that clear. I feel confident that the Government intend to uphold the promise that was made on that in the other place and that we shall see an amendment to clause 17(2) to that effect."[122]

Turning now to "electronic", this term is defined in section 178 of the CDPA 1988 as meaning "actuated by electric, magnetic, electromagnetic, electro-chemical, or electro-mechanical energy."[123] Moreover, "in electronic form" means in a form usable only by electronic means.[124]

Laddie, Prescott and Vitoria stated that the term "electronic" is defined widely in its legal interpretation.[125] "Electronic" is defined in the *Oxford English Dictionary* as "(of a device) having or operating with components such as microchips and transistors that control and direct electric currents: such as an electronic calculator, an electronic organ."[126] This is a very broad definition. The examples do not include a computer.

In relation to either the internal or the external perspective, it would appear that this subsection references hardware and the technical function of an electronic device, and therefore suggests an external perspective. This is confirmed by the understanding that the intention of the subsection was to include storing copyright protected material on a computer. However, the use of the term "storage" in this context is a metaphorical understanding of how a computer works, which suggests an internal perspective. Therefore, it is necessary to analyse the case law that applies section 17(2) in order to determine how the judges interpret and apply this regulation online.

In summary, it can be seen that this subsection of the CDPA 1988 was introduced without foresight or particular expertise in the understanding of computer function or technological development. Furthermore, the intended purpose of the subsection is not relevant to modern technology, and the circumstance may never have arisen. The case law relating to storing copyright works will be considered in Chapter 4, in order to determine whether judges apply this subsection with either an internal or an external perspective.

121 *Hansard*, Copyright, Designs and Patents Bill [Lords] HC Deb 28 April 1988 Vol 132 Cols 525–599, Order for Second Reading read, Miss Emma Nicholson (Torridge and Devon, West) at 578.

122 *Ibid.*

123 CDPA 1988, section 178.

124 These provisions are re-enactments of Copyright Act 1956, sections 2(5) and 3(5) as amended by the Copyright (Computer Software) Amendments Act 1985 and, as regards to reproducing in any material form, section 49(4).

125 *Laddie, Prescott and Vitoria*, 14.10.

126 *Oxford English Dictionary* (Oxford: Oxford University Press, 2010).

Making a three-dimensional copying

Section 17(3) of the CDPA 1988 states that it is an infringement to make a copy in a different dimension: "In relation to an artistic work copying includes the making of a copy in three dimensions of a two-dimensional work and the making of a copy in two dimensions of a three-dimensional work."

This section appears to be a codification of the law as determined in the case of *Bradbury, Agnew and Co v Day.* [127] In this case a play was performed using characters from a cartoon, which was deemed to be indirect copying of the original two-dimensional drawing.[128] This meant that the manner in which an artistic work can be copied depends primarily on form[129] and became statutory with the introduction of section 17(3) of the CDPA 1988.

The wording of this subsection has unusual implications in context of current technological developments. The terminology used in this section, taken at face value, read as a product of its time: it is intended to restrict adaptions, for example from a book to a play. However, read today it may well encompass activity such as printing a 3D model from a 3D CAD file.[130]

The application of the internal and external frameworks to this section, therefore, is not straightforward as the subsection was drafted with a specific analogue scenario in mind. Theoretically, applying this section online[131] could suggest that transforming an eBook into a computer game would be of parallel circumstance. From an external perspective, what dimension is copyright material online? Technically, the computer screen is displaying pixels, regardless of the type of material and therefore this might be considered two dimensional.

Categorising types of copyright works, from an external perspective, leads to the consideration of what type of copyright work is a digital file? Historically, in the UK, copyright law is organised into a list of different media:[132] written texts are literary works; still images are artistic works; moving images are films or broadcasting, and so on. However, from an external perspective, in multi-media, all of these different items are bundled together into a single product[133] or online file. On the other hand, from an internal perspective, a computer file

127 *Bradbury, Agnew and Co v Day* (1916) 32 TLR 349.

128 *Ibid.*

129 Merkin R., *Richards Butler on Copyright, Designs and Patents: The New Law* (London: Longman, 1989) p. 150.

130 CAD stands for Computer Aided Design: an image file format used to create 2D and 3D designs. CAD files hold information for these images, as well as drafting information.

131 WIPO Copyright Treaty 1996 (adopted in Geneva on 20 December 1996), agreed statements concerning Article 1(4): "The reproduction right, as set out in Article 9 of the Berne Convention, and the exceptions permitted thereunder, fully apply in the digital environment, in particular to the use of works in digital form."

132 As a strategy to bring clarity to the law, discussed above.

133 Oppenheim C., Copyright in the Electronic Age in Parrinder P. and Chernaik W., *Textual Monopolies: Literary Copyright and the Public Domain* (London: Office for Humanities Communication, 1997) p. 105.

would be considered as a piece of music, an image, or a film experienced online.[134]

Nevertheless, due to the technological specific nature of this subsection it has become irrelevant in the face of technological developments. Whilst the analysis of this subsection has contemplated how it might be applied to online circumstances, and considered the implications of the internal and external perspectives, it is ultimately not relevant in the context of this research to continue investigation. Therefore, this section will be excluded from the case law analysis undertaken in Chapter 4.

Broadcasting

Under section 17(5) of the CDPA 1988 it is deemed an infringement of copyright to broadcast a work without permission: "Copying in relation to a film or broadcast[135] includes making a photograph of the whole or any substantial part of any image forming part of the film or broadcast."

This section is another example of law that was carried forward from the Copyright Act 1956. The intended mischief that this section sought to remedy, was explained in the case of *Spelling Goldberg* [136] where the court held that taking a "still" from a film and publishing it in the form of a photograph was an infringement of the copyright in the film.[137]

When considering the application of this section to the current technology, such as the ability of a device to take screen-capture and screen-recording[138] as a modern parallel, would this be considered making a photograph? The exhibition of original works is not restricted by copyright,[139] which might suggest that the right to control digital reproduction should not enable the copyright owner to control the display of works on a computer monitor or a screen. However, a screenshot technically creates a copy of the work, which could therefore constitute an infringement.

134 Kerr O. S., The Problem of Perspective in Internet Law (2003) 91 *Georgetown Law Journal*, pp. 357–405, p. 379.

135 The definition of "broadcast" was later amended by Copyright and Related Rights Regulations 2003 (SI 2003/2498) regulations 2(1), 5(5), Sch 1 para 3(1)(a) (with regulations 31–40), resulting from Directive 93/98/EEC: "Section 3: Amendments to the definition of 'broadcast' section 17(4); for the words 'broadcast or cable programme' there shall be substituted 'or broadcast'."

136 *Spelling Goldberg v BPC Publishing* [1981] FSR 280.

137 *Ibid.*

138 Screen-capture or screenshot is image capturing by way of a digital photograph taken of the interface that the screen of the device is currently displaying, a common feature on smartphones, tablets or through the print screen option on a computer. Screen recording is a feature enabled on an iPhone device that allows the user to record the visuals appearing on the screen.

139 *Bookmaker's Afternoon Greyhound Services v Wilf Gilbert (Staffordshire) Ltd* [1994] FSR 723.

Minister for the Department of Culture, Media and Sport, Edward Vaizey, stated in March 2016 that taking a screenshot of an image on the social media app Snapchat would constitute infringement of copyright, even though Snapchat videos are only available for 24 hours: "Under UK copyright law, it would be unlawful for a Snapchat user to copy an image and make it available to the public without the consent of the image owner. The image owner would be able to sue anyone who does this for copyright infringement. Snapchat photos are automatically deleted after 10 seconds. The Snapchat Privacy Policy states that if Snapchat is able to detect that a recipient has taken a screenshot of an image, they will try to inform the original poster. However, Snapchat advises users to avoid sending messages which they would not want to be saved or shared."[140] Facebook and Instagram also include a "story" feature, which enables users to post a video that is available for other users to see for 24 hours. Unlike, Snapchat, Instagram stories are archived and can be featured on a user's profile. Instagram includes a number of in-app controls, such as not allowing videos that contain added music to be downloaded to the user's phone and a content ID system that restricts the upload of certain copyright content.[141]

This question was raised *inter alia* in the US matter of *Hoge v Schmalfeldt* (2014).[142] Blogger Mr Hoge sought an injunction against the defendant for sharing his work on social media platforms, including the use of image capturing.[143] The injunction was not granted. However, Tan argued that this could have been a policy decision to shield social media sites and services providers "given that the screenshot capturing function is made available by the operating systems of digital devices, users are inclined to take such functionalities for granted. If the specific injunction Mr Hoge sought was granted, it would have grave implications on how we may be compelled to turn away from the conveniences technological advancements have afforded us, and such counter-intuitive directives cannot be reasonable."[144]

In *England and Wales Cricket Board* a mobile phone app which used screen capture technology to record and share eight-second clips of sports events was considered to be copyright infringement.[145] This case demonstrates that, firstly,

140 Social Media: Photographs: Written question – 12484, asked by Jim Shannon (Strangford), 19 October 2015, answered by Rt Hon Edward Vaizey MP (Department for Culture, Media and Sport), 24 March 2016, https://www.parliament.uk/business/publications/written-questions-answers-statements/written-question/Commons/2015-10-19/12484/

141 For discussion on copyright and social media, see Bosher H. and Yesiloglu S., An Analysis of the Fundamental Tensions Between Copyright and Social Media: The Legal Implications of Sharing Images on Instagram (2018) 33(2) *International Review of Law, Computers & Technology*, pp. 164–186.

142 *Hoge v Schmalfeldt*, Civil Action No ELH-14–1683 (US District Court for the District of Maryland, July 1, 2014).

143 *Ibid.*, p. 4.

144 Tan C. H. Y., Technological "Nudges" and Copyright on Social Media Sites (2015) 1 *Intellectual Property Quarterly*, pp. 62–78, p. 76.

145 *England and Wales Cricket Board Ltd and Anor v Tixdaq Ltd and Anor* [2016] EWHC 575 (Ch) as per Arnold J at [29].

due to taking the external perspective and focusing specifically on the technology, Justice Arnold was forced to address each version of the app. He considered, in particular, versions 8.2, 8.3, 8.3.2 and 8.4, and versions 8.5 to 8.5.4.[146] This demonstrates one of the drawbacks of taking a purely external approach which focuses too closely on the specific nature of the technology. The result of this was that many cases had similar circumstances, which differed only slightly on a technicality.

Secondly, Justice Arnold considered that films and broadcasts were signal rights and not content rights.[147] He explained in an previous article that we need to distinguish between these two types of rights: "Thus we need to distinguish between a literary work (content) and the paper it is printed on (signal) between a musical work (content) and the sound recording which embodies it (signal); between an audio-visual work (content) and the celluloid which fixes it (signal); and between a dramatic work (content) and the broadcast which diffuses it (signal)."[148] Arnold suggested that, indeed, recognising these different types of rights in films and broadcasts could bring clarity to the system: "The solution … is to have a content right for any audiovisual work captured or capable of being captured in a film, and a signal right for the film itself as at present. It is suggested that this would not only be Berne-compliant, but also rather more clearly so than the current system."[149]

Sky successfully argued that the broadcast of its work had been infringed.[150] Crystal and Charalambous argued that this was "a significant victory for rights holders"[151] as it clarified that key moments of sporting events constituted a substantial part of the broadcast.[152]

In relation to the internal and external perspectives: again, this appears to be a clause focusing on a specific circumstance that does not directly relate to the use of the internet. As a result, the internal and external perspectives cannot be applied. This demonstrates the outdated nature of the law in the face of internet technologies as a result of attempting to carry regulation from 1956.

Facsimile copy

Under section 17(5) of the CDPA 1988 it is an infringement of copyright to copy a work by facsimile: "Copying in relation to the typographical arrangement of a published edition means making a facsimile copy of the arrangement."

146 *Ibid.*, Arnold J at [130]–[166].
147 *Ibid.*, Arnold J at [58].
148 Arnold R., Content Copyrights and Signal Copyrights: The Case for a Rational Scheme of Protection (2011) 1(3) *Queen Mary Journal of Intellectual Property*, pp. 272–279, p. 272.
149 *Ibid.*, p. 276.
150 *England and Wales Cricket Board Ltd and Anor v Tixdaq Ltd and Anor* [2016] EWHC 575 (Ch) as per Arnold J.
151 Crystal A. and Charalambous J., Copyright test Match – High Court Provides Guidance on Substantiality and Fair Dealing in Relation to Sports Clips (2016) *Entertainment Law Review*, pp. 214–217, p. 217.
152 *Ibid.*, p. 217.

Again, this section is a re-statement of the Copyright Act 1956, and in doing so repeats the specific and confined clause. *Laddie, Prescott and Vitoria* suggested that "presumably in these days of computer typesetting one might make a 'facsimile' by some sort of scanning process, such as a pdf file."[153] Their use of the word "presumably" demonstrates that the pace of technological development renders the law uncertain.

Thus, this is another example of a technologically obsolete and specific clause that would be difficult to apply to the digital landscape.

Incidental and transient copying

Section 17(6) of the CDPA 1988 states that incidental and transient copying as an infringement of copyright: "Copying in relation to any description of work includes the making of copies which are transient or are incidental to some other use of the work."

The mischief this subsection aimed to remedy was the act of loading or storing a computer program onto a computer as an act of copying. In particular, Lord Mattistone explained that the desired effect was that "incidental copying in the course of running a computer program, or viewing a work stored in a computer database, was no longer excluded from the restricted act of copying."[154]

The copying of a work through incidental storage on a computer was included in the Copyright Act 1956 when it was amended in 1985, but this was not brought forward in the original CDPA Bill.[155] At the time of the Bill, clause 17(6) originally stated that "storing a work in a computer does not amount to copying the work where done only incidentally in the course of viewing the work, or in the case of a computer program, running the program."[156] However, the Lords Committee argued that the excision of incidental storage in the course of viewing a work or, in the case of a computer programme, running it, as was proposed in the then clause 17(7) of the Bill, would undermine the basis of licensing in the software field.[157] Moreover, Lord Mottistone argued that "the information stored belongs to its originator in the same way that the text of a book belongs to its author. The author obtains royalties on the sale of his book. The originator of a database could reasonably expect the same … However, Clause 17(7) appears to have the opposite effect because it says that viewing a work stored in a computer is not

153 *Laddie, Prescott and Vitoria*, 14.22.
154 *Hansard*, Copyright, Designs and Patents Bill [HL], HL Deb 29 March 1988 Vol 495 Cols 607–696, Lord Mattistone at 647.
155 *Hansard*, Copyright, Designs and Patents Bill [HL], HL Deb 12 November 1987 Vol 489 Cols 1476–540, Lord Mottistone at 1501.
156 Groves P., *Copyright and Designs Law: A Question of Balance* (London: Graham and Trotman Ltd, 1991) p. 56.
157 *Ibid.*, p. 55, referring to *Hansard*, Copyright, Designs and Patents Bill [HL], HL Deb 3 December 1987 Vol 490 Cols 1149–1227, Lord Mottistone at 1177.

infringing copyright."[158] Thereafter, the clause was amended to appear as it does now that incidental and transient copying is an infringement of copyright.[159]

Originally, the Government's amendment within the Standing Committee which inserted this provision originally used the word "ephemeral" instead of "transient". Emma Nicholson MP explained that this word came from the Greek ephemeros, meaning lasting for one day. In addition, ephemera are mayfly and ephemomorph is a general term for the lowest forms of life. Applied to the software industry, the expression was ambiguous, and Nicholson, instead, suggested transient, from the past participle of the Latin verb *transire*, meaning to be passed over, not durable or not permanent. The Government agreed, and the word "transient" was used.[160]

This highlights the significance of word choice in legislation. On consideration, using the word "transient" to encapsulate the activity of "storing" on a computer appears to be an oxymoron. Whilst transient implies not durable or permanent, storage juxtaposes this as a term that implies some degree of permanency. As Merkin argued "it is difficult to see how storage could have been merely incidental to running and viewing the program."[161] Therefore, the term may actually be considered contradictory to its intended meaning.

The Information Society Directive, on the other hand, used the phrase "temporary or permanent reproduction"[162] instead of "transient or are incidental."[163] The implications of the Information Society Directive was that the CDPA 1988 must be interpreted in light of Article 2; which specifically referred to "temporary … reproduction by any means and in any form."[164] It could be argued that the Information Society Directive used more accurate language. *Laddie, Prescott and Vitoria* argued that these terms mean the same thing.[165]

Overall, section 17(6) exemplifies the legislators struggle with technologically specific language. In choosing this route, this section clearly displays an external perspective, *prima facia*, due to the use of technical terminology.

However, on closer inspection, the section also demonstrates the human condition in cognitively processing new technologies in light of past knowledge. For example "storage" is a term that already has a meaning in the analogue world and is being directly applied to the digital environment. The difficulty is that this metaphor does not transpose smoothly to new technology. The term "storage"

158 *Hansard*, Copyright, Designs and Patents Bill [HL], HL Deb 12 November 1987 Vol 489 Cols 1476–540, Lord Mottistone at 1501.

159 CDPA 1988, section 17(6).

160 Groves P., *Copyright and Designs Law: A Question of Balance* (London: Graham and Trotman Ltd, 1991) p. 55.

161 Merkin R., *Richards Butler on Copyright, Designs and Patents: The New Law* (London: Longman, 1989) p. 196.

162 The Information Society Directive, Recital 33.

163 CDPA 1988, section 17(6).

164 The Information Society Directive, Article 2.

165 *Laddie, Prescott and Vitoria*, 14.10.

brings with it connotations of long-term putting away, whereas in this section the law is including temporary storage, which may last only a matter of minutes.[166] Perhaps a more accurate wording would be "temporary existence".

Therefore, in order to further determine the meaning of this section and the perspective taken when it is applied online, the relevant case law will be considered in Chapter 4.

Conclusion

This chapter first considered the historical development of the CDPA 1988. This analysis uncovered the challenges faced when drafting copyright law, particularly due to the need to meet different stakeholder interests and to keep up with technological developments. The analysis of the consultation all the way through to the final 1988 Act demonstrated that the intention of the Government was to address specific technological developments. In particular, the copyright owners appeared to have the loudest voice during the debate, which can be seen throughout the consultation process.

The chapter demonstrated that the CDPA 1988 was a very long time coming[167] after a lengthy consultation process stretching back some fifteen years.[168] As Lord Willis exclaimed: "I feel rather like somebody who has been standing at a railway station on a cold winter morning for a very long time and when the train eventually arrives I do not care whether it has a buffet car or first class accommodation as long as it is there."[169] The concern is that the desire to complete the task and appease the strongest lobbyists might supersede the vigilance required to create a fair and a balanced copyright law.

However, it could be argued that the delays were not entirely without value, as this allowed for a great deal of debate,[170] but due to the nature of the law, the political and practical difficulties took their toll.[171]

The second part of the chapter specifically considered section 17 of the CDPA 1988. This analysis looked closely at the wording of the legislation and highlighted ambiguities and inconsistencies within the law. It was demonstrated that the original intention of the law did not always easily apply to the development of new technologies and behaviours in the modern landscape. Section 17 has been

166 Gralla P., *How the Internet Works* (Indiana: Que Corporation, 1999).

167 Merkin R., *Richards Butler on Copyright, Designs and Patents: The New Law* (London: Longman, 1989) p. 1.

168 *Ibid.*, p. 2.

169 *Hansard*, Copyright, Designs and Patents Bill [HL], HL Deb 12 November 1987 Vol 489 Cols 1476–540, Lord Willis at 1494.

170 See speech by Tony Blair at the Report Stage: *Hansard*, HC Deb 25 July 1988 Vol 138, Cols 37–73: https://api.parliament.uk/historic-hansard/commons/1988/jul/25/design-right#column_37.

171 *Hansard*, Legislative Drafting, HL Deb 11 November 1987 Vol 489 Cols 1417–1449, Lord Cameron of Lochbroom at 1442.

criticised for being poorly drafted as a result of the temptation to over-regulate, creating unintended consequences in how far the law can reach[172]

In view of this analysis, it was shown that whilst the external perspective may have been the intention to address the specific technology, internal perspectives were also found in understanding how that technology worked.

In order to develop the understanding of the internal and external perspectives within the meaning of section 17 of the CDPA 1988, Chapter 4 will consider in more detail the case law that interprets sections 17(2) and 17(6), particularly in cases of online activity.

As Lord Atkin stated: "When these ghosts of the past stand in the path of justice clanking their mediaeval chains, the proper course is for the judge to pass through them undeterred."[173] It has been argued that in relation to copyright, not only do the mediaeval chains remain, but they have also been reinforced with late 20th-century steel.[174]

Bibliography

Books

Cornish W. R., *Intellectual Property: Patents, Copyright, Trade Marks and Allied Rights* (London: Sweet & Maxwell, 1999).

Cucchi C., Vague Expressions in the European Parliament: A Marker of Cultural Identity? in Garzone G. and Archibald J., *Discourse, Identities and Roles in Specialized Communication* (Switzerland: Peter Lang, 2010).

Dale W., *Legislative Drafting: A New Approach a Comparative Study of Methods in France, Germany, Sweden and the United Kingdom* (London: Butterworths, 1977).

Davis G., *Copyright and the Public Interest*, 2nd edition (London: Sweet & Maxwell, 2002).

Drassinower A., *What's Wrong With Copying?* (Cambridge, MA: Harvard University Press, 2015).

Dworkin G. and Taylor R. D., *Blackstone's Guide to the Copyright, Designs and Patents Act 1988* (London: Blackstone Press Ltd, 1989).

Feather J., *Publishing, Piracy and Politics, An Historical Study of Copyright in Britain* (London: Mansell Publishing, 1994).

Gralla P., *How the Internet Works* (Indiana: Que Corporation, 1999).

Groves P., *Copyright and Designs Law: A Question of Balance* (London: Graham and Trotman Ltd, 1991).

Lester D. and Mitchell P., *Joynson-Hicks on UK Copyright Law* (London: Sweet & Maxwell, 1989).

Litman J., *Digital Copyright*, 2nd edition (New York: Prometheus Books, 2006).

172 Tappin M., et al (eds), *Laddie, Prescott and Vitoria: The Modern Law of Copyright*, 5th edition (London: Lexis Nexis, 2018) pp. 770–771.

173 *Liversidge v Anderson* [1941] AC 1 as per Lord Atkin at 29.

174 Laddie J., Copyright: Over-Strength, Over-Regulated, Over-Rated? (1996) 18(5) *European Intellectual Property Review*, pp. 253–260, p. 260.

Merkin R., *Richards Butler on Copyright, Designs and Patents: The New Law* (London: Longman, 1989).
Oppenheim C., Copyright in the Electronic Age in Parrinder P. and Chernaik W. (eds), *Textual Monopolies: Literary Copyright and the Public Domain* (London: Office for Humanities Communication, 1997).
Oxford English Dictionary (Oxford: Oxford University Press, 2010).
Speck A., et al (eds), *Laddie, Prescott and Vitoria: The Modern Law of Copyright and Designs*, 5th edition (London: Butterworths Law, 2018).
Vitoria M., et al (eds), *Laddie, Prescott and Vitoria: The Modern Law of Copyright and Designs*, 4th edition (London: Butterworths Law, 2011).

Case law

Apple Computer Inc v Computer Edge Pty Ltd [1984] FSR 487.
Bookmakers' Afternoon Greyhound Services v Wilf Gilbert (Staffordshire) Ltd [1994] FSR 723.
Bradbury, Agnew and Co v Day (1916) 32 TLR 349.
Data Cash Systems Inc v JS and A Group, 480 F Supp 1063 (ND) III (1979).
England and Wales Cricket Board Ltd and Anor v Tixdaq Ltd and Anor [2016] EWHC 575 (Ch).
Hoge v Schmalfeldt, Civil Action No ELH-14–1683 (US District Court for the District of Maryland, July 1, 2014).
Liversidge v Anderson [1941] AC 1.
Spelling Goldberg v BPC Publishing [1981] FSR 280.

Journals

Arnold R., Content Copyrights and Signal Copyrights: The Case for a Rational Scheme of Protection (2011) 1(3) *Queen Mary Journal of Intellectual Property*, pp. 272–279.
Arnold R., The Need for a New Copyright Act: A Case Study in Law Reform, The Herchel Smith Intellectual Property Lecture (2014) 5(2) *Queen Mary Journal of Intellectual Property*, pp. 110–131.
Bennion F., Review of Legislative Drafting: A New Approach by Sir William Dale KCMG – Reviewing the Reviewers (1980) *Statute Law Review*, pp. 61–76.
Bosher H. and Yesiloglu S., An Analysis of the Fundamental Tensions Between Copyright and Social Media: The Legal Implications of Sharing Images on Instagram (2018) 33(2) *International Review of Law, Computers & Technology*, pp. 164–186.
Crystal A. and Charalambous J., Copyright test Match – High Court Provides Guidance on Substantiality and Fair Dealing in Relation to Sports Clips (2016) *Entertainment Law Review*, pp. 214–217.
Kerr O. S., The Problem of Perspective in Internet Law (2003) 91 *Georgetown Law Journal*, pp. 357–405.
Laddie J., Copyright: Over-Strength, Over-Regulated, Over-Rated? (1996) 18(5) *European Intellectual Property Review*, pp. 253–260.
Leopold P. M., Reports of Committees, the Whitford Committee Report on Copyright and Designs Law (1977) 40(6) *Modern Law Review*, pp. 685–705.
Light S. N., Parody, Burlesque and the Economic Rationale for Copyright (1979) 11(4) *Connecticut Law Review*, pp. 615–636.

Reinbothe J., Martin-Prat M. and Lewinski S., The New WIPO Treaties: A First Resume (1977) *European Intellectual Property Review*, pp. 171–184.

Tan C. H. Y., Technological "Nudges" and Copyright on Social Media Sites (2015) 1 *Intellectual Property Quarterly*, pp. 62–78.

Legislation

Berne Convention for the Protection of Literary and Artistic Works 1886.

Copyright Act 1911.

Copyright (Computer Software) Amendment Act 1985.

Copyright and Related Rights Regulations 1996 (SI 1996/2967).

Copyright and Related Rights Regulations 2003 (SI 2003/2498).

Copyright, Designs and Patents Act 1988.

Council Directive 93/98/EEC of 29 October 1993 harmonizing the term of protection of copyright and certain related rights [1993] *OJ* L 290/9.

Directive 2001/29/EC of the European Parliament and of the Council of 22 May 2001 on the harmonisation of certain aspects of copyright and related rights in the information society [2001] *OJ* L 167/10.

WIPO Copyright Treaty 1996.

WIPO Performances and Phonograms Treaty 1996.

Official documents and reports

Department of Trade and Industry, *Reform of the Law Relating to Copyright, Designs and Performers' Protection*, Green Paper 1 (London: Her Majesty's Stationery Office, 1981) Cmnd 8302.

Department of Trade and Industry, *The Recording and Rental of Audio and Video Copyright Material*, Second Green Paper (London: Her Majesty's Stationery Office, 1985) Cmnd 9445.

Department of Trade and Industry, *Intellectual Property and Innovation*, White Paper (London: Her Majesty's Stationery Office, 1986) Cmnd 9712.

Hansard, Copyright (Computer Software) Amendment Bill, HL Deb 5 June 1985 Vol 464 Cols 823–829.

Hansard, Copyright, Designs and Patents Bill [HL], HL Deb 12 November 1987 Vol 489 Cols 1476–1540.

Hansard, Copyright, Designs and Patents Bill [HL], HL Deb 29 March 1988 Vol 495 Cols 607–696.

Hansard, Copyright, Designs and Patents Bill [Lords], HC Deb 28 April 1988 Vol 132 Cols 525–599, Order for Second Reading read.

Hansard, Copyright, Designs and Patents Bill [HL], HL Deb 3 December 1987 Vol 490 Cols 1149–1227.

Hansard, Copyright, Designs and Patents Bill [HL], HL Deb 30 November 1987 Vol 490 Cols 813–874.

Hansard, Infringement of Copyright by Copying, HC Deb 25 July 1988 Vol 138 Col 129.

Hansard, Legislative Drafting, HL Deb 11 November 1987 Vol 489 Cols 1417–1449.

Hansard, HC Deb 4 June 1956 Vol 553 Cols 715–811 (Second Reading).

Hansard, HC Deb 24 October 1956 Vol 558, Cols 665–685 (Report Stage).

Hansard, HC Deb 25 July 1988 Vol 138, Cols 37–73 (Report Stage): https://api.parliament.uk/historic-hansard/commons/1988/jul/25/design-right#column_37, speech by Tony Blair.

Hargreaves I., *Digital Opportunity, A Review of Intellectual Property and Growth*, May 2011.

Social Media: Photographs: Written question – 12484, asked by Jim Shannon (Strangford), 19 October 2015, answered by Rt HonEdwardVaizeyMP (Department for Culture, Media and Sport), 24 March 2016, https://www.parliament.uk/business/publications/written-questions-answers-statements/written-question/Commons/2015-10-19/12484/.

Gregory Committee, *The Board of Trade Report of the Copyright Committee* (London: Her Majesty's Stationery Office, 1952) Cmnd 8662.

Whitford Committee, *Copyright and Designs Law, Report of the Committee to Consider the Law on Copyright and Designs* (London: Her Majesty's Stationery Office, 1977) Cmnd 6732.

4 Online copyright infringement by storage and transient copying

Introduction

Chapter 3 analysed the historical development of the CDPA 1988 followed by a focus on the specific wording of section 17, leading to sections 17(2) and 17 (6) being recognised as the most relevant to the investigation of online copyright infringement. In particular, whilst the intention of section 17(2) was to protect copyright material on a computer from an external perspective, the use of the term "storage" in this context was metaphorical, which suggested an internal perspective. Similarly, in relation to section 17(6) the legislators struggled with technologically specific language taking an external perspective. However, the terminology used was also metaphorical in nature.

Therefore, this chapter looks at the case law that applies sections 17(2) and 17(6) in order to determine how the judges interpret and apply this regulation online, to further explore the meaning and to consider whether they take on an internal or external perspective when applied to cases of online infringement.

Four main tensions that are illuminated through this analysis. The first, as the chapter demonstrates, is that over time the legal definition of both "storage" and "transient copying" have developed as technological developments have occurred. As a result, the broadening of the law now also encompasses *access to* and *display of* copyright materials. This could contradict the closed lists of restricted acts and, perhaps, undermines the aim of copyright to uphold a fair balance between stakeholders.

Secondly, the analysis reveals that most often judges are seen to take an external perspective when describing the facts of the case as they take a considerable amount of time to understand in great detail the technical function of the process or program in question. This has led to a body of jurisprudence that is very technologically specific, and therefore judges are faced with many cases of similar circumstances that differ only slightly on the technicalities.

Thirdly, and in contrast to the second point, judges and counsel often attempt to map the law onto new technical circumstances with the use of analogy, taking an internal approach. The analogies used are often offline similes, metaphors or skeumorphs.[1] This demonstrates the attempt to understand new technologies, and how the law applies to them, through the use of previous knowledge and understanding. Whilst this is a natural human response to cognitively digesting a new experience or phenomenon,[2] there are disadvantages of using such an approach in the application of the law. The general drawbacks of using such an approach are set out in detail in Chapter 2. However, for the purpose of this chapter, the main arguments are that applying the law to online activity as if it were offline activity can be inaccurate, misleading and inappropriate.

Lastly, the analysis of the case law also reveals that there is no longer a clear distinction between "storage" and "transient copying", when applying these sections of the CDPA 1988 to the current technological landscape. There are some cases that clearly demonstrate the traditional view: that storage on a computer involves storage of material over time, whereas transient copying is only temporary. However, the recent case law focuses more on *temporary storage* within the Random Access Memory (RAM) of a computer or a server, demonstrating a clear overlap. From an external perspective, under both circumstances a copy is made in the memory of the computer. The only difference from a literal perspective would be that storage requires the passage of time. However, the courts do not appear to apply storage in this way in relation to transient storage which is temporary.

From an internal perspective, transient copying occurs automatically by the computer and without direct action, knowledge or perception of the user. However, long-term storage implies that the user has saved the work, taking a direct action with the knowledge and understanding that a copy has been made. The analysis in this chapter illuminates the courts' struggle with this tension.

In order to demonstrate these arguments, this chapter first considers the case law that relates to section 17(2): infringement by the storage of a copyright work, followed by a consideration of the case law that relates to section 17(6): infringement by transient and incidental copying.

1 A skeumorph is the reuse of old concepts for new phenomena; see Chapter 2 for more detail.

2 In psychology, this is understood as a schema. Schemas are mental structures that humans use to organise their knowledge about the world. Schema theory was developed by Bartlett, who argued that prior knowledge is stored in the brain in the form of schemas, which provide one of the main ways in which information in memory is organised. See Bartlett F. C., *Remembering: A Study in Experimental and Social Psychology* (Cambridge: Cambridge University Press, 1932). This was developed by Rumelhart and Norman, who suggested that schema learning occurs in three ways, including "accretion". This is where a new example of an existing schema is recorded and added to the relevant schematic information in long-term memory. See Rumelhart D. E. and Norman D. A., Analogical Processes in Learning in Anderson J. R. (ed) *Cognitive Skills and Their Acquisition* (Hillsdale: Lawrence Erlbaum Associates Inc, 1981).

Storing the work by any technical means: what does it mean?

As mentioned, this section analysis section 17(2) of the CDPA 1988, which provided that "copying in relation to a work means reproducing the work in any material form. This includes storing the work in any medium by electronic means."

The origin of storage: serendipity or misunderstanding?

Chapter 3 set out the circumstances under which this clause arose. This analysis revealed that the original intention of the clause was to protect stored work as an eligible copyright work in itself,[3] in the event that somebody else might try to steal the work and there was no other version of the work written down in a recorded form.[4]

This clause was first introduced prior to the CDPA 1988, by way of the Copyright (Computer Software) Amendment Act 1985 which amended the Copyright Act 1956. The suggestion came from Lord Coville, who admitted to having limited computer knowledge,[5] based on the idea that a work stored in a computer memory might be the only copy a creator could rely on – should the computer shut down and fail to save the work and in the meantime someone had stolen a copy of that work.[6] He stated that his intention was to make sure that where a work had "not yet been written down it is still protected",[7] contradicting the requirement that copyright only subsists in a literary, dramatic or musical work once it is recorded or written down.[8]

Nevertheless, the suggestion was accepted by Lord McIntosh for the Whitford Committee, who expressed gratitude for Lord Coville's expertise and also admitted to having "no particular knowledge of copyright law."[9] Lord Brabazon affirmed that the main motivation for the clause was to protect a new copyright work created and stored on a computer: "It will also apply, for example, to a novel or to any other sort of work being written directly into computer storage. In so far as there is any doubt now that such a work is 'fixed in material form', and therefore qualifies for copyright protection at the instant of its creation within the machine, the amendment will remove that doubt."[10] Lord Brabazon's language suggests a level of misunderstanding on the technical functioning of a computer, and what he meant by "written directly onto computer storage" is not clear.

3 *Hansard*, Copyright (Computer Software) Amendment Bill, HL Deb 5 June 1985 Vol 464 Cols 823–829, Viscount Colville of Culross at 824.

4 As required by CDPA 1988, section 3(2).

5 *Hansard*, Copyright (Computer Software) Amendment Bill, HL Deb 5 June 1985 Vol 464 Cols 823–829, Viscount Colville of Culross at 824.

6 *Ibid.*, Viscount Colville at 824.

7 *Ibid.*, Viscount Colville at 828.

8 CDPA 1988, section 3(2).

9 *Hansard*, Copyright (Computer Software) Amendment Bill, HL Deb 5 June 1985 Vol 464 Cols 823–829, Lord McIntosh at 825.

10 *Ibid.*, Lord Brabazon at 826.

It is suggested that the true intention at the root of the clause was simply that copyright should protect works that were created on a computer. However, in their confusion of the way a computer works and the choice of terminology used, it appeared as though the Lords were concerned about works that were only, or directly created, in computer storage. It is in fact unlikely that works of this description would ever exist. Nevertheless, the clause quickly extended the scope of copyright to encompass work stored on a computer.

The interpretation of the concept as it has been used in the case law was therefore not the main intended purpose when the clause was drafted, although it was mentioned as an afterthought.[11] Lord Brabazon argued that it was uncertain in cases where an existing work was copied into a computer, whether or not this would constitute a "reproduction in a material form" under copyright law.[12] He suggested that the copyright owner should be entitled to control this use of his work and that the amendment should also apply equally to the loading of works onto a computer.[13]

The Copyright (Computer Software) Amendment Act 1985 thus amended the Copyright Act 1956 to state that reproduction of any work in a material form included the storage of that work in a computer, which carried over into the CDPA 1988.[14] Elsom argued that whilst the amendment "partially clarified"[15] that storage of a work in a computer was a reproduction of the work, uncertainty remained. He stated that "the 1985 Amendment failed to clarify whether a copy stored in the machine-readable medium independent of the computer (for example, in or on a floppy disk, magnetic tape, etc.) is included. A residual uncertainty existed as to the status of copies in such machine-readable media."[16]

Recovering storage from lost property

The infringement of copyright by reproducing a work in the storage of a computer was omitted from the original CDPA 1988 Bill. There is no clear explanation or evidence as to why the clause was missing from the Bill, but there are only two possible motives: by mistake, or on purpose.

Either way, the Government was reminded by Miss Emma Nicholson, who declared a "professional interest"[17] in computer programming, of the policy developments of the

11 *Ibid.*, Viscount Colville at 827: "I had not actually thought of all those arguments."
12 *Ibid.*, Lord Brabazon at 826.
13 *Ibid.*, Lord Brabazon at 827.
14 Copyright (Computer Software) Amendment Act 1985, section 2.
15 Elsom S. M., Copyright Aspects of Information Technology: The Copyright, Designs and Patents Bill (1988) 10(11) *European Intellectual Property Review*, pp. 326–330, p. 327.
16 *Ibid.*, p. 327.
17 *Hansard*, Copyright, Designs and Patents Bill [Lords] HC Deb 28 April 1988 Vol 132 Cols 525–599, Order for Second Reading read, Miss Emma Nicholson (Torridge and Devon, West) at 576: "I was trained by ICL as a computer programmer. I went on to be an assistant analyst and computer consultant with 10 years hands-on experience in the industry. I am now enjoying an industry and Parliament fellowship with

Copyright (Computer Software) Amendment Act 1985.[18] As Litman put it: "No effected party is going to agree to support a bill that leaves it worse off than it is under [previous] law."[19] Accordingly, the Government was held to account on the keeping up of policy, and the clause was reintroduced to the CDPA 1988 Bill.

Furthermore, Miss Nicholson also highlighted that as a computer program was a literary work, it would fall within the scope of clause 29: fair dealing for the purposes of research and private study.[20] She suggested that this was an unintended consequence which would not be welcomed by the industry and therefore recommended that electronic reproduction be excluded from the fair dealing defence.[21] Indeed, section 29 of the CDPA 1988 can now be seen to reflect Miss Nicholson's request. Fair dealing for the purpose of research and private study explicitly states that it is not fair dealing to "incidentally … copy"[22] or even "observe"[23] a computer program in order to determine the ideas and principles which underlie it. However, section 50BA(1)[24] states that it is not an infringement to observe if it is done whilst loading, displaying, running, transmitting or storing the program.[25] This clause reflects Article 5(3) of the Information Society Directive, but appears to cause more confusion than clarity. As Onslow and Jamal argue, the section is a riddle: "if the loading and running has to be licensed in the first place, then art.5(3) serves no purpose. If the loading and running for testing does not have to be licensed in the first place, then why refer to a licence at all."[26]

Nevertheless section 17(2) of the CDPA 1988 has expanded the reach of copyright[27] by restricting the act of storing a work in an electronic form. The clause was originally introduced with a substantial lack of computer and copyright knowledge and the justifications for the clause were not entirely thought through.[28] In defence of the legislators, the use of computers at the time of drafting was limited.[29] It is

IBM, and I maintain links with my old colleagues who are now senior members of the British Computer Society."

18 *Ibid.*, Miss Emma Nicholson at 578.

19 Litman J., *Digital Copyright*, 2nd edition (New York: Prometheus Books, 2006) p. 23.

20 *Hansard*, Copyright, Designs and Patents Bill [Lords] HC Deb 28 April 1988 Vol 132 Cols 525–599, Order for Second Reading read, Miss Emma Nicholson at 578.

21 *Ibid.*, Miss Emma Nicholson at 578.

22 CDPA 1988, section 29(4)(b).

23 *Ibid.*, section 29(4A).

24 As inserted on 31 October 2003 by Copyright and Related Rights Regulations 2003 (SI 2003/2498), regulation 15(1) (with regulations 31–40).

25 CDPA 1988, section 50(BA)(1), reflecting Article 5(3) of the Information Society Directive.

26 Onslow R. and Jamal I., Copyright Infringement and Software Emulation – *SAS Inc v World Programming Limited* Case Comment (2013) 35(6) *European Intellectual Property Review*, pp. 352–356, pp. 354–355.

27 Vitoria M., et al (eds), *Laddie, Prescott and Vitoria: The Modern Law of Copyright and Designs* (London: Butterworths Law, 2011) (hereafter, *Laddie, Prescott and Vitoria*) 3.123.

28 *Hansard*, Copyright (Computer Software) Amendment Bill, HL Deb 5 June 1985 Vol 464 Cols 823–829, Lord McIntosh at 825.

29 *Ibid.*, Viscount Colville at 824.

unlikely that they could have ever foreseen the developments in technology that were to follow.[30] However, their lack of awareness of these limitations is the true criticism to be made. As Viscount Coville optimistically concluded, the clause "probably will work"[31] and did not expect any unforeseen consequences: "there will not be a nasty lacuna in the legal protection."[32]

Furthermore, the strong influence of stakeholders' interests is evident. Support for the policy to continue in the CDPA 1988 was given by the industry and Miss Nicholson had a particularly strong influence as an industry representative within the debate.[33] The discussions were dominated by members with interests in industry and there appeared to be little consideration for the public interest.[34]

Since 2001 temporary copying has been recognised at European level as an act that requires a copyright holder's permission, the reproduction right under Article 2 of the Information Society Directive required member states to "provide the exclusive right to authorise or prohibit direct or indirect, temporary or permanent reproduction by any means and in any form, in whole or in part."[35] Therefore, the protection of temporary copying is enforced at EU level and section 17 is read in light of Article 2 of the Information Society Directive.[36]

Application and interpretation of storage

The cases addressed in this section are considered in chronological order to demonstrate how the meaning of infringement by storage has developed over time. The focus of the analysis is how judges have determined the facts of the case in relation to the internet, and thereafter how they have mapped section 17(2) of the CDPA 1988 onto those facts. Therefore, the judgments where the meaning was defined, discussed or changed are explained in detail, although the knowledge and understanding of the full case law landscape is acknowledged and drawn upon where appropriate.

In order to begin this analysis, all of the relevant cases were collated. Firstly, it was found that there have been more than 90 cases that have referenced section

30 *Football Association Premier League Ltd and Others v QC Leisure and Others* [2008] EWHC 1411 (Ch), as per Kitchin J at [232]: "I entertain some doubt as to whether those who framed the CDPA ever contemplated that displaying an image on a television screen amounts to copying."

31 *Hansard*, Copyright (Computer Software) Amendment Bill, HL Deb 5 June 1985 Vol 464 Cols 823–829, Viscount Colville at 827.

32 *Ibid.*, Viscount Colville at 828.

33 *Hansard*, Copyright, Designs and Patents Bill [Lords] HC Deb 28 April 1988 Vol 132 Cols 525–599.

34 *Ibid.*

35 *Ibid.*, Article 2.

36 *Football Association Premier League Ltd and Others v QC Leisure and Others* [2008] EWHC 1411 (Ch), as per Kitchin J at [231].

17 since the CDPA 1988 came into force.[37] Within those cases there were more than 200 references to storage, made in 47 different cases.[38]

A reading of these 47 cases showed that some cases were completely irrelevant to the context of this investigation, as "storage" is a word with more than one meaning. Those cases were excluded from the analysis. In addition, many cases only mentioned section 17(2) in passing or referred to the CDPA 1988 in general and no discussion of its meaning or application took place. Those cases were also excluded. This left 25 cases of relevance, of which there were over 50 judgments.

Of those cases, four have been identified as the most significant in the development of the meaning of reproduction by way of storage by electronic means: *Ocular Sciences,* [39] *EasyInternetCafe,* [40] *Navitaire* [41] and *Meltwater.* [42] In these cases the judge gave particular consideration to the interpretation and meaning of section 17(2) of the CDPA 1988, whereas the majority of the other cases simply applied it without addressing the meaning.

These cases demonstrate the development of the meaning of copyright infringement under section 17(2) of the CDPA 1988 over a significant period of time, taking place in 1996,[43] 2003,[44] to 2010.[45] The first two cases focus on the meaning of "storage", the third case focuses on the meaning of "electronic means". The fourth and final case demonstrates the culmination of the

37 The CDPA 1988 received Royal Assent on 15 November 1988.

38 These figures were obtained by the researcher through searching Westlaw and Lexis Library databases for cases referring to CDPA 1988, section 17 as part of her PhD thesis, this data is accurate at 20 December 2015. The judgments from these cases were then uploaded to Nvivo – a qualitative software analysis program. Using the software, the researcher was able to trace every mention of the word "storage" in any case in which the word appeared.

39 *Ocular Sciences Ltd and Another v Aspect Vision Care Ltd and Others* (First Action); *Geoffrey Harrison Galley v Ocular Sciences Ltd* (Second Action) [1996] EWHC Patents 1, [1997] RPC 289.

40 *Sony Music Entertainment (UK) Ltd, Sony Music Entertainment Inc, Polydor Ltd, UMG Recordings Inc, Virgin Records Ltd v Easyinternetcafe Ltd* [2003] EWHC 62 (Ch).

41 *Navitaire Inc v EasyJet Airline Company Ltd, Bullet Proof Technologies Inc* [2003] EWHC 3487 (Ch).

42 *The Newspaper Licensing Agency Ltd, MGN Ltd, Associated Newspapers Ltd, Express Newspapers Ltd, Guardian News and Media Ltd, Telegraph Media Group Ltd, Independent Print Ltd v Meltwater Holding BV, Meltwater News UK Ltd, Public Relations Consultants Association Ltd* [2010] EWHC 3099 (Ch).

43 *Ocular Sciences Ltd and Another v Aspect Vision Care Ltd and Others* (First Action); *Geoffrey Harrison Galley v Ocular Sciences Ltd* (Second Action) [1996] EWHC Patents 1, [1997] RPC 289.

44 *Sony Music Entertainment (UK) Ltd, Sony Music Entertainment Inc, Polydor Ltd, UMG Recordings Inc, Virgin Records Ltd v Easyinternetcafe Ltd* [2003] EWHC 62 (Ch); *Navitaire Inc v EasyJet Airline Company Ltd, Bullet Proof Technologies Inc* [2003] EWHC 3487 (Ch).

45 *The Newspaper Licensing Agency Ltd, MGN Ltd, Associated Newspapers Ltd, Express Newspapers Ltd, Guardian News and Media Ltd, Telegraph Media Group Ltd, Independent Print Ltd v Meltwater Holding BV, Meltwater News UK Ltd, Public Relations Consultants Association Ltd* [2010] EWHC 3099 (Ch).

development of the law in this area, considering all aspects of section 17(2) of the CDPA 1988. These cases are discussed in detail below.

Case law analysis: section 17(2) of the CDPA 1988

This section analyses the case law that applies section 17(2) of the CDPA 1988, reproducing the work in any material form, including storing the work in any medium by electronic means.

Storage as a verb

In 1996 in the case of *Ocular Sciences*, [46] Mr Justice Laddie made the first significant judgment that considered the application and meaning of "storing" the work.

In this matter, the plaintiffs alleged the infringement of their contact-lens design program through reproduction and storage by electronic means.[47] The defendants conceded to reproduction but not to copying by storing, arguing that being *in* storage insufficient to amount to storage within the meaning of the CDPA 1988.[48]

Thus, Mr Justice Laddie considered the nature of the infringing act required to amount to copyright infringement in this context.[49] He emphasised that "act" is a verb, a "doing-word" that requires action taken by the alleged infringer: "the statute gives the copyright proprietor the exclusive right 'to do' certain 'acts'. Those acts include 'to copy'. The copyright is infringed by a person who 'does' any of those acts … in relation to a substantial part of the work. Furthermore, the concept of activity is consistent with the subsequent subsections in section 17."[50]

This interpretation suggested the need for a conscious and deliberate action by a person in order to constitute an infringement, as opposed to automatic copying by the computer system. Therefore, through this interpretation Mr Justice Laddie appeared to take a literal reading of the law.

He went on to describe the activity of putting something into computer storage which creates a digital copy of the work, from a technology perspective.[51] For example, he described the technical function of storing such as by magnetic floppy disk or hard drive. He then used this technological basis to apply the CDPA 1988 wording of "storing in any medium by electronic means" to confirm that copying by magnetic storage constitutes reproduction in a material form.[52] This

46 *Ocular Sciences Ltd and Another v Aspect Vision Care Ltd and Others* (First Action); *Geoffrey Harrison Galley v Ocular Sciences Ltd* (Second Action) [1996] EWHC Patents 1, [1997] RPC 289.
47 *Ibid.*, Laddie J at 417.
48 *Ibid.*, Laddie J at 417.
49 *Ibid.*, Laddie J at 418.
50 *Ibid.*, Laddie J at 418.
51 *Ibid.*, Laddie J at 418.
52 *Ibid.*, Laddie J at 418.

represented an external perspective by considering the technical function of the hardware and software.

Mr Justice Laddie concluded that in order to infringe by storing a work, an action must have been performed by the infringer; that action being retrieving the work out of storage or saving it to storage.[53] He supported this by highlighting the distinction between being in possession of a floppy disk which was not of itself an infringement, whereas using the disk to retrieve the data out of storage could be.[54] The facts of the case were such that it was clear that the defendants had altered the program in question. Mr Justice Laddie inferred from this that once the change had been made, the program would have been saved and that amounted to the act of storing and thus an infringement of copyright.[55]

This case demonstrated the judge taking a literal reading of the law and an external perspective when determining the facts of the case as he considered the technical process of copying by storage, specifically on a floppy disc.[56] In his application of the law he took a literal reading of section 17(2) of the CDPA 1988 in order to support his decision.

In relation to the meaning of "storage", Mr Justice Laddie interpreted the CDPA 1988 to grant a copyright holder the exclusive right to do certain acts, therefore infringement is an *act performed* without permission. He described infringement by storage as when a person saves a work or retrieves it from storage without permission.[57] Hence, at this stage, storage of a work could be described as a verb, since it required an action.

Storage as a voluntary verb

The meaning of storing the work under section 17(2) of the CDPA 1988 was again considered in 2003 by Mr Justice Peter Smith in the matter of *Sony Music v EasyInternetCafe.* [58]

In this case the judge was asked to consider the lawfulness of a CD burning service made available by an internet café.[59] At *EasyInternetCafe* customers could download files from the internet and save them onto a private directory on the café's server, identified by reference to the personal ID of the customer.[60] The customer could then request a member of *EasyInternetCafe* staff to download the files from the customer's "private area" on the server onto a CD.[61]

53 *Ibid.*, Laddie J at 418.
54 *Ibid.*, Laddie J at 418.
55 *Ibid.*, Laddie J at 418.
56 *Ibid.*, Laddie J at 418.
57 *Ibid.*, Laddie J at 418.
58 *Sony Music Entertainment (UK) Ltd, Sony Music Entertainment Inc, Polydor Ltd, UMG Recordings Inc, Virgin Records Ltd v Easyinternetcafe Ltd* [2003] EWHC 62 (Ch).
59 *Ibid.*, Peter Smith J at [1].
60 *Ibid.*, Peter Smith J at [6].
61 *Ibid.*, Peter Smith J at [7].

The defendant's evidence, which was accepted by the judge, was that staff were prohibited from looking at the contents of any files, unless the customer agreed.[62] In addition, the log-on process displayed a significant number of copyright infringement warnings to customers.[63]

The then Mr Richard Arnold QC argued for the defence that the circumstances were comparable to a situation where A sends an infringing copy of a literary or artistic work to B by fax or email; the copy is made by B's machine but the person who caused it to be made was A. Therefore, the person who did the restricted act was A, and not B.[64] He drew a similar analogy with an internet service provider (ISP) whose computer stored an infringing copy being transmitted from A to B, but was not responsible for that act of copying.[65]

Mr Arnold QC anticipated that the claimants would argue that the situation was different because the defendant's employee operated the machine so there had been human intervention.[66] However, he argued that this made no difference because the files were anonymous and therefore the human being was an automaton.[67] To demonstrate this, he drew a further analogy where A asks a blind person B to photocopy a piece of paper, which contains a copyright work; the blind person had no knowledge of what was being copied and acts as an automaton carrying out A's instructions, so would be liable.[68]

Mr Arnold QC's argument built upon the reasoning set out in *Ocular Sciences* [69] discussed above. As did Mr Justice Laddie, Arnold interpreted the CDPA 1988 to require an *act* of infringement as a verb, whereby the infringer physically does something. Arnold used this argument on its head to suggest that his clients were not guilty as the act was done blindly or in a robotic, unconscious manner.[70] Arnold's arguments were metaphoric, using offline similes in attempt to map copyright law onto new technologies. This approach is a clear example of using the internal perspective.

However, the judge in this matter, Mr Justice Peter Smith, did not accept Mr Arnold QC's arguments, for two reasons. Firstly, the liability for infringement under section 17 of the CDPA 1988 is strict so there is no defence for copying without knowledge.[71] Importantly, though, he did distinguish between copying

62 *Ibid.*, Peter Smith J at [8].
63 *Ibid.*, Peter Smith J at [8].
64 *Ibid.*, Peter Smith J at [31].
65 *Ibid.*, Peter Smith J at [31].
66 *Ibid.*, Peter Smith J at [32].
67 *Ibid.*, Peter Smith J at [32]. An automaton is a moving mechanical device made in imitation of a human being.
68 *Ibid.*, Peter Smith J at [32].
69 *Ocular Sciences Ltd and Another v Aspect Vision Care Ltd and Others* (First Action); *Geoffrey Harrison Galley v Ocular Sciences Ltd* (Second Action) [1996] EWHC Patents 1, [1997] RPC 289.
70 *Sony Music Entertainment (UK) Ltd, Sony Music Entertainment Inc, Polydor Ltd, UMG Recordings Inc, Virgin Records Ltd v Easyinternetcafe Ltd* [2003] EWHC 62 (Ch), as per Peter Smith J at [32].
71 *Ibid.*, Peter Smith J at [33].

without knowledge and involuntary copying: "Obviously, when strict liability is pushed to its boundaries absurd results can arise. It would be absurd if the recipient of a fax over which he has no control could be said to be infringing it merely because his machine is the one that prints the transmission. Generally, the owner of a fax machine cannot stop material being sent. He is an involuntary copier. The same occurs in relation to the Internet Service Provider."[72]

Here the judge has used the idea of a fax machine as a skeumorph to understand how the law relates to ISP liability, also using an internal perspective in the application of copyright law to online activity. However, in his case comment, Garnett disagreed with the judge's arguments, stating that "there is no potential absurdity. In both these cases the recipient is not an involuntary copier: he is not a copier at all. The copier is the person who is the proximate cause of the copy being made, which in each case is the sender. The rule of strict liability can sometimes produce harsh results but not, it is suggested, absurd ones since the question is always: who is the copier?"[73]

Nevertheless, on this first point relating to strict liability, the judge stated that the decision to keep the information confidential was voluntary.[74] To expand, he used the analogy of a high street printer who photocopies a PhD thesis that contained infringing material – he would not be aware of the infringing material, but he would still be liable.[75] The judge concluded that to accept the arguments of Mr Arnold QC would be to introduce a *mens rea* defence where none was available in primary copyright infringement.[76]

The second reason that the judge disagreed with Mr Arnold QC's argument was in relation to the analogy, described above, of the blind person making an infringing photocopy without knowledge. The judge rebutted Arnold's argument by stating that if a blind person was asked to copy something without taking precautions to check whether or not the matter potentially infringed copyright, he could not see how that would avoid the strict liability of infringement.[77]

The judge found that on the evidence, the material was downloaded in an unauthorised way by the customers,[78] and having rejected the defence argument, EasyInternetCafe was liable.[79]

In relation to the Framework for Constructing Digital Perspectives, this judgment took a literal reading of the law and rejected Arnold's internal perspective when determining the facts of the case. The scope of infringement by storage was

72 *Ibid.*, Peter Smith J at [33].
73 Garnett K., The Easyinternetcafe Decision Case Comment (2003) 25(9) *European Intellectual Property Review*, pp. 426–427, p. 426.
74 *Sony Music Entertainment (UK) Ltd, Sony Music Entertainment Inc, Polydor Ltd, UMG Recordings Inc, Virgin Records Ltd v Easyinternetcafe Ltd* [2003] EWHC 62 (Ch), as per Peter Smith J at [35].
75 *Ibid.*, Peter Smith J at [35].
76 *Ibid.*, Peter Smith J at [35].
77 *Ibid.*, Peter Smith J at [36].
78 *Ibid.*, Peter Smith J at [25].
79 *Ibid.*, Peter Smith J at [37].

defined to include copying without knowledge; however, the judge did suggest that there would not be liability for involuntary copying.[80]

On the other hand, the judge and counsel both used analogies in order to support their arguments for how the law should apply to this situation; this metaphorical approach is in line with the internal perspective. Ritchie argued that the potential copying by a passive third party ISP, or fax machine, and that of the defendants is essentially the same.[81] She stated that "the difference in the acts carried out in each case can be viewed as only a matter of scale and automation, in terms of the volume of data processing/copying carried out, and in each case profits are intended to be made from the service."[82]

This case developed the meaning of infringement by way of storage to exclude involuntary copying. Although strict liability applied and no *mens rea* was introduced, the judge found that it was relevant that the action was voluntary. In the next key judgment that considered the meaning of section 17(2) of the CDPA 1988, the focus moved from the meaning of "storage" to the meaning of "reproduction in any material form".

Reproducing in any material form

In the case of *Navitaire v EasyJet* [83] the meaning of section 17(2) of the CDPA 1988 continued to develop, focusing on reproducing the work in any material form. In this case the claimants argued that their airline booking software, OpenRes, was infringed by the defendant's software, eRes, which replaced its own as the booking service for EasyJet Airline Company Limited.[84]

In the first instance, Mr Justice Pumfrey was asked to strike out the allegations of infringement on the grounds that the allegations were so incoherent that they were not triable.[85] Mr Justice Pumfrey found that there was a legitimate case for trial:[86] whilst there was no dispute that the actual code in the eRes had no resemblance to that of OpenRes,[87] he stated that "from the user's point of view"[88] the eRes system operated in the same way as OpenRes, for example, the functions available to the user, the screens which were displayed to the user, the steps which the user took to book a passenger onto a flight and clear a credit card payment.[89] The applicants gave examples of this by way of "walk-throughs" which

80 *Ibid.*, Peter Smith J at [33].
81 Ritchie M., *Sony Music Entertainment (UK) Ltd v Easyinternetcafe Ltd* January 28, 2003 (2003) 14(6) *Entertainment Law Review*, pp. 155–156, p. 156.
82 *Ibid.*, p. 156.
83 *Navitaire Inc v EasyJet Airline Company Ltd, Bullet Proof Technologies Inc* [2003] EWHC 3487 (Ch).
84 *Ibid.*, Pumfrey J at [1]–[3].
85 *Ibid.*, Pumfrey J at [1].
86 *Ibid.*, Pumfrey J at [47].
87 *Ibid.*, Pumfrey J at [4].
88 *Ibid.*, Pumfrey J at [5].
89 *Ibid.*, Pumfrey J at [6].

followed a customer through the system who books and purchases a ticket, is checked in and then boards a flight.[90]

As such, it was held that the functional structure of the OpenRes system was copied by eRes.[91] Mr Justice Pumfrey acknowledged that the coding of the programs was different, but that the outcome on the screen, from the user's perspective, appeared the same.[92] To support this, the analogy of taking the plot of a book was used.[93] Mr Justice Pumfrey explained that "in the same way that copyright subsisting in a literary work may be infringed by a change in medium in which all that is taken is the plot, so also, it is said, may the copyright in computer software be infringed when the functional structure of the code is appropriated by writing different code which, put crudely, works in the same way."[94]

Mr Justice Pumfrey acknowledged that an allegation of infringement of copyright is fact-sensitive.[95] As was discussed in Chapter 2, the law is contingent on the facts, and the facts are contingent on the perspective.

Stokes argued that Mr Justice Pumfrey took the correct approach in balancing the stakeholder's interests: "The judge was signalling that it is not the place of copyright law to protect the functionality produced by running code where the code has itself not been copied … Whilst this decision will alarm some in the IT industry, it is submitted that in this case the judge got the balance right."[96]

On the other hand, Heritage and Jones argued that the decision left software developers vulnerable: "It appears that competitors can now copy the general 'look and feel' of a program's function and 'business logic' with relative confidence, provided they do not have access to the original program's source code."[97]

From the perspective of the Framework for Constructing Digital Perspectives, Mr Justice Pumfrey therefore considered there to be no similarities from an external perspective, but many from an internal perspective. Taking the internal perspective in this matter, he determined that the screen displayed for the user could be copyright infringement.

The case proceeded to trial before Mr Justice Pumfrey, who eventually decided that the claim could not be substantiated.[98] He explained that whilst he was

90 *Ibid.*, Pumfrey J at [31].
91 *Ibid.*, Pumfrey J at [7].
92 *Ibid.*, Pumfrey J at [7].
93 *Ibid.*, Pumfrey J at [8].
94 *Ibid.*, Pumfrey J at [7].
95 *Ibid.*, Pumfrey J at [8].
96 Stokes S., The Development of UK Software Copyright Law: From John Richardson Computers to Navitaire (2005) 11(4) *Computer and Telecommunications Law Review*, pp. 129–133, p. 133.
97 Heritage M. and Jones P., The End of "Look and Feel" and the Invasion of the Little Green Men? UK Copyright and Patent Protection for Software After 2005 (2006) 12 (3) *Computer and Telecommunications Law Review*, pp. 67–70, p. 69.
98 *Navitaire Inc v EasyJet Airline Company Ltd, Bullet Proof Technologies Inc* [2004] EWHC 1725 (Ch), as per Pumfrey J at [321].

impressed by the amount of programming effort that went into the display of every layout on the screen, the defendants manipulated the data in a different way and displayed it in a different way; therefore, this did not amount to a substantial part.[99] This judgment utilised the literal approach, steering away from a purposive approach, such as the mischief rule. For example, it could have been argued that the mischief the regulation sought to remedy was the copying of work, and the new website achieved a copy of the original, albeit with different coding.

Whilst this case was fundamentally about copyright infringement in computer software, it is relevant on the points of its application of section 17(2) of the CDPA 1988. Firstly, the threshold of "reproducing in any material form" was not reached despite the similarities of interface and functionality when the coding behind the scenes was original; and, secondly, in relation to how the courts considered both the technical function and the user perspective, which produced different outcomes. The case highlighted examples of analogies used to understand how copyright can be mapped onto new technological circumstances. The analogy supported the applicant's claim originally; however, as the matter proceeded to trial, Mr Justice Pumfrey took a very technical approach. He considered closely the coding and technical process of creating the software, on which basis he found that there had been no copyright infringement.

The discussion now turns to the final key case in the analysis of section 17(2) of the CDPA 1988, which brings together all the elements discussed so far of infringement by reproducing a work in any material form, including storage.

Reproduction by storing a cache copy: Meltwater

In 2010 the meaning and application of section 17(2) of the CDPA 1988 culminated in the matter of *Meltwater*, [100] where Mrs Justice Proudman considered whether the receivers[101] of a news service provided by Meltwater[102] required a licence from the copyright holders.[103]

The applicants[104] claimed that without a licence the end-users of Meltwater's service infringed their copyright because "by receiving and reading Meltwater

99 *Ibid.*, Pumfrey J at [321].

100 *The Newspaper Licensing Agency Ltd, MGN Ltd, Associated Newspapers Ltd, Express Newspapers Ltd, Guardian News and Media Ltd, Telegraph Media Group Ltd, Independent Print Ltd v Meltwater Holding BV, Meltwater News UK Ltd, Public Relations Consultants Association Ltd* [2010] EWHC 3099 (Ch).

101 *Ibid.*, Proudman J at [4]: the third defendant was the Public Relations Consultants Association Ltd, which represented the interests of its members who are UK public relations providers using the Meltwater News service.

102 *Ibid.*, Proudman J at [3]: the first defendant was Meltwater, which provided a commercial media monitoring service called "Meltwater News" to business customers online.

103 *Ibid.*, Proudman J at [6] and [22].

104 *Ibid.*, Proudman J at [1]: the first claimant was the Newspaper Licensing Agency Limited and the other claimants are publishers of national newspapers and are shareholder members of NLA.

News the end user will be making a copy of it,"[105] and that by clicking on the link to the article the end-user would make a further copy of the article.[106]

Mrs Justice Proudman agreed that when an end-user received an email containing Meltwater News, a copy was made on their computer and remained there until deleted.[107] Further, when the end-user viewed Meltwater News via the website onscreen, another copy was made on the end-user's computer.[108] Thus, she stated that this was more likely than not to infringe copyright.[109]

The defendants sought to rely on the exception set out in section 28A of the CDPA 1988, which required the following to be achieved:

> (i) the act must be temporary, (ii) it must be transient or incidental, (iii) it must be an integral and essential part of the technological process, (iv) the sole purpose of the process must be to enable a transmission network between third parties by an intermediary or the lawful use of the work or protected subject matter; and (v) the act must have no independent economic significance.[110]

The court added that the act of making the temporary and transient copy must not exceed what is necessary for the proper completion of the technological process and that the storage and deletion must not be dependent on human intervention; it must be automated.[111]

The defendants in the *Meltwater* case argued that the user's actions were incidental to online browsing and therefore fell within the exception.[112] They relied on Recital 33 of the Information Society Directive, which permitted "acts which enable browsing as well as acts of caching to take place."[113]

Mrs Justice Proudman clarified that the purpose of the exception was to ensure that the incidental storage of copies of a work on, for example, intermediate computer servers between a web-server and the computer running a web-browser used by an end-user would be exempt.[114] The test was whether the temporary reproduction had no "independent economic significance."[115] This meant that

105 *Ibid.*, Proudman J at [45] bullet point 1.
106 *Ibid.*, Proudman J at [45] bullet point 2.
107 *Ibid.*, Proudman J at [101].
108 *Ibid.*, Proudman J at [101].
109 *Ibid.*, Proudman J at [103].
110 *Ibid.*, Proudman J at [106] set out the requirements which were established by the CJEU in *Infopaq International AS v Danske Dagblades Forening* (Case C-5/08) ECLI:EU:C:2009:465 at 54.
111 As set out in *Infopaq International AS v Danske Dagblades Forening* (Case C-5/08) ECLI:EU:C:2009:465 at 61–64.
112 *The Newspaper Licensing Agency Ltd, MGN Ltd, Associated Newspapers Ltd, Express Newspapers Ltd, Guardian News and Media Ltd, Telegraph Media Group Ltd, Independent Print Ltd v Meltwater Holding BV, Meltwater News UK Ltd, Public Relations Consultants Association Ltd* [2010] EWHC 3099 (Ch), as per Proudman J at [107].
113 *Ibid.*, Proudman J at [107] referring to Information Society Directive, Recital 33.
114 *Ibid.*, Proudman J at [108].
115 *Ibid.*, Proudman J at [108] referring to *Football Association Premier League Ltd and Others v QC Leisure and Others* [2008] EWHC 1411 (Ch), as per Kitchin J at [241]–

any act of reproduction that in effect was a "consumption of the work",[116] including temporary copying into memory in order to use or access such works required the permission of the right holder.[117]

Therefore, the exception was concerned only with incidental and transient copies which had no value in themselves and any copy which was a consumption of the work, whether temporary or not, required the permission of the copyright holder. Mrs Justice Proudman stated that "a person making a copy of a webpage on his computer screen will not have a defence under s. 28A CDPA simply because he has been browsing."[118]

The judge found that the exception was inapplicable in the present case[119] and as a result, the end-users infringed the applicant's copyright when receiving and using the Meltwater service. She stated that "the whole point of the receipt and copying of Meltwater News is to enable the end user to receive and read it. Making the copy is not an essential and integral part of a technological process but the end which the process is designed to achieve. Storage of the copy and the duration of that storage are matters within the end user's control."[120] Thus, the exception cannot be used to legitimise copies made in the course of browsing.[121]

Hobson criticised the judgment, arguing that it created uncertainty and illustrated an inconsistency in the application of the law of copyright infringement. He doubted the expertise of the judge, highlighting that the case had not been listed before one of the four specialist IP judges in the Chancery Division.[122] Hart appeared to be more understanding of Mrs Justice Proudman's approach, but nevertheless also disagreed with her decision: "Piracy greatly concerned Proudman J who felt that the exception cannot have been intended to legitimise all copies made in the course of browsing as otherwise users would be permitted to watch pirated films and listen to pirated music … However viewing and watching protected works are not restricted copyright acts."[123]

Evidently, the case proceeded to the Court of Appeal on the grounds that what resulted from Mrs Justice Proudman's judgment would require double-licensing.[124] To support this argument the second defendants (PRCA) used the

[242] who provided that "the opinion of the Economic and Social Committee (of September 9, 1998) on an early draft of the Directive explained the purpose of the exception as follows … The test is whether the temporary reproduction has no independent economic significance."

116 *Ibid.*, Proudman J at [109].
117 *Ibid.*, Proudman J at [109].
118 *Ibid.*, Proudman J at [109].
119 *Ibid.*, Proudman J at [112].
120 *Ibid.*, Proudman J at [109].
121 *Ibid.*, Proudman J at [110].
122 Hobson A., *Newspaper Licensing Agency Ltd v Meltwater Holdings BV* (2011) 22(3) *Entertainment Law Review*, pp. 101–104, p. 101.
123 Hart M., The Legality of Internet Browsing in the Digital Age (2014) 36(10) *European Intellectual Property Review*, pp. 630–639, p. 633.
124 *The Newspaper Licensing Agency Ltd, MGN Ltd, Associated Newspapers Ltd, Express Newspapers Ltd, Guardian News and Media Ltd, Telegraph Media Group Ltd, Independent Print Ltd v Meltwater Holding BV, Meltwater News UK Ltd, Public Relations Consultants Association Ltd* [2011] EWCA Civ 890, before Jackson LJ (The Chancellor of the High Court) and Elias LJ, judgment: Jackson LJ at [6].

analogy of the press clippings agency, which requires a licence from the publishers to make "hard" copies, but does not require a licence to receive and read them. The PRCA thus argued that Meltwater's licence should encompass copies made when received and read by the end-user.[125]

In relation to the section 28A of the CDPA 1988 exception argument put forward by PRCA, the Court of Appeal agreed with Mrs Justice Proudman and further commented that "the acts of reproduction are those occasioned by the voluntary human process of accessing that webpage."[126]

The court dismissed the appeal, agreeing with Mrs Justice Proudman and her original judgment. However, the court did consider Mrs Justice Proudman to have gone too far in her declaration and clarified that it is not the case that every recipient and/or user of Meltwater News would inevitably infringe the copyright so as to require a licence or consent from the publisher.[127]

The concept of "voluntary human process"[128] builds on the comments found in the above mentioned cases of *Ocular Sciences* [129] and *EasyInternetCafe.* [130] The case law shows the court's finding that by the "act" of "accessing" a webpage, which by the inherent technical process makes a copy in the computer's memory, a user can infringe copyright. However, did this extend the scope of reproduction too far?

The matter went before the Supreme Court in February 2013, which recognised that this appeal raised some important questions about the application of copyright law to the technical processes involved in viewing copyright material on the internet.[131]

The Supreme Court agreed that viewing or reading is not an act of infringement: "A person who reads a pirated copy of a protected book or views a forgery of a protected painting commits no infringement."[132] This statement appears to contradict the case law analysed above, which stated that accessing unlawful content was an infringement. However, the difficulty with the statement given by the Supreme Court is that it is an analogy: it uses the example of reading a book or viewing a painting, which is not infringement, *per se.* [133] However, when a person views or reads a book or a painting online, a copy is made in the memory of the

125 *Ibid.*, Jackson LJ at [6].
126 *Ibid.*, Jackson LJ at [35].
127 *Ibid.*, Jackson LJ at [48].
128 *Ibid.*, Jackson LJ at [35].
129 *Ocular Sciences Ltd and Another v Aspect Vision Care Ltd and Others* (First Action); *Geoffrey Harrison Galley v Ocular Sciences Ltd* (Second Action) [1996] EWHC Patents 1, [1997] RPC 289.
130 *Sony Music Entertainment (UK) Ltd, Sony Music Entertainment Inc, Polydor Ltd, UMG Recordings Inc, Virgin Records Ltd v Easyinternetcafe Ltd* [2003] EWHC 62 (Ch).
131 *Public Relations Consultants Association Ltd v The Newspaper Licensing Agency Ltd and Others* [2013] UKSC 18 before Lord Neuberger, President Lord Kerr, Lord Clarke, Lord Sumption and Lord Carnwathas, as per Lord Sumption at [1].
132 *Ibid.*, Lord Sumption at [1].
133 The act of reading or viewing does not create a copy of the work, *per se.* It could be argued, for the sake of highlighting the obscurity of the argument, that a copy is made in the memory of the person's brain who is viewing or reading. This is not a tangible, or necessarily a retrievable or sustainable copy, but these are not required in order to constitute "material form" as explained above.

computer. This exemplifies the tension between applying offline concepts online. The difference between reading online is significantly different to reading offline.

Stokes and Reeves highlight the disadvantage of attempting to apply copyright law to modern technology by using a skeumorph, or offline metaphor in this way: "… it begs a lot of questions. Not least, why the Supreme Court felt so strongly that a web page should be equated to a printed book? A printed book has limited circulation. A web page can receive millions of hits. And this case was about the commercial use of copyrighted material where the rights owners were willing to offer licences to end users."[134]

The Supreme Court acknowledged that as part of the ordinary technical process of the internet, temporary copies are made at several stages. It described in detail the technical process of "caching", whereby copies are made without downloading, noting that "it is a universal feature of current internet browsing technology."[135] The Supreme Court stated that these copies, along with the display of the work on the screen, are an incidental consequence to using a computer online and sets out to consider if these copies constitute infringement.[136]

The Supreme Court took an internal perspective by considering the experience of the user. Furthermore, it found that the technical function that occurred in order to facilitate this experience was irrelevant. In doing so, the Supreme Court disagreed with the approach taken by Mrs Justice Proudman. As Hart explained: "Unlike Proudman J, who considered that the making of the copy was the objective of the end-user, Lord Sumption stressed that the end-user in this case does not set out to make a copy of the web page and that, unless he chooses to download or print it, his objective is simply to view the material."[137]

Nevertheless, the Supreme Court recognised that the issues at hand had a transnational dimension and resolved to refer to the European Union for guidance. The referral questioned whether acts of reproduction need to be temporary, transient or incidental and an integral part of the technological process, taking into consideration that copies are made in the ordinary use of the internet.[138]

134 Stokes S. and Reeves S., UK Supreme Court Decides Web-Browsing Doesn't Infringe Copyright But Nevertheless Refers the Matter to the CJEU: *PRCA Ltd v The NLA* (2013) 24(5) *Entertainment Law Review*, pp. 174–176, p. 175.

135 *Public Relations Consultants Association Ltd v The Newspaper Licensing Agency Ltd and Others* [2013] UKSC 18 as per Lord Sumption at [2].

136 *Ibid.*, at [2].

137 Hart M., The Legality of Internet Browsing in the Digital Age (2014) 36(10) *European Intellectual Property Review*, pp. 630–639, p. 635.

138 *Public Relations Consultants Association Ltd v The Newspaper Licensing Agency Ltd and Others* [2013] UKSC 18 as per Lord Sumption at [38].

Meltwater in the CJEU: moving away from the UK approach

The Court of Justice of the European Union (CJEU) was satisfied that the temporary cache copying of material online met the five requirements of the exception, as set out above and addressed in the first instance by Mrs Justice Proudman. The CJEU confirmed that onscreen copies and cached copies made by an end-user in the course of viewing a website satisfied the conditions that those copies must be temporary, that they must be transient or incidental in nature and that they must constitute an integral and essential part of a technological process, and that they may therefore be made without the authorisation of the copyright holders.[139]

In its reasoning, the CJEU steered away from the UK understanding of voluntary copying by the act of accessing discussed above. Instead, the CJEU stated that onscreen copies and cached copies are created and deleted by the technological process[140] and therefore it was irrelevant that the process was "activated by the internet user."[141] This reasoning encompassed both the internal and external perspectives. Firstly, the CJEU considered the technical function of the process, taking the external perspective, but ultimately it acknowledged the user experience as prevailing, as the copying was made irrelevant to the user by the technical process.

This decision has been considered as the prevailing of a "common sense."[142] As a result, the CJEU avoided "potentially causing irreparable damage to the operation of the internet in Europe."[143] Therefore, it appears that the CJEU has offered the UK some relief from the restrictions of the overly technical approach taken in the case law. However, the implications of the *Meltwater* decision remain to be seen,[144] but it appears that the copies made during internet browsing fall within the exception of section 28A of the CDPA 1988.

139 *Newspaper Licensing Agency Ltd and others v Meltwater Holding BV and others* (Case C-360/13) ECLI:EU:C:2014:1195, at 63.

140 *Ibid.*, at 29.

141 *Ibid.*, at 30.

142 Baker A., EU Copyright Directive: Does Internet Browsing Require Copyright Licences? *Public Relations Consultants Association Ltd v Newspaper Licensing Agency Ltd* (C-360/13) (the *Meltwater* case) Case Comment (2014) 25(7) *Entertainment Law Review*, pp. 257–261 at p. 261.

143 James S., And Breathe ... You Can Continue Browsing the Internet, as The CJEU Hands Down its Decision in *PRCA v NLA* (2014) 20(6) *Computer and Telecommunications Law Review*, pp. 169–171, p 169.

144 Baker A., EU Copyright Directive: Does Internet Browsing Require Copyright Licences? *Public Relations Consultants Association Ltd v Newspaper Licensing Agency Ltd* (C-360/13) (the *Meltwater* case) Case Comment (2014) 25(7) *Entertainment Law Review*, pp. 257–261 at p. 261.

The verdict on reproduction by storage

Overall, the above case law analysis suggests that unlawful use can take many forms, it is a broad concept[145] and it is applied strictly.[146] In light of this, copyright law appears to have developed from protecting *copying* of works to restricting the *use* of and *access* to copyright works.[147]

So far, this chapter has demonstrated examples of cases which suggested that accessing copyright work can be an infringement, such as Lord McIntosh suggested in the process of drafting the CDPA 1988: "it is the accessing of the work which makes the act relevant to copyright restrictions."[148]

Laddie, Prescott and Vitoria argued that the approach taken by the UK Courts was "surely to defy common sense … [because] … machines do not infringe copyright; only persons do."[149] It supports this argument with the analogy of copying by hand as the person is "doing it … he whose hand guides the pen, and not he who happens to be the owner of the paper."[150] It recognised that the wording of the act does not identify the person who is responsible for the act and whilst there is no defence for being unaware, it does not mean that a person can be liable for an act he did not perform.[151]

Nevertheless, as the case law analysis has demonstrated, strict liability has been applied by the UK courts as to find liability where copying was made automatically by a machine without the requirement for knowledge. Mr Justice Smith made a distinction between copying without knowledge and involuntary copying;[152] however, the subsequent case law essentially found that any person using a computer could be said to be taking a voluntary action by viewing, accessing or using a work via a computer.[153]

Perhaps, though, Lessig would argue that this is not a bad thing, and is indeed the future of copyright regulations: "Copyright law has got to give up its obsession with 'the copy.' The law should not regulate 'copies' or 'modern

145 *Indicii Salus Ltd (In Receivership) v Garu Paran Chandrasekaran, Vanessa Chandrasekaran, Ssaneva Security Technologies* [2007] EWHC 406 (Ch), as per Warren J at [25].

146 *Sony Music Entertainment (UK) Ltd, Sony Music Entertainment Inc, Polydor Ltd, UMG Recordings Inc, Virgin Records Ltd v Easyinternetcafe Ltd* [2003] EWHC 62 (Ch) at 33.

147 CDPA 1988, section 16(1)(a)–(e); the acts restricted by copyright.

148 *Hansard*, Copyright (Computer Software) Amendment Bill, HL Deb 5 June 1985 Vol 464 Cols 823–829, Lord McIntosh of Haringey at 825.

149 *Laddie, Prescott and Vitoria*, 14.14.

150 *Ibid.*, 14.14

151 *Ibid.*, 14.14

152 *Sony Music Entertainment (UK) Ltd, Sony Music Entertainment Inc, Polydor Ltd, UMG Recordings Inc, Virgin Records Ltd v Easyinternetcafe Ltd* [2003] EWHC 62 (Ch) at 33.

153 *The Newspaper Licensing Agency Ltd, MGN Ltd, Associated Newspapers Ltd, Express Newspapers Ltd, Guardian News and Media Ltd, Telegraph Media Group Ltd, Independent Print Ltd v Meltwater Holding BV, Meltwater News UK Ltd, Public Relations Consultants Association Ltd* [2010] EWHC 3099 (Ch) at 109.

reproductions' on their own. It should instead regulate uses – like public distributions of copies of copyrighted work – that connect directly to the economic incentive copyright law was intended to foster."[154]

However, this approach was retracted to some extent by the CJEU in the *Meltwater* case.[155] It remains to be seen how the UK courts will take on board the distinction in the reasoning made in order to reach this conclusion.[156]

In relation to the Framework for Constructing Digital Perspectives, the analysis demonstrated that both judges and counsel used both the internal and external perspectives in their interpretation and application of copyright law. In particular, the external perspective was used to understand the technical function of the network or process in question. On the other hand, a metaphorical approach was often taken to map the law onto the circumstances of the case, applying the law to old offline concepts to justify how it should apply to the new technology online.

The case of *Navitaire v EasyJet* [157] in particular demonstrated clearly the uncertainty and inconsistency in the law that transpires as a result of the changing of perspective. In the first instance, Mr Justice Pumfrey took an internal perspective in favour of the applicants, stating that the works were the same "from the user's point of view."[158] However, his final decision took the external perspective as he recognised that the interface of the software was the same but the technical process behind the interface was different and therefore no copying had taken place.[159]

Further, the *Meltwater* [160] case also amplified how taking a purely external perspective, by only considering the technical function of the process can lead to obscure copyright law that encompasses all activity online. This also demonstrates the limitations of taking a purely literal approach, which can lead to absurdities. However, the CJEU was able to take both the internal and external perspectives to bring the law back into balance.[161]

154 Lessig L., *Remix: Making Art and Commerce Thrive in the Hybrid Economy* (New York: Penguin Press, 2008) p. 268.

155 *Newspaper Licensing Agency Ltd and others v Meltwater Holding BV and others* (Case C-360/13) ECLI:EU:C:2014:1195.

156 Baker A., EU Copyright Directive: Does Internet Browsing Require Copyright Licences? *Public Relations Consultants Association Ltd v Newspaper Licensing Agency Ltd* (C-360/13) (the *Meltwater* case) Case Comment (2014) 25(7) *Entertainment Law Review*, pp. 257–261 at p. 261.

157 *Navitaire Inc v EasyJet Airline Company Ltd, Bullet Proof Technologies Inc* [2003] EWHC 3487 (Ch).

158 *Ibid.*, Pumfrey J at [5].

159 *Navitaire Inc v EasyJet Airline Company Ltd, Bullet Proof Technologies Inc* [2004] EWHC 1725 (Ch), as per Pumfrey J at [321].

160 *The Newspaper Licensing Agency Ltd, MGN Ltd, Associated Newspapers Ltd, Express Newspapers Ltd, Guardian News and Media Ltd, Telegraph Media Group Ltd, Independent Print Ltd v Meltwater Holding BV, Meltwater News UK Ltd, Public Relations Consultants Association Ltd* [2010] EWHC 3099 (Ch).

161 *Newspaper Licensing Agency Ltd and others v Meltwater Holding BV and others* (Case C-360/13) ECLI:EU:C:2014:1195.

Case law analysis: section 17(6) of the CDPA 1988

This chapter now turns to consider the case law that considers section 17(6) of the CDPA 1988 in order to determine how judges interpret and apply this part of the regulation online.

Transient and incidental copying

Chapter 3 established that the purpose of section 17(6) of the CDPA 1988 was to restrict the loading or storing of a computer program so that incidental copying in the course of running a computer program, or viewing a work stored in a computer database, was a restricted act of copying.[162] As a result, loading or running a computer program constitutes reproduction.[163]

Section 17(6) of the CDPA 1988 states that: "copying in relation to any description of work includes the making of copies which are transient or are incidental to some other use of the work." This section will now consider some of the key cases which determine the meaning of section 17(6).[164]

The case selection and methodology are the same as for the above section; all of the relevant cases were collated by reference to section 17 of the CDPA 1988. These cases were searched for using the terms "transient" and "incidental", which provided 122 references within 29 cases. The most relevant are analysed below to demonstrate the court's interpretation and application of section 17(6). In particular, three cases were identified as the most significant in the development of the meaning of transient and incidental copying, namely *Cantor Gaming*,[165] *R v Higgs*[166] and *Gilham.*[167]

In these cases, the judge gave particular consideration to the interpretation and meaning of section 17(6) of the CDPA 1988. As with the previous section, these cases are addressed in chronological order so as to demonstrate the development of the section over time. The first case in particular sees the court demonstrate the limitations of taking the external perspective too far in relation to running a computer program. The second and third cases discuss and develop transient copying in the RAM and onscreen.

162 *Hansard*, Copyright, Designs and Patents Bill [HL], HL Deb 29 March 1988 Vol 495 Cols 607–696, Lord Mattistone at 647.

163 *Kabushiki Kaisha Sony Computer Entertainment Inc Also Trading As Sony Computer Entertainment Inc (A Company Incorporated Under The Law Of Japan), Sony Computer Entertainment Europe Ltd, Sony Computer Entertainment UK Ltd v Gaynor David Ball, Gary Edmunds, Boris Baikov, Ina Sorokovich, Igor Tiporov, K Shashkov, Stepan Gvozdeff* [2004] EWHC 1738 (Ch), as per Laddie J at [17]: "playing of an unauthorised copy of a PS2 game or a 'foreign' authentic game on a PS2 console involves copying a substantial part of the copyright work into RAM and, questions of licence aside, amounts to infringement."

164 The case selection and methodology is the same as above for storage. The search terms used were "transient" and "incidental", this provided 122 references in 29 cases.

165 *Cantor Gaming Ltd v Gameaccount Global Ltd* [2007] EWHC 1914 (Ch).

166 *R v Higgs* [2008] EWCA Crim 1324.

167 *Christopher Paul Gilham v The Queen* [2009] EWCA Crim 2293.

The limitations of taking the external perspective in transient copying

In 2007, transient copying was considered in the case of *Cantor Gaming.* [168] In its application of the law the court took an external perspective. It explained in detail the technical process which took place when a program was "executed by a computer"[169] to create copies from a hard drive into the computer's memory. The court went further to explain that the copies made inside the computer were expressed in "machine code rather than high level programming language",[170] which were constantly being copied and recopied as the computer performed logical operations. Therefore, the court recognised that it was not possible to say, with any confidence, precisely what transient reproduction would occur. The best it could say with any confidence was that it was "highly likely" that, in the circumstances, the work would have been partially or completely copied.[171]

This is an example of how taking the external perspective too far can result in confusion. The court recognised the technical function of the network and considered in detail how the computer makes copies. However, the court's justification is limited by its understanding of the functioning of a computer. Once the court reaches this point, it can say only that it is highly likely the computer made copies but cannot support this by continuing with the external perspective.

In making its decision, the court considered that under UK copyright law, infringement by copying is a broad concept and that this is consistent with EU law,[172] which states that the permanent or temporary reproduction of a computer program is the exclusive right of the copyright holder.[173] Therefore, despite the uncertainty, the court found that, on the balance of probabilities, at least some of the applicant's work would have been copied.[174]

In this matter, the court took an external perspective to determine the facts of the case. However, it was unable to continue with this perspective in order to use the technical process as evidence to support substantial copying. Therefore, the court determined that copying had occurred simply on balance that it probably did.

The subsequent case also demonstrates the court taking an external perspective, where it determined that transient and incidental copying encompass copying on the RAM of a computer or game console.

168 *Cantor Gaming Ltd v Gameaccount Global Ltd* [2007] EWHC 1914 (Ch), before Mr Daniel Alexander QC sitting as a Deputy High Court Judge (Chancery Division). The case primarily concerned breach of contract, where the defendant's actions fell outside the contract and the claimants argued that this was an infringement of their copyright.
169 *Ibid.*, Mr Daniel Alexander QC at [39].
170 *Ibid.*, Mr Daniel Alexander QC at [39].
171 *Ibid.*, Mr Daniel Alexander QC at [94].
172 Referring to Council Directive 91/250/EEC of 14 May 1991 on the Legal Protection of Computer Programs [1991] OJ L 122/42, Article 4.
173 *Cantor Gaming Ltd v Gameaccount Global Ltd* [2007] EWHC 1914 (Ch), as per Mr Daniel Alexander QC at [81].
174 *Ibid.*, as per Mr Daniel Alexander QC at [94].

Random access memory as transient copying

In 2008, Mr Higgs ran a business selling modchips,[175] fitting modchips to customers' computer games consoles and selling games consoles into which he had already fitted modchips.[176]

The case against Mr Higgs was not the playing of pirated material,[177] but that by selling the modchips and modified consoles he encouraged and exploited a market for pirate games.[178]

When considering section 17(6) of the CDPA 1988, Mr Macdonald for the Crown highlighted to the court that the language of the Act was not exactly the same as that in the Directive:

Directive: "Designed to prevent or restrict acts, in respect of works or other subject-matter, which are not authorized by the rightholder."
UK Act: "prevention or restriction of acts that are not authorised by the copyright owner of that work and are restricted by copyright."

The UK Act adds the words "and are restricted by copyright."[179]

Mr MacDonald suggested that the words that were not in the Directive should be disregarded, which would have the effect of a wider meaning.[180] However, the court did not appreciate the inconsistency,[181] and disagreed with Mr MacDonald, stating that the "the words add nothing."[182] The court went on to explain that "when speaking of 'acts which are not authorised' it is implicit that one is considering only acts which need authorization, i.e. acts which are otherwise restricted. To 'authorise' a man to do something he is free to do anyway – something which needs no authority – is a meaningless concept."[183]

This is interesting in light of the previous analysis, which highlighted the significance of word choice in the drafting of legislation as it demonstrates that a literal reading of the law can lead to inconsistencies when the law has been transposed from an EU Directive using different wording. The reason for this change in the wording is unknown, although this is a common characteristic of UK implementation of EU Directives.[184] Whilst there may have been a reason

175 A modchip (a modification chip) is a small electronic device used to alter or disable artificial restrictions of computers or entertainment devices. Modchips are mainly used in videogame consoles, but also in some DVD or Blu-ray players.
176 *R v Higgs* [2008] EWCA Crim 1324, as per Jacob LJ at [2].
177 *Ibid.*, Jacob LJ at [11].
178 *Ibid.*, Jacob LJ at [12].
179 *Ibid.*, Jacob LJ at [31].
180 *Ibid.*, Jacob LJ at [31]–[32].
181 *Ibid.*, Jacob LJ at [31] and concluding at [32]: "the UK draftsman was merely making explicit that which was implicit in the Directive – and indeed in the original 1966 Treaty obligations."
182 *Ibid.*, Jacob LJ at [32].
183 *Ibid.*, Jacob LJ at [32].
184 *Laddie, Prescott and Vitoria*, 17.7.

behind the change, Lord Justice Jacob did not appreciate it in this case, as he stated: "Why, oh why do statutory draftsman persist in trying to gloss Directives which are specific about what is to be implemented?"[185] Nevertheless, Lord Justice Jacob argued that the draftsman's only intention could have been to make clearer the same meaning expressed in the Directive: "The UK draftsman was merely making explicit that which was implicit in the Directive – and indeed in the original 1966 Treaty obligations."[186] This interpretation follows the golden rule discussed in Chapter 1, where Lord Justice Jacob is determining that although the specific words are different, the meaning intended by those words is the same.

Secondly, Lord Justice Jacob stated, albeit *obiter*, that the making of transient copies of copyright material into a RAM was a restricted act.[187] The court recognised that Mr Justice Laddie had held in *Sony Entertainment v Ball* [188] that a transient copy in a games console was an infringing copy of a work, and that the facts of the case in hand were "near identical to those in this case, that there was infringement."[189] In these circumstances, the court explained, even a single frame of a cinematograph film could constitute infringement.[190] Therefore, the playing of an unauthorised game on a console would also be an infringement. This shows the court taking a purely external perspective, which resulted in a broad application of copyright law that effectively encompasses all online activity.

However, in Mr Higgs's case, the prosecution failed to put forward any evidence relating to whether or not his modchip enabled a transient copy.[191] This left the court unable to uphold the conviction against Mr Higgs as it had not seen any evidence in this case that a transient copy was made. Lord Justice Jacob described Mr Higgs as a "fortunate man"[192] in this regard, stating that if the legislation had been less complex and/or the Crown had considered the details of copyright law to a greater extent, the case would have been proved on the basis that merely playing a pirated game involved making a copy in the console.[193]

Nevertheless, this case demonstrated the court taking an external perspective and determining that transient and incidental copying encompassed copying on

185 *R v Higgs* [2008] EWCA Crim 1324, as per Jacob LJ at [31].

186 *Ibid.*, Jacob LJ at [32].

187 *Ibid.*, Jacob LJ at [9].

188 *Kabushiki Kaisha Sony Computer Entertainment Inc Also Trading As Sony Computer Entertainment Inc (A Company Incorporated Under The Law Of Japan), Sony Computer Entertainment Europe Ltd, Sony Computer Entertainment UK Ltd v Gaynor David Ball, Gary Edmunds, Boris Baikov, Ina Sorokovich, Igor Tiporov, K Shashkov, Stepan Gvozdeff* [2004] EWHC 1738 (Ch).

189 *R v Higgs* [2008] EWCA Crim 1324, as per Jacob LJ at [10].

190 *Ibid.*, Jacob LJ at [9] referring to *Spelling Goldberg v BPC Publishing* [1981] RPC 225.

191 *Ibid.*, Jacob LJ at [29].

192 *Ibid.*, Jacob LJ at [36].

193 *Ibid.*, Jacob LJ at [36].

the RAM of a computer or game console. This point was recognised and relied upon in *R v Gilham*, [194] discussed below.

Displaying images shown on the screen as infringement

Subsequently, in 2009, the restricted act of transient copying in the RAM of a games console was developed further in the matter of *Gilham*. In this case, the Court of Appeal considered in detail the technical process of copying a work into the RAM of a computer console and whether this amounted to a substantial part of the work.[195]

The court noted that Lord Justice Jacob had stated in the matter of *R v Higgs*, [196] that copying into RAM would be infringement of copyright.[197] Indeed, it was proved in the present case that during the playing of a game from a counterfeit DVD, data was copied into the RAM of the games console.[198]

However, the appellant in this case argued that although there was such copying, it did not represent at any one time the whole or a substantial part of the game's data on the DVD, and therefore did not amount to the copying of a substantial part of the work.[199]

Lord Justice Burton stated that even if the contents of the RAM of a game console were not a substantial copy, the image displayed on screen would be.[200] This was because, as he stated, "the various drawings that result in the images shown on the television screen or monitor are themselves artistic works protected by copyright. The images shown on the screen are copies, and substantial copies, of those works."[201] He even went on to explain that the images need not have been an exact copy of the artistic work because the software may move the image,

194 *Christopher Paul Gilham v The Queen* [2009] EWCA Crim 2293, before Stanley Burnton LJ, Penry Davey J and Sharpe J, DBE, 9 November 2009.

195 *Ibid.*, Stanley Burnton LJ at [18] and [30]. In the first instance the appellant had been convicted of copyright infringement by a jury – as this case had been brought under criminal proceedings. However, the court stated that this was not appropriate: "We repeat with emphasis what Jacob LJ said in Higgs about the trial of cases involving recondite issues of copyright law before a jury. Cases that, for example, involve determination of difficult questions whether a copy is of a substantial part of a copyright work, can and should be tried in the Chancery Division before specialist judges." See further: Sharp C. and Smith J., The Interplay Between Civil and Criminal IP Litigation in the UK (2012) 7(8) *Journal of Intellectual Property Law and Practice*, pp. 573–579.

196 *R v Higgs* [2008] EWCA Crim 1324, as per Jacob LJ at [4].

197 *Christopher Paul Gilham v The Queen* [2009] EWCA Crim 2293, as per Stanley Burton LJ at [7].

198 *Ibid.*, Stanley Burton LJ at [16]. However, the expert evidence explained that when a game is played on a console using a counterfeit DVD, the RAM in the console will copy a very small amount (less than 3 per cent) of the whole of the counterfeit DVD at any one time, but it cannot be predicted what data will be being copied and then overwritten in the RAM at any time because that depended on the way that the game is played.

199 *Ibid.*, Stanley Burton LJ at [17].

200 *Ibid.*, Stanley Burton LJ at [25].

201 *Ibid.*, Stanley Burton LJ at [24].

but nonetheless would be recognisable. He supported this argument by stating that when the "pause" button on a game console is pressed, what is shown on screen constitutes an image that is a copy of an artistic work generated by the digital data in RAM.[202]

He also referred to the judgment of Mr Justice Kitchin in the *Football Association Premier League* case,[203] where he doubted that "those who framed the CDPA ever contemplated that displaying an image on a television screen amounts to copying. However, s.17 must be construed in the light of the Directive and, despite my reservations, I have reached the conclusion that it is indeed this broad."[204] Mr Justice Kitchin had supported his decision by drawing on a much earlier case,[205] which held that the defendants infringed the copyright subsisting in race cards by showing them on television monitors in their shops.[206]

The defence argued that display on a screen could not be a substantial copy of a copyright work, as it only appeared for an instant. However, the court found this to be irrelevant, as section 17(6) of the CDPA 1988 expressly provided that a transient copy is a copy, adding that the fact that players do not normally pause the game is immaterial.[207]

To some it was considered "common sense"[208] that the playing of an illegally created game or DVD on a games console should be copyright infringement, on the basis that it made a copy of at least a substantial part of the game whether in the RAM, or on the screen even though it only exists at any one time for a fraction of a second.[209] Therefore, the judgment went beyond the literal reading of the words in the statute, in order to remedy the mischief it intended to address by restricting this act, in line with the mischief rule discussed in Chapter 1. In this regard, the judgment was considered "welcome news for copyright owners in the digital age."[210] Ormerod argued that the court's approach in this case was "entirely right."[211] Although Massey noted that the court seemed to skip over the point, as mentioned above, when not ruling in relation to the RAM copying: "It seems a shame,

202 *Ibid.*, Stanley Burton LJ at [25].
203 *Football Association Premier League Ltd and Others v QC Leisure and Others* [2008] EWHC 1411 (Ch).
204 *Ibid.*, Kitchin J at [232].
205 *Bookmakers' Afternoon Greyhound Services v Wilf Gilbert (Staffordshire) Ltd* [1994] FSR 723, as per Aldous J (a decision under the Copyright Act 1956).
206 *Football Association Premier League Ltd and Others v QC Leisure and Others* [2008] EWHC 1411 (Ch), as per Kitchin J at [232].
207 *Christopher Paul Gilham v The Queen* [2009] EWCA Crim 2293, as per Stanley Burton LJ at [25] and [27].
208 Massey R., *R. v Gilham (Christopher Paul)* – Pirates Beware! Transient Copying to RAM is Sufficient for Infringement of Copyright (2010) 21(3) *Entertainment Law Review*, pp. 107–108, p. 108.
209 *Ibid.*
210 *Ibid.*
211 Ormerod D., *R. v Gilham*: Copyright – Copyright, Designs and Patents Act 1988 s.296ZB (2010) 5 *Criminal Law Review*, pp. 407–409, p. 408.

however, that the Court of Appeal did not rule, as opposed to merely comment, on Mr Gilham's 'little and often' defence which after all was the focus of the case at trial. This would have taken *Sony v Ball* up a notch and set Jacob L.J.'s *dicta* in stone."[212]

In relation to the Framework for Constructing Digital Perspectives, it is clear that in this matter the court used the external perspective when determining the facts of the case by considering the technical process of the RAM and the game console. However, when it then attempted to map these circumstances onto the relevant copyright law, in this literal manner, it appears that it did not fit. The difficulty was that, as the analysis demonstrated, "common sense" assured the court that playing a counterfeit game should be illegal, but it was unable to find a way within the external perspective to reason this decision. This demonstrates the limitations of taking a literal approach in interpreting the law. As a result, the judges took a purposive approach in order to achieve the intended outcome, or the mischief that the legislation aimed to remedy.

The judge instead took the internal perspective, and considered that the user could see the images on the screen, therefore the *display* of the copyright work was infringement.[213] However, the court still struggled to justify this as a reason for infringement, suggesting that the image was "generated by the digital data in RAM."[214]

Therefore, this case clearly exemplified the tensions that occur when attempting to map copyright law onto new technologies. Further, it demonstrated the difficulties that can occur when taking the external perspective too far – the law becomes too narrow and specific and defies common sense. In these circumstances, the courts appear to be fumbling for a justification to bring the law back in line with its purpose, as the external perspective, and lack of awareness thereof, had failed to accommodate the intention of the law. The court finally used the internal perspective to find its way to infringement in these circumstances, taking a purposive approach to remedy the mischief.

The verdict on transient copying

Overall, the case law analysis in this section has demonstrated that the law in relation to section 17(6) of the CDPA 1988 is broad and encompasses activity such as display of the work on a screen.[215]

Accordingly, storage in computer memory infringes copyright, including cloud storage[216] and even in dynamic RAM where the information would perish almost

212 Massey R., *R. v Gilham (Christopher Paul)* – Pirates Beware! Transient Copying to RAM is Sufficient for Infringement of Copyright (2010) 21(3) *Entertainment Law Review*, pp. 107–108, p. 108.

213 *Christopher Paul Gilham v The Queen* [2009] EWCA Crim 2293, as per Stanley Burton LJ at [25].

214 *Ibid.*, Stanley Burton LJ at [25].

215 *Christopher Paul Gilham v The Queen* [2009] EWCA Crim 2293.

216 *VCAST Ltd v RTI SpA* (Case C-265/16), ECLI:EU:C:2017:913

instantaneously but for being constantly refreshed.[217] Therefore, loading or running a computer program would constitute infringement,[218] as could online browsing or access to any copyright material online. *Laddie, Prescott and Vitoria* suggests that the precise way in which the program works may affect the question of whether there has been reproduction;[219] however, this research demonstrates that is unlikely since courts have tended to take a metaphorical and purposive approach.

Whilst the drafters of the law may have had specific circumstances in mind, the law has been developed to encompass new technological developments which could not have been envisaged.[220]

Generally, judges appear to take an external perspective when considering the law of transient copying, in line with the drafting of the subsection. However, this can be problematic, as demonstrated in *Gilham*.

The problem of applying the law from the external perspective is that it can result in the law going much further than originally intended, for example, to include *display* of a copyright work instead of merely a copy of a copyright work. At its extreme this approach can lead to results that appear to disregard common sense. For example, *Laddie, Prescott and Vitoria* argued that with this reasoning reading a newspaper over somebody's shoulder could be infringement by "electronic means" because "electronic" could include actuated by electro-magnetic or electro-chemical energy and light is a form of electromagnetic energy:[221] an image of the page is formed on the retina of the eye, and through neurons transmitted in the brain a person will experience the conscious sensation of viewing the page, by way of biochemical processes which are actuated by electrochemical energy, which is then stored in the brain. This interpretation leads to an absurdity in the law: "All this reasoning is uncontroversial in scientific terms, but totally absurd all the same."[222]

Conclusion

As detailed at the beginning of this chapter, section 17(2) of the CDPA 1988 was first envisaged by Viscount Coville, who argued that it was necessary to protect a work stored on a computer in case this was the only copy on which a creator could rely.[223] A reading of the relevant case law demonstrated that in 27 years since the enactment, in over 90 cases that referred to this section, not one was applied in these

217 Speck A., et al (eds), *Laddie, Prescott and Vitoria: The Modern Law of Copyright*, 5th edition (London: Lexis Nexis, 2018) p. 769.

218 *Sony Computer Entertainment Inc v Ball* [2005] FSR 9 at 16; *R v Gilham* [2010] ECDR 5 at 15.

219 Speck A., et al (eds), *Laddie, Prescott and Vitoria: The Modern Law of Copyright* (London: Lexis Nexis, 2018) p. 769.

220 *Football Association Premier League Ltd and Others v QC Leisure and Others* [2008] EWHC 1411 (Ch), as per Kitchin J at [232].

221 *Laddie, Prescott and Vitoria*, 14.12.

222 *Ibid.*, 14.12.

223 *Hansard*, Copyright (Computer Software) Amendment Bill, HL Deb 5 June 1985 Vol 464 Cols 823–829, Viscount Colville of Culross at 824.

circumstances. This does not mean that the section is necessarily redundant. It does, however, demonstrate that Viscount Coville's justification for the introduction of the law was unfounded. The circumstances within which he envisaged the section being of use never occurred. This is not to say that the law should be restricted to the circumstances envisioned at the time of drafting, or that the committee debates constitute law. However, considering the history of the development of the legislation is helpful in unearthing the mysteries of why the law appears as it does. It also provides helpful context for understanding purposive interpretations of the law, such as by way of the mischief, golden or *Pepper v Hart* rules.

Analysis of the case law which interprets these sections of the CDPA 1988 revealed four main tensions in the application of copyright law online. Firstly, the chapter demonstrated that, over time, the legal definition of "storage" and "transient copying" has developed as the technological developments have occurred, for example encompassing activity such *display* of a copyright work.[224] This is to be expected in light of technological developments of course, and could be argued to be a strength of the drafting that it encapsulates circumstances never envisaged at the time of drafting. However, this approach can lead to the law going too far, beyond its intended purpose. Moreover, as this development has occurred in the courts and not in the statutory law, it may have gone under the radar. As demonstrated in Chapter 3, this will cause challenges for legislators in the future, as it is unlikely stakeholders will support new policy that leaves them worse off.

Secondly, judges spent a long time going into great detail on establishing the technical function or process of the computer program or technology in question. The judges spend pages explaining each technical step that the process takes, often relying on expert evidence provided to the court, clearly taking an external perspective. Some judges went even further to include an explanation not only of the program or system at hand, but also the technical function of a computer in general. For example, in the *IBCOS Computers* [225] case Mr Justice Jacob stated: "computers only work in binary code, a code made up of 0's and 1's. So all data held in a computer or held on a computer storage device (such as a RAM, disc, or tape) must be so coded."[226] However, the use of technologically specific justifications for decisions can lead to restrictions in the law that are contrary to common sense. It can also lead the court down a road of no return whereby it is seen to switch to the internal perspective without awareness or coherence in order to allow the law to fulfil its intended purpose. This shows that in these cases, the law is insufficient to allow judges to take a purely literal reading without creating an absurdity. This, therefore, encourages judges to lean towards a more purposive interpretation of the law in order to, for example, remedy the mischief that it intended to deal with.

224 *Christopher Paul Gilham v The Queen* [2009] EWCA Crim 2293, as per Stanley Burton LJ at [27].

225 *IBCOS Computers Ltd and Another v Barclays Mercantile Highland Finance* [1994] FSR 275.

226 *Ibid.*, as per Jacob J at 285.

Thirdly, another drawback of this approach is that similar cases are bought before the court, and the legal application has to be considered all over again because of a slight mechanical difference between the technologies in question. For example, Lord Penrose stated in the *Beta Computers* [227] case "the case is concerned with one type of software only and one form of contractual relationship for supply. It would be misleading to generalise."[228] Furthermore, in the case of *R v Higgs*, the judge referred back to *Sony Entertainment v Ball* [229] and stated that "on facts near identical to those in this case … The only factual difference is that, unlike this case, it was asserted that transient copying into the console took place – and the Defendant so admitted."[230]

Fourthly, judges and counsel tend to use analogue, offline, or historical analogies to understand and apply the law of copyright to the new technology. As discussed in Chapter 2, this is one way in which people, and the law, can process and deal with the development of new technologies. However, the difficulty of using this approach is that, at times, the skeumorph does not accurately portray the technological circumstance.

Lastly, from this analysis the relationship between section 17(2) and 17(6) of the CDPA 1988 can be considered. The cases appear to overlap or, at least, be interconnecting the two sections. The majority of cases that fully engage with section 17(2) also engage with section 17(6). This may be due to the circumstances of the cases being brought to court. There are some cases that clearly demonstrate that storage on a computer can be over time, whereas transient copying is only temporary copying. Although the more recent case law focuses more on the temporary storage within the RAM of a computer, or a server, transient copying is the temporary storage of a work, so there is a clear overlap.

This chapter completes the analysis of copyright infringement by way of copying as applied to online activity, through the lens of the Framework for Constructing Digital Perspectives. This investigation first considered the development of the statutory law, considering the context within which the law was created, including the long and complex development of the CDPA 1988, which in turn created long and complex legislation.[231] Moreover, the law was clearly influenced by human factors such as lack of copyright knowledge,[232]

227 *Beta Computers (Europe) Ltd v Adobe Systems* [1996] SLT 604.

228 *Ibid.*, as per Lord Penrose at 608.

229 *Kabushiki Kaisha Sony Computer Entertainment Inc Also Trading As Sony Computer Entertainment Inc (A Company Incorporated Under The Law Of Japan), Sony Computer Entertainment Europe Ltd, Sony Computer Entertainment UK Ltd v Gaynor David Ball, Gary Edmunds, Boris Baikov, Ina Sorokovich, Igor Tiporov, K Shashkov, Stepan Gvozdeff* [2004] EWHC 1738 (Ch).

230 *R v Higgs* [2008] EWCA Crim 1324, as per Jacob LJ at [10].

231 Merkin R., *Richards Butler on Copyright, Designs and Patents: The New Law* (London: Longman, 1989) pp. 1–2.

232 *Hansard*, Copyright (Computer Software) Amendment Bill, HL Deb 5 June 1985 Vol 464 Cols 823–829, Lord McIntosh at 825.

lack of understanding of the technology[233] and the competing stakeholder interests.[234]

In considering the details of section 17 of the CDPA 1988, the analysis looked closely at each subsection. This revealed that as one of the main goals in the law reform was to simplify the legislation,[235] many of the subsections were restatements of the previous Act, meaning that much of the law applied to modern technology today dates back to 1956. The statutory analysis identified that the legislator appeared to intend the law to be drafted from an external perspective, focusing on addressing new technology and the use of technological terminology. Nevertheless, evidence of the internal perspective was found in the wording of the law.

Thereafter, the case law relating to sections 17(2) and 17(6) of the CDPA 1988 was considered in order to determine how the judges interpreted and applied the law to cases of online copyright infringement. This analysis highlighted the tensions created in the application of copyright law to the internet, in view of the fact that there are two different ways in which online activity can be perceived.

The subsequent chapters continue the examination of online copyright infringement by considering the law relating to communication to the public. The analysis is undertaken using the same methodology and so the structure that follows in Chapter 5 and Chapter 6 mirrors that of Chapter 3 and Chapter 4.

Bibliography

Books

Bartlett F. C., *Remembering: A Study in Experimental and Social Psychology* (Cambridge: Cambridge University Press, 1932).

Tappin QCM., et al (eds) *The Modern Law of Copyright*, 5th edition (London: Lexis Nexis, 2018).

Lessig L., *Remix: Making Art and Commerce Thrive in the Hybrid Economy* (New York: Penguin Press, 2008).

Litman J., *Digital Copyright*, 2nd edition (New York: Prometheus Books, 2006).

Merkin R., *Richards Butler on Copyright, Designs and Patents: The New Law* (London: Longman, 1989).

Rumelhart D. E. and Norman D. A., Analogical Processes in Learning in Anderson J. R. (ed) *Cognitive Skills and Their Acquisition* (Hillsdale: Lawrence Erlbaum Associates Inc, 1981).

Speck A., et al (eds), *Laddie, Prescott and Vitoria: The Modern Law of Copyright and Designs*, 5th edition (London: Butterworths Law, 2018).

Vitoria M., et al (eds), *Laddie, Prescott and Vitoria: The Modern Law of Copyright and Designs*, 4th edition (London: Butterworths Law, 2011).

233 *Ibid.*, Viscount Colville of Culross at 824.

234 Laddie J., Copyright: Over-Strength, Over-Regulated, Over-Rated? (1996) 18(5) *European Intellectual Property Review*, pp. 253–260, p. 256.

235 Whitford Committee, *Copyright and Designs Law, Report of the Committee to Consider the Law on Copyright and Designs* (London: Her Majesty's Stationery Office, 1977) Cmnd 6732, para 16.

Case law

Beta Computers (Europe) Ltd v Adobe Systems [1996] SLT 604.
Bookmakers' Afternoon Greyhound Services v Wilf Gilbert (Staffordshire) Ltd [1994] FSR 723.
Cantor Gaming Ltd v Gameaccount Global Ltd [2007] EWHC 1914 (Ch).
Christopher Paul Gilham v The Queen [2009] EWCA Crim 2293.
Football Association Premier League Ltd and Others v QC Leisure and Others [2008] EWHC 1411 (Ch), [2008] FSR 32.
IBCOS Computers Ltd and Another v Barclays Mercantile Highland Finance [1994] FSR 275.
Indicii Salus Ltd (In Receivership) v Garu Paran Chandrasekaran, Vanessa Chandrasekaran, Ssaneva Security Technologies [2007] EWHC 406 (Ch).
Infopaq International AS v Danske Dagblades Forening (Case C-5/08) ECLI:EU:C:2009:465.
Kabushiki Kaisha Sony Computer Entertainment Inc Also Trading As Sony Computer Entertainment Inc (A Company Incorporated Under The Law Of Japan), Sony Computer Entertainment Europe Ltd, Sony Computer Entertainment UK Ltd v Gaynor David Ball, Gary Edmunds, Boris Baikov, Ina Sorokovich, Igor Tiporov, K Shashkov, Stepan Gvozdeff [2004] EWHC 1738 (Ch).
Navitaire Inc v EasyJet Airline Company Ltd, Bullet Proof Technologies Inc [2003] EWHC 3487 (Ch).
Navitaire Inc v EasyJet Airline Company Ltd, Bullet Proof Technologies Inc [2004] EWHC 1725 (Ch).
Newspaper Licensing Agency Ltd and others v Meltwater Holding BV and others (Case C-360/13) ECLI:EU:C:2014:1195.
Ocular Sciences Ltd and Another v Aspect Vision Care Ltd (First Action); *Geoffrey Harrison Galley v Ocular Sciences Ltd* (Second Action) [1996] EWHC Patents 1, [1997] RPC 289.
Public Relations Consultants Association Ltd v The Newspaper Licensing Agency Ltd and Others [2013] UKSC 18.
R v Gilham [2010] ECDR 5.
R v Higgs [2008] EWCA Crim 1324.
Sony Computer Entertainment Inc v Ball [2005] FSR 9.
Sony Music Entertainment (UK) Ltd, Sony Music Entertainment Inc, Polydor Ltd, UMG Recordings Inc, Virgin Records Ltd v Easyinternetcafe Ltd [2003] EWHC 62 (Ch).
Spelling Goldberg v BPC Publishing [1981] RPC 225.
The Newspaper Licensing Agency Ltd, MGN Ltd, Associated Newspapers Ltd, Express Newspapers Ltd, Guardian News and Media Ltd, Telegraph Media Group Ltd, Independent Print Ltd v Meltwater Holding BV, Meltwater News UK Ltd, Public Relations Consultants Association Ltd [2010] EWHC 3099 (Ch).
The Newspaper Licensing Agency Ltd, MGN Ltd, Associated Newspapers Ltd, Express Newspapers Ltd, Guardian News and Media Ltd, Telegraph Media Group Ltd, Independent Print Ltd v Meltwater Holding BV, Meltwater News UK Ltd, Public Relations Consultants Association Ltd [2011] EWCA Civ 890.
VCAST Ltd v RTI SpA (Case C-265/16), ECLI:EU:C:2017:913.

Journals

Bainbridge D. I, Legislation: The Copyright (Computer Software) Amendment Act (1986) 49(2) *The Modern Law Review*, pp. 214–224.

Baker A., EU Copyright Directive: Does Internet Browsing Require Copyright Licences? *Public Relations Consultants Association Ltd v Newspaper Licensing Agency Ltd* (C-360/13) (the *Meltwater* case) Case Comment (2014) 25(7) *Entertainment Law Review*, pp. 257–261.

Elsom S. M., Copyright Aspects of Information Technology: The Copyright, Designs and Patents Bill (1988) 10(11) *European Intellectual Property Review*, pp. 326–330.

Garnett K., The Easyinternetcafe Decision Case Comment (2003) 25(9) *European Intellectual Property Review*, pp. 426–427.

Hart M., The Legality of Internet Browsing in the Digital Age (2014) 36(10) *European Intellectual Property Review*, pp. 630–639.

Heritage M. and Jones P., The End of "Look and Feel" and the Invasion of the Little Green Men? UK Copyright and Patent Protection for Software After 2005 (2006) 12(3) *Computer and Telecommunications Law Review*, pp. 67–70.

Hobson A., *Newspaper Licensing Agency Ltd v Meltwater Holdings BV* (2011) 22(3) *Entertainment Law Review*, pp. 101–104.

James S., And Breathe … You Can Continue Browsing the Internet, as The CJEU Hands Down its Decision in *PRCA v NLA* (2014) 20(6) *Computer and Telecommunications Law Review*, pp. 169–171.

Kerr O. S., The Problem of Perspective in Internet Law (2003) 91 *Georgetown Law Journal*, pp. 357–405.

Laddie J., Copyright: Over-Strength, Over-Regulated, Over-Rated? (1996) 18(5) *European Intellectual Property Review*, pp. 253–260.

Massey R., *R. v Gilham (Christopher Paul)* – Pirates Beware! Transient Copying to RAM is Sufficient for Infringement of Copyright (2010) 21(3) *Entertainment Law Review*, pp. 107–108.

Onslow R. and Jamal I., Copyright Infringement and Software Emulation – *SAS Inc v World Programming Limited* Case Comment (2013) 35(6) *European Intellectual Property Review*, pp. 352–356.

Ormerod D., *R. v Gilham*: Copyright – Copyright, Designs and Patents Act 1988 s.296ZB (2010) 5*Criminal Law Review*, pp. 407–409.

Ritchie M., *Sony Music Entertainment (UK) Ltd v Easyinternetcafe Ltd* January 28, 2003 (2003) 14(6) *Entertainment Law Review*, pp. 155–156.

Sharp C. and Smith J., The Interplay Between Civil and Criminal IP Litigation in the UK (2012) 7(8) *Journal of Intellectual Property Law and Practice*, pp. 573–579.

Stokes S., The Development of UK Software Copyright Law: From John Richardson Computers to Navitaire (2005) 11(4) *Computer and Telecommunications Law Review*, pp. 129–133.

Stokes S. and Reeves S., UK Supreme Court Decides Web-Browsing Doesn't Infringe Copyright But Nevertheless Refers the Matter to the CJEU: PRCA Ltd v The NLA (2013) 24(5) *Entertainment Law Review*, pp. 174–176.

Legislation

Berne Convention for the Protection of Literary and Artistic Works 1886.

Copyright (Computer Software) Amendment Act 1985.

Copyright and Related Rights Regulations 2003 (SI 2003/2498).

Copyright, Designs and Patents Act 1988.

Council Directive 91/250/EEC of 14 May 1991 on the Legal Protection of Computer Programs [1991] *OJ* L 122/42.
Directive 2001/29/EC of the European Parliament and of the Council of 22 May 2001 on the harmonisation of certain aspects of copyright and related rights in the information society [2001] *OJ* L 167/10.
WIPO Copyright Treaty 1996.

Official documents and reports

Hansard, Copyright (Computer Software) Amendment Bill, HL Deb 5 June 1985 Vol 464 Cols 823–829.
Hansard, Copyright, Designs and Patents Bill [HL], HL Deb 29 March 1988 Vol 495 Cols 607–696.
Hansard, Copyright, Designs and Patents Bill [Lords], HC Deb 28 April 1988 Vol 132 Cols 525–599, Order for Second Reading read.
Whitford Committee, *Copyright and Designs Law, Report of the Committee to Consider the Law on Copyright and Designs* (London: Her Majesty's Stationery Office, 1977) Cmnd 6732.

5 The human element in communication to the public

Introduction

This chapter moves to applying the Framework for Constructing Digital Perspectives to copyright infringement by way of communication to the public. This right was initially designed to address broadcasting, but has expanded and become instrumental in the development of jurisprudence relating to online copyright infringement. The meaning of the concept of communication to the public is of fundamental importance in determining the circumstances in which the rights are infringed.[1] The right to control the communication of the work is considered as one of the most controversial and contentious developments in copyright law. It is imperative to the future of copyright,[2] as Keane argued "the right of communication to the public … lies at the heart of modern copyright law."[3] However, the development of the communication to the public right has been fragmented and with inconsistent application by the courts. Koo argues that this has had a chilling effect on the development of new technologies and business models and is prejudicial towards the end users.[4]

This chapter therefore, first looks at the historical development of the communication right, considering the context of the current statutory law in order to understand the intention behind it. Thereafter, a detailed analysis of section 20 of the CDPA 1988 is undertaken in order to establish the statutory meaning of communication to the public. The discussion focuses on the key elements of the right including the public and electronic transmission. There are many unanswered questions as to what constitutes a "communication" and indeed who are the "public". The Framework is applied where relevant to determine if the internal or

1 Rizzuto F., The European Union law Concept of Communication to the Public and the Protection of Copyright in Electronic Transmissions (2012) 18(6) *Computer and Telecommunications Law Review*, pp. 179–197, p. 179.

2 Haque H., Is the Time Ripe for Another Exclusive Right? A Proposal (2008) 30(9) *European Intellectual Property Review*, pp. 371–378, p. 376.

3 Keane B., Ill Communication? The Concept of a Communication to the Public Under EU Copyright Law (2013) 24(5) *Entertainment Law Review*, pp. 165–171, p. 165.

4 Koo J., *The Right of Communication to the Public in EU Copyright Law* (Oxford: Hart, 2019) p. 2.

external perspective was taken in the drafting of the regulation and what the impact of each perspective has on the law. The third step in the method, the analysis of the case law, takes place in Chapter 6.

The origin of the communication right

This section considers the first appearance of the communication right, looking at the international and European influences. There was no communication right when the CDPA 1988 was first enacted. The closest equivalent was the right to prevent broadcasting or inclusion of a work in a cable programme service.[5] The communication right was introduced into the CDPA 1988 by the Copyright and Related Rights Regulations 2003.[6]

The origins of communication to the public are found in the development of the copyright holder's right to restrict performance of his work. The recognition that authors should be paid for the communication of their works to the public was an extension of the performance right onto modern communication systems,[7] as such it was conceptualised from the right of public performance.[8]

The right was established in Article 11*bis*(1) of the Berne Convention,[9] with a view to enhancing protection for rights-holders in the digital age, as Advocate General Sharpston stated: "The history of Article 11*bis*(1) ... can be seen as a series of attempts to enhance protection of authors' rights in the light of technological developments. The author's right to authorise a performance of his dramatic or musical work had been granted from the outset in 1886."[10]

The first appearance of a communication right was in the 1928 Rome revision of the Berne Convention.[11] Previously, at the Berlin Revision, the Convention only included Article 11 which stipulated that the Convention applies to public representation of dramatic works and public performance of music works.[12] The Rome revision introduced the concept, providing that: "Authors of literary and artistic works shall enjoy the exclusive right of authorizing the communication of their works to the public by radio-diffusion."[13] However,

5 Vitoria M., et al (eds), *Laddie, Prescott and Vitoria: The Modern Law of Copyright and Designs* (London: Butterworths Law, 2011) (hereafter, *Laddie, Prescott and Vitoria*) 17.3.
6 Copyright and Related Rights Regulations 2003 (SI 2003/2498).
7 Keane B., Ill Communication? The Concept of a Communication to the Public Under EU Copyright Law (2013) 24(5) *Entertainment Law Review*, pp. 165–171, p. 165.
8 Mysoor P., Unpacking the Right of Communication to the Public: A Closer Look at International and EU Copyright law (2013) 2 *Intellectual Property Quarterly*, pp. 166–185, p. 173. See also Reinbothe J. and Von Lewinski S., *The WIPO Treaties 1996* (London: Butterworths, 2002) p. 105.
9 Berne Convention for the Protection of Literary and Artistic Works 1886 (hereafter, the Berne Convention).
10 *Sociedad General de Autores y Editores de Espana (SGAE) v Rafael Hoteles SA* (Case C-306/05) ECLI:EU:C:2006:764, Opinion of Advocate General Sharpston at 47.
11 Berne Convention, as amended by the Rome Act 1928.
12 Berlin Act 1908, Revised Berne Convention 13 November 1908, Article 11.
13 Berne Convention, as amended by the Rome Act 1928, Article 11*bis.*

it was undeveloped at this stage, as the WIPO *Guide to the Berne Convention* [14] stated, it was: "Slightly muddled in its terms, the text was like broadcasting itself – in its infancy."[15]

The word "radiodiffusion" is not a word in English but "radiodiffusion" is a word in French. The text was originally drafted in French and then translated into English. In French, the word "radiodiffusion" refers to the emission of signals through of electromagnetic waves. Furthermore, the word "radiodiffusion" translates directly into English as "broadcasting". In fact, the translators evidently did not translate the word "radiodiffusion" into broadcasting and decided instead to leave us with the word "radiodiffusion", although the WIPO *Guide to the Copyright and Related Rights Treaties* stated that "radiodiffusion" was a synonym of "broadcasting".[16] In which case, why not simply use the word "broadcasting"? This demonstrates the impact of the process of transposing regulation from international levels into UK law.

Radio and television offline transmissions and broadcast

As such, the transposing and translating of international and European documents into UK legislation is something of a controversy.[17] This highlights the impact of international legislative drafting and the difficulties thereof.

During the Brussels revision of 1948, the right was more fully considered in order to take account of the various ways and techniques by which it might be exploited. The Brussels revision consolidated the previous developments and provided authors with the right to authorise communication by way of three separate acts:

(i) the broadcasting of their works or the communication thereof to the public by any other means of wireless diffusion of signs, sounds or images;
(ii) any communication to the public by wire or by rebroadcasting of the broadcast of the work, when this communication is made by an organization other than the original one;
(iii) the public communication by loudspeaker or any other analogous instrument transmitting, by signs, sounds or images, the broadcast of the work.[18]

The Berne Convention did not provide a definition of communication to the public as such. However, judges have been seen to distinguish between the

14 Which the European Court has explained is "without being legally binding, nevertheless assists in interpreting Convention", *Sociedad General de Autores y Editores de Espana (SGAE) v Rafael Hoteles SA* (Case C-306/05) ECLI:EU:C:2006:764 at 41.
15 WIPO, *Guide to the Berne Convention for the Protection of Literary and Artistic Works, Paris 1971* (Geneva; WIPO: 1978) p. 66.
16 WIPO, *Guide to the Copyright and Related Rights Treaties Administered by WIPO and Glossary of Copyright and Related Rights Terms* (Geneva: WIPO, 2003) p. 69.
17 *Laddie, Prescott and Vitoria*, 17.7.
18 Brussels Act 1948, Article 11*bis*.

different types of act.[19] In the *FAPL* cases[20] the CJEU treated the three acts as different forms of communication to the public,[21] and in his Opinion the Advocate General suggested the third act may not amount to communication to the public at all.[22] This provision has sparked heated debate, and is said to have made more ink flow than any other rule formulated at the Brussels Conference.[23]

The Brussels revision took the scope of Article 11*bis*(1)(ii) back to "rebroadcasting" of the broadcast of the work. In the WIPO *Guide to the Berne Convention* Article 11*bis* was titled "right to broadcast", which included radio and television, stating that "what matters is the emission of signals."[24] Thereby, the rights-holder had the exclusive right to emit the signal that carried their work, to authorise the communication of the broadcast to the public by wire or otherwise, and by loudspeaker or on a television screen.[25]

No changes were made to Article 11*bis* by the Stockholm Act 1967 despite the UK proposing two changes. Firstly, the UK proposed deleting the condition in paragraph (3) that ephemeral recordings should be made by the broadcasting organisation "by means of its own facilities."[26] Secondly, it was proposed that the right of recording be restricted to cases where "for technical or other reasons, the broadcast cannot be made at the time of the performance of the work."[27] However, all the proposals were withdrawn at the session of the Committee which discussed Article 11*bis*. [28]

Subsequently, the Paris Act 1971 amended the word radio-diffusion to broadcasting in Article 11*bis*(1)(i). It also broadened the scope of Article 11*bis*(1)(ii) from "any communication to the public *by wire or by rebroadcasting* of the broadcast of the work" to "any communication to the public, *whether over wires or not*, of the radiodiffusion of the work." The WIPO *Guide to the Berne Convention* stated that

19 *Football Association Premier League Ltd, NetMed Hellas SA, Multichoice Hellas SA v QC Leisure (a trading name), David Richardson, AV Station Plc, Malcolm Chamberlain, Michael Madden, Sanjay Raval, David Greenslade, SR Leisure Ltd, Phillip George Charles Houghton, Derek Owen* [2008] EWHC 1411 (Ch) as per Kitchin J at 259.
20 *Football Association Premier League Ltd and Others v QC Leisure and Others* (Cases C-403/08 and 429/08) ECLI:EU:C:2011:631.
21 Ross A. and Livingstone C., Communication to the Public: Part 1 (2012) 23(6) *Entertainment Law Review*, pp. 169–173, p. 169.
22 *Karen Murphy v Media Protection Services Ltd* (Case C-429/08) [2012] 1 CMLR 29, Opinion of Advocate General Kokott at 121–143.
23 Bergström S., Problèmes actuels en matière de Radiodiffusion dans le domaine international (Current Problems Concerning Broadcasting in the International Field) (1959) 25 *RIDA* 148.
24 WIPO, *Guide to the Berne Convention for the Protection of Literary and Artistic Works, Paris 1971* (Geneva: WIPO, 1978) p. 66.
25 *Ibid.*, pp. 66–67.
26 Bergström S., Records of the Intellectual Property Conference of Stockholm June 11 to July 14, 1967 Volume II, Report on the Work of Main Committee I, at para 218: http://global.oup.com/booksites/content/9780198259466/15550029.
27 *Ibid.*, at 218.
28 *Ibid.*, at 221.

the Stockholm and Paris amendments were not changes in the law, but merely, a more suitable English translation.[29]

Ultimately, the Berne Convention was understood to restrict the mischief of "carrying of content to a different place with or without using wires, regardless of the distance separating the origin and the designation."[30] The WIPO *Guide to the Berne Convention* specifically stated that the ultimate aim of Article 11*bis* was to give the rights-holder the exclusive right to authorise to broadcast his work and to restrict the listening or seeing of unauthorised broadcasts by the eyes and ears of unpaying costumers.[31] However, the Paris Act 1971 was still considered in adequate in covering the right of communication to the public "incompletely and imperfectly through a tangle of occasionally redundant or self-contradictory provisions."[32]

Ricketson and Ginsburg raised the concern that the right covered "push" technologies, where the broadcast or wired transmission is from the transmitting entity to passive recipients.[33] However, the WIPO *Guide to the Berne Convention* stated that Article 11*bis* was a matter of transmission intended to be received by the general public: "The idea of transmission to the public is all important. Amateur radio and television communications are excluded."[34]

The purpose of the right consolidated under the Berne Convention was clearly to protect the offline communication of their work through broadcast. As the WIPO *Guide to the Berne Convention* said, Article 11 allowed for the regulation of television and radio broadcasts, as well as through loudspeakers such as in a café, restaurants, tea rooms, hotels, shops, trains and aircrafts.[35] Hague argued, in light of this that "the communication right conferred by Berne Convention became obsolete in the context of new technology."[36] The words chosen in legislative drafting define the ability of that regulation to remain fit for purpose. The application of these rights to an online context has a very different effect, because online digital transmission differs from the traditional categories in many ways.[37]

29 WIPO, *Guide to the Berne Convention for the Protection of Literary and Artistic Works, Paris 1971* (WIPO: Geneva, 1978) p. 66.

30 Mysoor P., Unpacking the Right of Communication to the Public: A Closer Look at International and EU Copyright Law (2013) 2 *Intellectual Property Quarterly*, pp. 166–185, p. 168.

31 WIPO, *Guide to the Berne Convention for the Protection of Literary and Artistic Works, Paris 1971* (WIPO: Geneva, 1978) p. 68.

32 Ginsburg J. C., The (New?) Right of Making Available to the Public in Vaver D. and Bently L. (eds) *Intellectual Property in The New Millennium, Essays in Honour of William R. Cornish* (Cambridge: Cambridge University Press, 2004) pp. 234–247, p. 234.

33 Ricketson S. and Ginsburg J., *International Copyright and Neighbouring Rights* (New York: Oxford University Press, 2006) p. 739.

34 WIPO, *Guide to the Berne Convention for the Protection of Literary and Artistic Works, Paris 1971* (WIPO: Geneva, 1978) p. 67.

35 *Ibid.*, p. 68.

36 Haque H., Is the Time Ripe for Another Exclusive Right? A Proposal (2008) 30(9) *European Intellectual Property Review*, pp. 371–378, p. 376.

37 Frame R., The Protection and Exploitation of Intellectual Property Rights on the Internet: The Way Forward for the Music Industry (1999) 4 *Intellectual Property Quarterly*, pp. 443–470, p. 444.

These rights where implementation into Europe in the form of the Satellite Broadcasting and Cable Retransmission Directive.[38] On 21 February 1990 in a Communication to the Council and Parliament on Audiovisual Policy, the Commission stated that the law required updating in order to respond to technological developments in satellite and television: "The entire audio-visual sector is being shaken up by constant innovations in terms of new technologies, particularly the new generation of satellites and the development of high definition television."[39] Accordingly, in order to draft a proposal for a new Directive, the Discussion Paper "Broadcasting and Copyright in the Internal Market" activated the process of consultation.[40] The most important feature for the Council by unanimity – with France abstaining – related to the issue of communication to the public by satellite.[41]

The Satellite Directive 1993 provided that communication to the public by satellite required "the act of introducing, under the control and responsibility of the broadcasting organization, the programme-carrying signals intended for reception by the public into an uninterrupted chain of communication leading to the satellite and down towards the earth."[42]

It was therefore crucial that the programme-carrying signals must be *intended* for public reception.[43] In the case of *Lagardère* the CJEU explained that: "A comparison of the wording of the various language versions of that provision, in particular the English ('programme-carrying signals intended for reception by the public'), the German ('die programmtragenden Signale, die für den öffentlichen Empfang bestimmt sind'), the Spanish ('las señales portadoras de programa, destinadas a la recepción por el público') or the Dutch version ('programmadragende signalen voor ontvangst door het publiek'), shows that it is the signals which must be intended for the public and not the programmes that they carry."[44]

38 Council Directive 93/83/EEC of 27 September 1993 on the Coordination of Certain Rules Concerning Copyright and Rights Related to Copyright Applicable to Satellite Broadcasting and Cable Retransmission [1993] OJ L 248/15 (hereafter, the Satellite Directive 1993).

39 Communication from the Commission to the Council and European Parliament on Audiovisual Policy COM (90) 78 final, Brussels, 21 February 1990, p. 29.

40 Broadcasting and Copyright in the Internal Market. Discussion Paper prepared by the Commission of the European Communities on Copyright Questions concerning Cable and Satellite Broadcasts, III/F/5263/80-EN, Brussels, November 1990.

41 Kern P., The EC "Common Position" on Copyright Applicable to Satellite Broadcasting and Cable Retransmission (1993) 15(8) *European Intellectual Property Review*, pp. 276–283, p. 276.

42 Satellite Directive 1993, para 14.

43 Schwarz M. and Hansen G., Current Misguided Developments in the Interpretation of the Term 'Initial Transmission' as a Prerequisite for the Right of Retransmission by Cable: An Analysis Proceeding from Section 20b of the German Copyright Act (2011) 42(2) *International Review of Intellectual Property and Competition Law*, pp. 201–213, p.209.

44 *Lagardère Active Broadcast v Société pur la Perception de la remuneration Équitable (SPRE) and Gesellschaft zur Verwertung von Eistungsschutzrechten MBH (GVL)* (Case C-192/04) ECLI:EU:C:2005:475, at 35.

This filled the gap in the law relating to cross-border broadcasting and dealt with the "problems raised respectively by satellite broadcasting and cable retransmission."[45] However, McKnight commented that although the wording of the UK law may have had to change in order to implement the act of communication to the public by satellite that occurred where the chain of communication commenced, the amendment was not, in practice, likely to require broadcasters to substantially change their copyright licensing practices.[46]

Therefore, whilst the Berne Convention and the Satellite Directive 1993 introduced the concepts of communication to the public into UK law, at this point it was only in relation to broadcasting and not yet challenged by online technologies. However, the contextual and historical development of the law enables a better understanding of why the law appears as it does today. In these circumstances, it has been demonstrated that the law of communication to the public, although relatively new, has rapidly and dramatically developed. At this stage communication only related to offline technologies. It is shown in the next section how this was later expanded to include online technologies. This is important in relation to the internal and external perspectives because it could explain why a particular perspective was taken, not as a conscious choice but merely as a development of extending existing law to apply to online technologies. This demonstrates the impact of attempting to apply law that was created in response to offline technologies to online technologies.

Updating communication for the digital age

As mentioned, following the development of new digital online technologies it was clear that the rights established under the Berne Convention needed to be updated. In 1995 at the Fifth Session of the International Bureau of WIPO, the USA submitted a comment that the Convention failed to recognise the right of digital transmission.[47] Australia argued that the Convention was fragmented, and made a proposal that would update it to enable the inclusion of digital transmission.[48] At the Sixth Session the USA proposed that digital transmission would be covered by the right of communication to the public, where transmission would not result in a copy.[49] Lastly, in the Seventh Session the delegation of the Commission of the European Council presented a proposal for a broad communication right, extending the Convention to cover digital transmission.[50]

45 Murray A., Copyright: Directive Co-ordinating Rules on Copyright and Rights Related to Copyright Applicable to Satellite Broadcasting and Cable Retransmissions (1993) 4(6) *Entertainment Law Review*, pp. 123–124, p. 124.

46 McKnight E., Exclusive Licensing of Television Programmes: The Cable and Satellite Directive (1995) 6(7) *Entertainment Law Review*, pp. 287–291, p. 288.

47 International Bureau of WIPO, *Memorandum for the Fifth Session, Industrial Property and Copyright* (1995) pp. 299, 308, para 8.

48 *Ibid.*, p. 313, para 27–32.

49 International Bureau of WIPO, *Comparative Table for the Sixth Session*, WIPO doc BCP/CE/VI/12, pp. 24–30.

50 International Bureau of WIPO, *Report on the Seventh Session*, WIPO doc BCP/CE/VII/4-INR/CE/VI/4 pp. 4 and p. 12.

Thereafter, the WIPO Copyright Treaty 1996[51] rationalised and synthesised protection by establishing full coverage of the communication right for all protected works of authorship.[52] The intention was to provide a technology-neutral right, where the technical means by which the communication was made was irrelevant, in order that any future technical development be included within the provision.[53] The aim of the WCT 1996 was to address the new forms of communication offered by the internet. Referring to the provisions of the Berne Convention set out above, the WCT 1996 granted authors of literary and artistic works the exclusive right of authorising any communication to the public of their works, by wire or wireless means, including the making available to the public of their works in such a way that members of the public could access them from a place and at a time individually chosen by them.[54] Article 8 of the WCT 1996 also extended the scope of the communication right that was provided under the Berne Convention, in that it now applies all kinds of works.[55]

Therefore, the WCT 1996 significantly expanded the subject matter coverage of the Berne Convention's communication to the public right.[56] Although at the time, in the agreed statement adopted by the Diplomatic Conference on Article 8, it was clarified that the purpose of the provision was not to include the facilities for enabling communication: "It is understood that the mere provision of physical facilities for enabling or making a communication does not in itself amount to communication within the meaning of this Treaty or the Berne Convention."[57]

Furthermore, during the discussions at the Diplomatic Conference in 1996, Australia proposed a technical amendment of the words "wire or wireless means" rather than just "making available",[58] in order to clarify that the right did *not* cover a display right.[59]

The provision was an attempt at filling the gaps and adapting communication to the digital age.[60] In particular, the right was framed in a way that gave it a unique status as a

51 Hereafter, WCT 1996.

52 Ginsburg J. C., The (New?) Right of Making Available to the Public in Vaver D. and Bently L. (eds) *Intellectual Property in The New Millennium, Essays in Honour of William R. Cornish* (Cambridge: Cambridge University Press, 2004) pp. 234–247, p. 234.

53 Reinbothe J. and Von Lewinski S., *The WIPO Treaties 1996* (London: Butterworths, 2002) pp. 105–109.

54 WCT 1996, Article 8.

55 Von Lewinski S., WIPO Diplomatic Conference Results in Two New Treaties (1997) 28(2) *International Review of Intellectual Property and Competition Law*, pp. 203–208, p. 205.

56 Ginsburg J. C., The (New?) Right of Making Available to the Public in Vaver D. and Bently L. (eds) *Intellectual Property in The New Millennium, Essays in Honour of William R. Cornish* (Cambridge: Cambridge University Press, 2004) pp. 234–247, p. 246.

57 WIPO, *Agreed statements concerning the WIPO Copyright Treaty adopted by the Diplomatic Conference on December 20, 1996* (Geneva: WIPO, 1978) Concerning Article 8.

58 WIPO, *Records of the Diplomatic Conference on Certain Copyright and Neighbouring Rights Questions* (Geneva: WIPO, 1996) Summary of Minutes of Main Committee II, para 307.

59 *Ibid.*

60 Reinbothe J. and Von Lewinski S., *The WIPO Treaties 1996* (London: Butterworths, 2002) pp. 333–364.

new general right for creators, including the more specific right of making a work available to the public from a place and at a time individually chosen by the public in question.[61] The specific right of "making available" was intended to regulate on-demand digital transmission,[62] despite the fact that the intention was to provide a technology-neutral right[63] to encompass any future technical developments.[64]

These updates were implemented in European law by way of the 2001 Information Society Directive.[65] Whilst the Information Society Directive also avoided specifying a definition of communication to the public, the scope of protection granted by the right was elaborated upon in the Recitals. Recital 23 states that the right should be understood in a "broad sense"[66] and it covered "any such transmission or retransmission of a work to the public by wire or wireless means."[67] Furthermore, Recital 25 states that all right-holders should have the "exclusive right to make available to the public copyright works or any other subject-matter by way of interactive on-demand transmissions."[68]

The Explanatory Memorandum accompanying the proposal for the Information Society Directive stated that: "The expression 'communication to the public' of a work covers any means or process other than the distribution of physical copies ... If, at any point of a transmission or at the end of a transmission the work is communicated to the public, including through public display on screen, each such communication to the public requires authorisation of the author."[69]

Furthermore, Article 3(1) of the Information Society Directive did not begin with the same Without Prejudice provision as Article 8 of the WCT 1996. Mysoor argued that as a result the CJEU is subsequently able to adopt an interpretation of the Directive that is not true to the words of the WCT 1996.[70] Therefore, dispensing with the historical context in the implementation of the Directive has resulted in a

61 Mysoor P., Unpacking the Right of Communication to the Public: A Closer Look at International and EU Copyright law (2013) 2 *Intellectual Property Quarterly*, pp. 166–185, at p. 168.
62 Reinbothe J. and Von Lewinski S., *The WIPO Treaties 1996* (London: Butterworths, 2002) p. 108.
63 *Ibid.*, p. 105.
64 *Ibid.*, p. 109.
65 Directive 2001/29/EC of the European Parliament and of the Council of 22 May 2001 on the Harmonisation of Certain Aspects of Copyright and Related Rights in the Information Society [2001] OJ L 167/10 (hereafter, the Information Society Directive).
66 *Ibid.*, Recital 23.
67 *Ibid.*, Recital 23.
68 *Ibid.*, Recital 25.
69 Proposal for a Directive on the Harmonisation of Certain Aspects of Copyright and Related Rights in the Information Society, COM 97 (628), Brussels, 10 December 1997, p. 25.
70 Mysoor P., Unpacking the Right of Communication to the Public: A Closer Look at International and EU Copyright law (2013) 2 *Intellectual Property Quarterly*, pp. 166–185, p. 173.

skewed interpretation.[71] This interpretation was broad and considered to go beyond the Berne definition of communication to the public.[72]

The Explanatory Memorandum also referred to the agreement made during the WIPO Diplomatic Conference whereby the act of offering a work on a publicly accessible website, prior to its actual transmission, would be captured by "making available", irrespective of whether any person actually accesses the work.[73] Again, this is a clear development in the scope of the meaning of the right from that in the Berne Convention, which, as stated above, emphasised the importance of the public receiving the work.

The CJEU has since stated that the concept of a communication to the public is the same across all the EU Directives and should be given the same meaning in accordance with "the European Union legal order and its coherence."[74] This meaning was considered to be broad and systematic to uphold the right of communication to the public.[75]

Neither the WCT 1996, nor the Information Society Directive provided a definition of communication to the public. The first definition of communication to the public appeared in the WIPO Performances and Phonograms Treaty 1996, which stated that: "Communication to the public of a performance or a phonogram means the transmission to the public by any medium, otherwise than by broadcasting, of sounds of a performance or the sounds or the representations of sounds fixed in a phonogram. For the purposes of Article 15, communication to the public includes making the sounds or representations of sounds fixed in a phonogram audible to the public."[76] However, the definition did not define the words "transmission" and "public" and therefore it remains vague.[77] It also remains unclear whether the making available of protected works over the internet is a unitary restricted act, or a series of restricted acts performed individually by the owner of the website, the service provider (host) and the access provider.[78]

71 *Ibid.*, p. 173.

72 Ross A. and Livingstone C., Communication to the Public: Part 1 (2012) 23(6) *Entertainment Law Review*, pp. 169–173, p. 170.

73 Proposal for a Directive on the Harmonisation of Certain Aspects of Copyright and Related Rights in the Information Society, COM 97 (628), Brussels, 10 December 1997, p.26.

74 *Football Association Premier League Ltd and Others v QC Leisure and Others* (Cases C-403/08 and 429/08) ECLI:EU:C:2011:631, at 188. The meaning of communication to the public by way of interpretation of the courts is dealt with in the following chapter.

75 Keane B., Ill Communication? The Concept of a Communication to the Public Under EU Copyright Law (2013) 24(5) *Entertainment Law Review*, pp. 165–171, p. 170; see also Bonadio E. and Santo M., "Communication to the Public" in *FAPL v QC Leisure* and *Murphy v Media Protection Services* (C-403/08 and C-429/08) (2012) 4 *European Intellectual Property Review*, pp. 277–279.

76 WIPO Performances and Phonograms Treaty 1996, Article 2(g).

77 Ross A. and Livingstone C., Communication to the Public: Part 1 (2012) 23(6) *Entertainment Law Review*, pp. 169–173, p. 170.

78 Hugenholtz B., Caching and Copyright: The Right of Temporary Copying (2000) 22 (10) *European Intellectual Property Review*, pp. 482–493, p. 489.

The development of the communication right from regulating offline broadcast to online activity created a new right to make the work available to the public by electronic transmission, in such a way that members of the public may access it from a place and at a time individually chosen by them.[79] Dixon and Hansen argued that this was beneficial for rights-holders: "Regardless of the manner or medium in which a protected work is accessed, authors would continue to enjoy the right to control economically meaningful exploitation of their works in the digital world."[80]

The legal drafting took an external perspective due to the use of technology-related terms within the drafting of the law, for example by "wire or wireless means."[81] Furthermore, the internal perspective was explicitly not included, for example when it was clarified that the right did not cover display.[82] This seems natural in light of the fact that the law developed from an offline regulation and, at the time of drafting, online technologies, activities and behaviours were still considered novel and not yet advanced.

This discussion now turns to consider the transposing of communication to the public into UK law and thus undertakes a statutory analysis of section 20 of the CDPA 1988.

The challenges of transposing EU directives into UK legislation

The Information Society Directive was transposed into UK law by way of the Copyright and Related Rights Regulations 2003,[83] which came into force on 31 October 2003. The content of the Directive was considered somewhat vague and, as a result, political compromise and debate were required in the drafting of the Regulations.[84] Implementation theory[85] stresses three important considerations when analysing the transposition of the law.[86] Firstly, the institutional factors, taking into consideration the number and strength of decision points required in the process; secondly, the political and policy agendas; and, thirdly, the substantive factors that concern the nature of the objective pursued.[87] These factors are borne in mind as the discussion now considers the transposing of the Information Society Directive into UK law.

79 *Laddie, Prescott and Vitoria*, 17.4.

80 Dixon A. N. and Hansen M. F., The Berne Convention Enters the Digital Age (1996) 18(11) *European Intellectual Property Review*, pp. 604–612, p. 610.

81 WCT 1996, Article 8.

82 WIPO, *Records of the Diplomatic Conference on Certain Copyright and Neighbouring Rights Questions* (Geneva: WIPO, 1996) Summary of Minutes of Main Committee II, para 307.

83 Copyright and Related Rights Regulations 2003 (SI 2003/2498).

84 Dimitrakopoulos D. G., The Transposition of EU Laws Post-Decisional Politics and Institutional Autonomy (2001) 7(4) *European Law Journal*, pp. 442–458, pp. 445–446.

85 Pressman J. L. and Wildavsky A., *Implementation, How Great Expectations in Washington are Dashed in Oakland* (California: University of California Press, 1984).

86 Dimitrakopoulos D. G., The Transposition of EU Laws Post-Decisional Politics and Institutional Autonomy (2001) 7(4) *European Law Journal*, pp. 442–458, p. 445.

87 *Ibid.*

Firstly, in relation to the institutional factors, the involvement of member states in the formation of EU Law cannot be forgotten. However, Page argued that the legislative output of the UK remained largely unaffected by EU membership.[88] Furthermore, it has been observed that there can be pressure on the officials who transpose EU law into UK regulation to mitigate, or defeat, unwanted consequences of EU law.[89]

Ramey argues that the implementation of Directives has been extremely onerous for the UK due to the volume of Directives adopted by the European Commission.[90] Moreover, in the UK the issues regarding transposition are considered technical, and drafters are often administration officials, not lawyers.[91] The characteristics of EU Directives can be stylistically and functionally different from UK legislation, which creates problems for the drafters.[92] Drafters must ensure that the implementing legislation achieves the Directive's objectives and attempt to do this by elaborating it into a common law style.[93] The UK tends to create variations when transposing rules from EU Directives. As a result, it has come to be expected, and it was therefore no surprise that the wording of section 20 of the CDPA 1988 is not the same as that of Article 3 of the Information Society Directive.[94]

For example, Article 3(1) of the Directive referred to communication by wire or wireless means[95] but, in contrast, the UK drafters replaced these words with *electronic transmission.* [96] It has been suggested that this was because the term "wire" had English historical connotations of telegraphy.[97] Larusson suggested that the drafter should have used the words "by electronic means" instead, which, he argued, were more passive and could have avoided the current uncertainty.[98]

Understanding why the language of the law changes in the transposition of the EU Directive into UK law is important in understanding what new meaning may be invoked from the revised words. Without this knowledge, the change in words are not always appreciated; for example as Jacob LJ stated: "Why, oh why do statutory draftsman persist in trying to gloss Directives which are specific about what is to be implemented?"[99]

88 Page E. C., The Impact of European Legalisation on British Public Policy Making: A Research Note (1998) 76 (4) *Public Administration*, pp. 803–809.
89 *Ibid.*
90 Ramsey L. E., The Copy out Technique: More of a Cop Out Than a Solution? (1996) 17(3) *Statute Law Review*, pp. 218–228, p. 221: for example "282 measures were required to be adopted in order to complete the internal market."
91 Dimitrakopoulos D. G., The Transposition of EU Laws Post-Decisional Politics and Institutional Autonomy (2001) 7(4) *European Law Journal*, pp. 442–458, p. 447.
92 Ramsey L. E., The Copy out Technique: More of a Cop Out Than a Solution? (1996) 17(3) *Statute Law Review*, pp. 218–228, p.221.
93 *Ibid.*, p. 222.
94 *Laddie, Prescott and Vitoria*, 17.7.
95 Information Society Directive, Article 3(1).
96 CDPA 1988, section 20.
97 Larusson H. K., Uncertainty in the Scope of Copyright: The Case of Illegal File-Sharing in the UK (2009) 31(3) *European Intellectual Property Review*, pp. 124–134, p. 126: "A technology which has been superseded by the internet and other modern communication technologies."
98 *Ibid.*, p. 126.
99 *R v Higgs* [2008] EWCA Crim 1324, as per Jacob LJ at [31].

In determining meaning from this change, Jacob LJ concluded that the draftsmen must have been attempting to make the same meaning expressed in the Directive clearer: "The UK draftsman was merely making explicit that which was implicit in the Directive."[100]

The Explanatory Notes stated that the Regulations implement the Information Society Directive with the view to harmonise (among other things) the right to communication to the public.[101] The Regulations redefined section 20 of the CDPA 1988, granting an exclusive right to the copyright owner to control the broadcasting of their work, and provided greater certainty that the copyright owner had the right to control any communication to the public by electronic transmission, including by means of a broadcast, but also in respect of the making available to the public of works in such a way that members of the public may access them from a place and at a time individually chosen by them.[102]

Subsequently, the Regulations clearly provided the copyright holder with the exclusive right to control any electronic communication to the public.[103] Haque argued that this expanded the copyright holder's rights too far, allowing them control over the individual.[104] Moreover, Koelman argued that this extended copyright law to new levels not seen before: "An action against non-commercial individual access to, or consumption of a work, constitutes a revolution in copyright law, which traditionally covers acts related to commercial exploitation performed by potential competitors rather than acts carried out by individual end users."[105]

On the other hand, Gillen recognised that the new right to communication was designed to fill the gaps in the other provisions, and that it was clear that this new right went further than the performance right –where it was usually expected that the public will be present, allowing communication to occur at any place or time of the receiver's choosing[106] – whilst the original intention of the right was to enable copyright holders to control the television and radio broadcast of their work. Subsequently, it encapsulated on-demand television broadcasts accessed at a different time or place by the user.

The external perspective appeared to take precedent in the drafting of the law, developed as a response to new technologies,[107] and therefore was drafted in a

100 *Ibid.*, Jacob LJ at [32].
101 Copyright and Related Rights Regulations 2003 (SI 2003/2498), Explanatory Note.
102 *Ibid.*
103 *Ibid.*, Article 6.
104 Haque H., Is the Time Ripe for Another Exclusive Right? A Proposal (2008) 30(9) *European Intellectual Property Review*, pp. 371–378, p. 376.
105 Koelman K. J., A Hard Nut to Crack: The Protection of Technological Measures (2000) 22 (6) *European Intellectual Property Review*, pp. 272–288, p. 6.
106 Gillen M., File-Sharing and Individual Civil Liability in the United Kingdom: A Question of Substantial Abuse? (2006) 17(1) *Entertainment Law Review*, pp. 7–14, p. 11.
107 International Bureau of WIPO, *Memorandum for the Fifth Session, Industrial Property and Copyright* (1995) p. 308.

technologically specific manner, despite the intention for it to remain technologically neutral.[108]

An analysis of section 20 of the CDPA 1988

As mentioned, there is no statutory definition of communication to the public *per se*. Herein lies the first challenge of this Regulation. This new right granted copyright holders the power to govern the use of copyright-protected content online and, therefore, it is imperative that a clear understanding of what constitutes an act of communication online is established.

The Information Society Directive provided that the right of communication to the public should be interpreted in a broad sense covering all communication to the public not present at the place where the communication originates.[109]

It was recognised that this is a highly contentious area[110] and that the concept of communication to the public is uncertain.[111] The challenges that arise in the process of transposing the right[112] raised questions about whether the current set of rights is sufficient or appropriate.[113]

Therefore, the discussion now turns to a consideration of the key elements of the right to communication as per section 20 of the CDPA 1988 in order to decipher the meaning of the right, before applying the internal and external perspectives. In particular, this section considers in detail the wording of the statutory law in relation to three key elements of the right: the categories, the public and electronic transmission. The analysis of the case law that relates to section 20 follows in Chapter 6.

Communicating subject matter

Section 20(1) of the CDPA 1988 stated that communication to the public of the work is an act restricted by the copyright in: (a) literary, dramatic, musical or artistic works; (b) sound recordings or film; or (c) broadcasts. This suggested that the question of whether a particular act constitutes a communication to the public may depend on the nature of the copyright work under consideration. This is relevant to the current investigation as the internal and external perspectives of the internet have a dramatic effect on the categorisation of works online. From the external perspective, it could be argued that all types of work online, or on a computer, are files of some technical description. From this perspective, it does not matter what form of art the file holds, such as a film or

108 Reinbothe J. and Von Lewinski S., *The WIPO Treaties 1996* (London: Butterworths, 2002) p. 105.
109 Information Society Directive, Recital 23.
110 Communication from the Commission to the European Parliament, the Council, the European Economic and Social Committee and the Committee of the Regions, Towards a Modern, More European Copyright Framework, COM (2015) 626, Brussels, 9 December 2015, p. 10.
111 *Ibid.*, p. 9.
112 *Ibid.*, p. 9.
113 *Ibid.*, p. 10.

a song, it is simply digital data. On the other hand, the internal perspective would view the different types of work as they are consumed, by the experience of something being listened to, read or watched, and therefore categorisation of works is relevant.

This highlights a tension in the way that the law has been applied to online activities. For example, according to the CJEU, although a graphic user interface of a computer program can be protected by copyright, television broadcasting of the graphic user interface will not constitute communication to the public of that work.[114] The CJEU justified this on the basis that television viewers received the graphic user interface solely in a passive manner, without the possibility of intervening.[115] *Laddie, Prescott and Vitoria* argued that the difference between a graphic interface and a television broadcast was that the user could not interact with a television broadcast, submitting that insofar as a graphic user interface consisted of graphics in addition to interactivity, these aspects of the work are communicated to the public.[116]

One key issue with the separation of works into categories in the modern digital age is that the distinction between the characteristics of each type of work is becoming indistinguishable. Technological developments are resulting in the overlap of such categories, which ultimately leads to greater confusion in the meaning of the law. For example, as a result of Smart Television technology, it is now possible for a television broadcast to be interactive. For example, a viewer can select different cameras to watch or interact with the broadcast through the internet or social media, on the television itself.[117]

A second example demonstrating this point is the use of gaming techniques in the development of non-gaming contexts such as webpages or social media to mimic the characteristics of games. Games and game technologies are increasingly transcending the traditional boundaries of their medium.[118] Deterding et al. explained that: "Recent years have seen a rapid proliferation of mass-market consumer software that takes inspiration from video games. Usually summarized as gamification."[119] They define gamification as the use of game elements for purposes other than their normal expected use[120] with the aim to retain visitors on the website for longer, for example by using reward techniques.[121] As such, website developers

114 *Bezpečnostní softwarová asociace - Svaz softwarové ochrany v Ministerstvo kultury* (Case C-393/09) ECLI:EU:C:2010:816 at 57.
115 *Ibid.*
116 *Laddie, Prescott and Vitoria*, 17.16.
117 Foged T., Danish licences for Europe (2015) 37(1) *European Intellectual Property Review*, pp. 15–24, p. 15.
118 Deterding S., Sicart M., Nacke L., O'Hara K. and Dixon D., Gamification: Using Game-Design Elements in Non-Gaming Contexts (2011) In *CHI'11 Extended Abstracts on Human Factors in Computing Systems*, ACM, pp. 2425–2428, p. 2425.
119 Deterding S., Dixon D., Khaled R. and Nacke L., From Game Design Elements to Gamefulness: Defining "Gamification" (2011) *Proceedings of the 15th International Academic MindTrek Conference: Envisioning Future Media Environments*, ACM, pp. 9–15, p. 9.
120 *Ibid.*, p. 12.
121 Mullan J., Re-Emerging Technologies: What's Hot and What's Not! (2014) 14(3) *Legal Information Management*, pp. 168–173, p. 172.

have been inspired by gaming to develop an application which stores the memory representation of what is displayed on the HTML[122] page and then executes codes to draw elements on the page, checking against the Virtual Document Object Model (DOM)[123] to match up the display.[124] This application minimises the need for redrawing and therefore costs of resources are reduced.[125]

From an external perspective, the technology behind the website mimics that of a game and therefore suggests that the website be regulated as such. However, from an internal perspective the experience of the product is as a webpage. This highlights that developing software engineering in this way clearly blurs the boundaries between different types of copyright material.[126] As such, if technology continues to develop in this manner, attempting to regulate online activity by defining categories of works could become redundant.

The discussion now turns to consider the second key element of the statutory analysis of communication to the public, i.e. the meaning of "the public."

Who are the public?

There is no clear definition of the meaning of "the public" in statutory law, intentionally: "The need to define the notion of public had been successfully avoided."[127]

However, it is argued that most national laws have struggled, and continue to find it difficult, to formulate a clear meaning as to the "in public" requirement.[128] This has become a challenge[129] and the lack of clarity has left many questions open in critically important areas concerning copyright in the digital networked world.[130] There is a need for the communication right to be clearer.[131]

122 Hypertext Markup Language, this is a standardised system for tagging files to font, colour, graphics and hyperlink effects on the World Wide Web.

123 This is an application programming interface (API) for HTML documents.

124 For example, 'React' is a library application for creating user interfaces by rendering the UI and responding to events. It is revolutionary in the way that it build components, not templates, as websites are traditionally coded, see https://facebook.github.io/react/index.html

125 *Ibid.*

126 Deterding S., Sicart M., Nacke L., O'Hara K. and Dixon D., Gamification: Using Game-Design Elements in Non-Gaming Contexts (2011) In *CHI'11 Extended Abstracts on Human Factors in Computing Systems*, ACM, pp. 2425–2428, p. 2425.

127 International Bureau of WIPO, Report on the Seventh Session, WIPO doc BCP/CE/VII/4-INR/CE/VI/4, pp. 4 and 12.

128 Makeen M. F., Rationalising Performance "in Public" Under UK Copyright Law (2016) 2 *Intellectual Property Quarterly*, pp. 117–134, p. 122.

129 Frame R., The Protection and Exploitation of Intellectual Property Rights on the Internet: The Way Forward for the Music Industry (1999) 4 *Intellectual Property Quarterly*, pp. 443–470, p. 443.

130 Hart M., The Copyright in the Information Society Directive: An Overview (2002) 24(2) *European Intellectual Property Review*, pp. 58–64, p. 64

131 Mysoor P., Unpacking the Right of Communication to the Public: A Closer Look at International and EU Copyright Law (2013) 2 *Intellectual Property Quarterly*, pp. 166–185, p. 166.

It was previously considered that the access of information online was not to the public, but to a private individual. As the WIPO *Guide to the Copyright and Related Rights Treaties* stated, the opposite of public was private and therefore private communication would not constitute communication to the public: "The Convention does not provide a definition of the concept of 'public', either as an adjective or as a noun. It is, however, quite obvious that, as regards the adjective 'public', it is the opposite of the adjective 'private' and, thus, what may not be characterized as 'private' is supposed to be regarded 'public.'"[132] For example, Article 8 of the WCT 1996 excluded family members, but included school or company intranet as public communications.[133]

However, the new right blurred the distinction between public and private communication, creating confusion at a technological level.[134] For example, the meaning of "the public" in relation to communication of copyright work has been held by the CJEU to make no distinction between the making available in the private context of a hotel room and in public areas in the hotel. The important question was whether a new section of the public sees or hears the work.[135]

Therefore, when applying the concept of public online, even though there may be only one person accessing the information, he or she qualifies as the public.[136] Arezzo agreed that as in general users would receive the communication within the privacy of their own homes, the notion of the public in this context appears peculiar.[137] However, some case law has suggested that it is not the economic relevance of the user but the cumulative effect[138] created by the number of people who could simultaneously, or in succession, access the work.[139]

Nevertheless, it is argued by many that this is an exceptionally wide interpretation of "the public", which gives the words virtually no meaning at all.[140] For example, the meaning of the words "in public" in relation to section 19 of the

132 WIPO, *Guide to the Copyright and Related Rights Treaties Administered by WIPO and Glossary of Copyright and Related Rights Terms* (Geneva: WIPO, 2003) p. 69.

133 Reinbothe J. and Von Lewinski S., *The WIPO Treaties 1996* (London: Butterworths, 2002) p. 111.

134 Haque H., Is the Time Ripe for Another Exclusive Right? A Proposal (2008) 30(9) *European Intellectual Property Review*, pp. 371–378.

135 *Sociedad General de Autores y Editores de España (SGAE) v Rafael Hoteles SA* (Case C-306/05) ECLI:EU:C:2006:764 at 41.

136 Frame R., The Protection and Exploitation of Intellectual Property Rights on the Internet: The Way Forward for the Music Industry (1999) 4 *Intellectual Property Quarterly*, pp. 443–470, p. 443.

137 Arezzo E., Hyperlinks and Making Available Right in the European Union – What Future for the Internet After Svensson? (2014) 45(5) *International Review of Intellectual Property and Competition Law*, pp. 524–555, p. 534.

138 *Sociedad General de Autores y Editores de Espana (SGAE) v Rafael Hoteles SA* (Case C-306/05) ECLI:EU:C:2006:764 at 39.

139 *Società Consortile Fonografici (SCF) v Marco Del Corso* (Case C-135/10) ECLI:EU:C:2012:140 at 87.

140 *Laddie, Prescott and Vitoria*, 17.13.

CDPA 1988 have been interpreted with a far narrower scope. Indeed, it has been suggested that some limitation must be imposed, for example by excluding family and close friends.[141]

The CJEU has also specified that the public must be a "new public", meaning a public which was not taken into account by the authors of the protected works when they authorized their use by the communication to the original public.[142] This could be seen to reflect the original wording, as stated above, of granting the copyright holders control of any "rebroadcasting". Thus, when this communication is made by an organisation other than the original one[143] and thereby, to a new public.

In relation to the Framework for Constructing Digital Perspectives it is not possible to be certain of a perspective in the statutory law where the aim has been to avoid defining meaning. The term "public" has been deliberately left vague for the court's interpretation. However, the notion of the public as opposed to a private individual differs depending on the perspective. As stated, from an offline perspective the distinction between these two audiences is clear; however, when applying this to the online environment it is confused by technology that allows many individual users to access a work at any one time. From an external perspective, this would be difficult to consider as a public as technically the people are individually accessing the work in a private setting. However, from an internal perspective, it could be suggested that together the individuals form an online community which constitutes a public.

Nevertheless, the legislature has made it clear that the issue of defining the public was better left to the courts.[144] Therefore, the concept of the "public" will be addressed in more detail in Chapter 6, which considers the case law relating to communication to the public.

This discussion now turns to the final consideration of the statutory analysis of communication to the public, i.e. the meaning of "electronic transmission".

Electronic transmission

Section 20 of the CDPA 1988 granted the copyright holder the right to control communication to the public by "electronic transmission". The identification of the

141 *Sociedad General de Autores y Editores de España (SGAE) v Rafael Hoteles SA* (Case C-306/05) ECLI:EU:C:2006:764, Opinion of the Advocate-General at 64. See also Reinbothe J. and Von Lewinski S., *The WIPO Treaties 1996* (London: Butterworths, 2002) Commentary to art 8 WCT, at para 21.

142 *Football Association Premier League Ltd and Others v QC Leisure and Others* (Cases C-403/08 and 429/08) ECLI:EU:C:2011:631; *Karen Murphy v Media Protection Services Ltd* (Case C-429/08) [2012] 1 CMLR 29, at 197. See also, *Airfield NV and Canal Digitaal BV v Belgische Vereniging van Auteurs, Componisten en Uitgevers CVBA (Sabam)* (Case C-431/09) and *Airfield NV v Agicoa Belgium BVBA* (Case C-432/09) Judgment of the Court, Third Chamber, 13 October 2011 [2011] ECR I-09363, at 76.

143 Berne Convention, Article 11*bis*.

144 *Hansard*, HL, Copyright, Designs and Patents Bill [HL], 5th Ser, Col 268, 2 November 1988.

legal concept of communication to the public with the technical notion of transmission of the work is crucial to properly understanding the contours of this right.[145]

As mentioned, the words "electronic transmission" did not appear in Article 3 of the Information Society Directive. The reason for this change may have come from the fact that "by wire" had historical connotations to telegraphy.[146] However, the draftsmen could have used the more passive "by electronic means". Nevertheless, it appeared that the intention of these words remained to ensure that the communication right restricted the communication of a copyright work to a public not present at the place where the communication originated.[147]

However, the term "electronic transmission" does not necessarily suggest that the members of the public are not present at the time of transmission. For example, *Laddie, Prescott and Vitoria* suggested the example of a transmission by loudspeaker as a form of electronic communication where the public may be present at the place where the communication originates.[148] Nevertheless, the book suggested that section 20 must only be interpreted to mean forms of communication where the public is not present where the communication originated.[149]

Another controversial uncertainty in the wording of the CDPA 1988 was that there appeared to be no requirement that any transmission actually takes place before infringement can occur. Particularly, in relation to the making available of the work, which may only require that members of the public *could* access it.[150] In light of this, the communication right differs significantly from the other rights granted to copyright holders where infringement implies an actual exploitation or enjoyment of the work. Conversely, the right of communication to the public has been interpreted as covering acts of transmission not followed by any actual enjoyment of the work.[151]

This interpretation has been confirmed by the CJEU, which explicitly stated that transmission simply involved *an act of intervention* which made the work available to the public in such a way that the persons forming the public *may access*

145 Arezzo E., Hyperlinks and Making Available Right in the European Union – What Future for the Internet After Svensson? (2014) 45(5) *International Review of Intellectual Property and Competition Law*, pp. 524–555, p. 532.

146 Larusson H. K., Uncertainty in the Scope of Copyright: The Case of Illegal File-Sharing in the UK (2009) 31(3) *European Intellectual Property Review*, pp. 124–134, p. 126.

147 *Football Association Premier League Ltd, NetMed Hellas SA, Multichoice Hellas SA v QC Leisure (a trading name), David Richardson, AV Station Plc, Malcolm Chamberlain, Michael Madden, Sanjay Raval, David Greenslade, SR Leisure Ltd, Phillip George Charles Houghton, Derek Owen*, as per Kitchin J at 261, in line with Information Society Directive, Recital 23.

148 *Laddie, Prescott and Vitoria*, 17.12.

149 *Ibid.*

150 Caddick N., Davies G. and Harbottle G., *Copinger and Skone James on Copyright* (London: Sweet & Maxwell, 2016) paras 7–116.

151 Arezzo E., Hyperlinks and Making Available Right in the European Union – What Future for the Internet After Svensson? (2014) 45(5) *International Review of Intellectual Property and Competition Law*, pp. 524–555, p. 532.

it: what mattered was that the work was put in a position to be *potentially* accessed by the public.[152]

In applying the Framework for Constructing Digital Perspectives, it is clear that the words "electronic transmission" fall within the external perspective as it applies to the technological function of the hardware and software involved in the communication of the copyright work. In analysing the intention of the right, again the external perspective was taken in order to create a new right to deal specifically with a technological development of television and radio broadcast.

Conclusion

The historical analysis of the development of the right to communication revealed that the original purpose of the right was to allow copyright holders to control television and radio broadcasts. However, the scope of the right expanded dramatically over the course of its development through international, European and UK legislation.

The statutory analysis revealed that despite the importance of this right being defined, there was no clear definition of the boundaries or meaning of "communication to the public". A clearer understanding of the terms "communication" and "public" are still needed.[153]

As a result, the right of communication to the public has struggled to find a predictable interpretation[154] and the potential scope of communication is unlimited. The scope of the right widened quickly and dramatically, particularly in light of new technological and behaviour developments. This right now allows copyright holders to essentially control any communication of their work.[155] In 1999, Russell Fame predicted that "the internet is a new and as yet, a relatively unregulated medium for communication."[156] However, with the development of the right to communication, this would suggest that it is possible for rights-holders' to control everything on the internet. This risk is increased by the potential

152 *Mediakabel BV v Commissariaat voor de Media* (Case C-89/04) Judgment of the Court, Third Chamber, 2 June 2005, ECLI:EU:C:2005:348, at 30; *Lagardère Active Broadcast v Société pur la Perception de la remuneration Équitable (SPRE) and Gesellschaft zur Verwertung von Eistungsschutzrechten MBH (GVL)* (Case C-192/04) ECLI:EU:C:2005:475, at 31.

153 Mysoor P., Unpacking the Right of Communication to the Public: A Closer Look at International and EU Copyright Law (2013) 2 *Intellectual Property Quarterly*, pp. 166–185, p. 167.

154 *Ibid.*, p. 167.

155 Gillen M., File-Sharing and Individual Civil Liability in the United Kingdom: A Question of Substantial Abuse? (2006) 17(1) *Entertainment Law Review*, pp. 7–14, p. 11: arguing that the new right addresses the latest challenges to copyright, "making available is the essence of file-sharing."

156 Frame R., The Protection and Exploitation of Intellectual Property Rights on the Internet: The Way Forward for the Music Industry (1999) 4 *Intellectual Property Quarterly*, pp. 443–470, p. 443.

implementation of Article 17 of the DSM Copyright Directive,[157] which provides the basis for an upload filter. The aim of this article was to solve a power struggle between YouTube and the content industry. However, the impact is more than likely an over-regulation of the internet at the expense of the fair balance copyright law is supposed to maintain between all the stakeholders – including the public and other rights such as freedom of speech. In its current state of requiring "best efforts", the regulation will have little obstruction to the YouTube monopoly, which would have been more appropriately addressed through competition law. At the time of writing, after two and a half years in the making, the European Parliament adopted the latest version of the Directive which formally came into effect 17 April 2019 and will now need to be transposed into the domestic law of Member States by 7 June 2021.

In relation to the Framework for Constructing Digital Perspectives originally, at the stage of the Berne Convention there was a suggestion of an internal perspective as the WIPO *Guide to the Berne Convention* discussed the need for the work to be received by the eyes or ears of a person.[158] However, it appeared that the scope of the right has extended so far that the making available of the work is enough to constitute communication, and therefore only the potential to access the material is needed, no eyes or ears necessarily need to receive it. As the ALAI Report stated, the making available right covers all kinds of on-demand access "whether or not the access results in a retention copy."[159]

Thereafter, the statutory law took on an external perspective due to the use of technology-related terms within the drafting. Furthermore, the internal perspective was explicitly not included, for example, when Australia clarified that the right did not cover display.[160] This perspective appeared to be a consequence of the fact that the law developed from an offline regulation. The regulation surrounding communication to the public clearly highlighted the tensions that arise when attempting to apply laws created for specific analogue technological purposes onto activity conducted online. This was highlighted by drawing attention to the problem of regulating different types of copyright materials online.

As demonstrated, much of the statutory law in relation to communication to the public was deliberately broad and vague, with the intention that further

157 Directive (EU) 2019/790 of the European Parliament and of the Council of 17 April 2019 on Copyright and Related Rights in the Digital Single Market and Amending Directives 96/9/EC and 2001/29/EC [2019] OJ L 130/92.

158 WIPO, *Guide to the Berne Convention for the Protection of Literary and Artistic Works, Paris 1971* (WIPO: Geneva, 1978) p. 68.

159 Association Littéraire et Artistique Internationale (ALAI), *Report and Opinion on the Making Available and Communication to the Public in the Internet Environment – Focus on Linking Techniques on the Internet*, Paris, 16 September 2013: http://www.alai.org/en/assets/files/resolutions/making-available-right-report-opinion.pdf Point (i).

160 WIPO, *Records of the Diplomatic Conference on Certain Copyright and Neighbouring Rights Questions* (Geneva: WIPO, 1996) Summary of Minutes of Main Committee II, para 307.

clarification be defined through the courts.[161] This leads the courts towards a purposive interpretation as the literal meaning of the words used were deliberately ambiguous. As such, Chapter 6 considers this in more detail, by making an analysis of the case law which interprets and applies the statutory regulation.

Bibliography

Books

Broom H., *A Selection of Legal Maxims: Classified and Illustrated* (London: The Lawbook Exchange, 1864).

Caddick, N., Davies G. and Harbottle G., *Copinger and Skone James on Copyright* (London: Sweet & Maxwell, 2016).

Ginsburg J. C., The (New?) Right of Making Available to the Public in Vaver D. and Bently L. (eds) *Intellectual Property in The New Millennium, Essays in Honour of William R. Cornish* (Cambridge: Cambridge University Press, 2004) pp. 234–247.

Koo J., *The Right of Communication to the Public in EU Copyright Law* (Oxford: Hart, 2019).

Pressman J. L. and Wildavsky A., *Implementation, How Great Expectations in Washington are Dashed in Oakland* (California: University of California Press, 1984).

Reinbothe J. and Von Lewinski S., *The WIPO Treaties 1996* (London: Butterworths, 2002).

Ricketson S. and Ginsburg J., *International Copyright and Neighbouring Rights* (New York: Oxford University Press, 2006).

Vitoria M., et al (eds), *Laddie, Prescott and Vitoria: The Modern Law of Copyright and Designs*, 4th edition (London: Butterworths Law, 2011).

Case law

Airfield NV and Canal Digitaal BV v Belgische Vereniging van Auteurs, Componisten en Uitgevers CVBA (Sabam) (Case C-431/09) and *Airfield NV v Agicoa Belgium BVBA* (Case C-432/09) Judgment of the Court, Third Chamber, 13 October 2011 [2011] ECR I-09363.

Bezpečnostní softwarová asociace - Svaz softwarové ochrany v Ministerstvo kultury (Case C-393/09) ECLI:EU:C:2010:816.

Football Association Premier League Ltd, NetMed Hellas SA, Multichoice Hellas SA v QC Leisure (a trading name), David Richardson, AV Station Plc, Malcolm Chamberlain, Michael Madden, Sanjay Raval, David Greenslade, SR Leisure Ltd, Phillip George Charles Houghton, Derek Owen [2008] EWHC 1411 (Ch), [2008] FSR 32.

Football Association Premier League Ltd and Others v QC Leisure and Others (Cases C-403/08 and 429/08) ECLI:EU:C:2011:631.

ITV Broadcasting Ltd, ITV 2 Ltd, ITV Digital Channels Ltd, Channel 4 Television Corporation, Four Ventures Ltd, Channel 5 Broadcasting Ltd, ITV Studios Ltd v TVCatchup Ltd, The Secretary of State for Business, Innovation and Skills [2011] EWHC 1874 (Pat), [2011] FSR 16.

Karen Murphy v Media Protection Services Ltd (Case C-429/08) [2012] 1 CMLR 29.

161 *Hansard*, HL, Copyright, Designs and Patents Bill [HL], 5th Ser, Col 268, 2 November 1988.

Lagardère Active Broadcast v Société pur la Perception de la remuneration Équitable (SPRE) and Gesellschaft zur Verwertung von Eistungsschutzrechten MBH (GVL) (Case C-192/04) ECLI:EU:C:2005:475.

Mediakabel BV v Commissariaat voor de Media (Case C-89/04), Judgment of the Court, Third Chamber, 2 June 2005, ECLI:EU:C:2005:348.

R v Higgs [2008] EWCA Crim 1324.

Sociedad General de Autores y Editores de Espana (SGAE) v Rafael Hoteles SA (Case C-306/05) ECLI:EU:C:2006:764.

Società Consortile Fonografici (SCF) v Marco Del Corso (Case C-135/10) ECLI:EU:C:2012:140.

Journals

Arezzo E., Hyperlinks and Making Available Right in the European Union – What Future for the Internet After Svensson? (2014) 45(5) *International Review of Intellectual Property and Competition Law*, pp. 524–555.

Bergström S., Problèmes actuels en matière de Radiodiffusion dans le domaine international (Current Problems Concerning Broadcasting in the International Field) (1959) 25*RIDA* 148.

Bonadio E. and Santo M., "Communication to the Public" in *FAPL v QC Leisure* and *Murphy v Media Protection Services* (C-403/08 and C-429/08) (2012) (4) *European Intellectual Property Review*, pp. 277–279.

Deterding S., Dixon D., Khaled R. and Nacke L., From Game Design Elements to Gamefulness: Defining "Gamification" (2011) *Proceedings of the 15th International Academic MindTrek Conference: Envisioning Future Media Environments*, ACM, pp. 9–15.

Deterding S., Sicart M., Nacke L., O'Hara K. and Dixon D., Gamification: Using Game-Design Elements in Non-Gaming Contexts (2011) *CHI'11 Extended Abstracts on Human Factors in Computing Systems*, ACM, pp. 2425–2428.

Dimitrakopoulos D. G., The Transposition of EU Laws Post-Decisional Politics and Institutional Autonomy (2001) 7(4) *European Law Journal*, pp. 442–458.

Dixon A. N. and Hansen M. F., The Berne Convention Enters the Digital Age (1996) 18 (11) *European Intellectual Property Review*, pp. 604–612.

Foged T., Danish licences for Europe (2015) 37(1) *European Intellectual Property Review*, pp. 15–24.

Frame R., The Protection and Exploitation of Intellectual Property Rights on the Internet: The Way Forward for the Music Industry (1999) 4 *Intellectual Property Quarterly*, pp. 443–470.

Gillen M., File-Sharing and Individual Civil Liability in the United Kingdom: A Question of Substantial Abuse? (2006) 17(1) *Entertainment Law Review*, pp. 7–14.

Haque H., Is the Time Ripe for Another Exclusive Right? A Proposal (2008) 30(9) *European Intellectual Property Review*, pp. 371–378.

Hart M., The Copyright in the Information Society Directive: An Overview (2002) 24(2) *European Intellectual Property Review*, pp. 58–64.

Hugenholtz B. P., Caching and Copyright: The Right of Temporary Copying (2000) 22 (10) *European Intellectual Property Review*, pp. 482–493.

Keane B., Ill Communication? The Concept of a Communication to the Public Under EU Copyright Law (2013) 24(5) *Entertainment Law Review*, pp. 165–171.

Kern P., The EC "Common Position" on Copyright Applicable to Satellite Broadcasting and Cable Retransmission (1993) 15(8) *European Intellectual Property Review*, pp. 276–283.

Koelman K. J., A Hard Nut to Crack: The Protection of Technological Measures (2000) 22(6) *European Intellectual Property Review*, pp. 272–288.

Larusson H. K., Uncertainty in the Scope of Copyright: The Case of Illegal File-Sharing in the UK (2009) 31(3) *European Intellectual Property Review*, pp. 124–134.

Makeen M. F., Rationalising Performance "in Public" Under UK Copyright Law (2016) 2 *Intellectual Property Quarterly*, pp. 117–134.

McKnight E., Exclusive Licensing of Television Programmes: The Cable and Satellite Directive (1995) 6(7) *Entertainment Law Review*, pp. 287–291.

Mullan J., Re-Emerging Technologies: What's Hot and What's Not! (2014) 14(3) *Legal Information Management*, pp. 168–173.

Murray A., Copyright: Directive Co-ordinating Rules on Copyright and Rights Related to Copyright Applicable to Satellite Broadcasting and Cable Retransmissions (1993) 4(6) *Entertainment Law Review*, pp. 123–124.

Mysoor P., Unpacking the Right of Communication to the Public: A Closer Look at International and EU Copyright law (2013) 2 *Intellectual Property Quarterly*, pp. 166–185.

Page E. C., The Impact of European Legalisation on British Public Policy Making: A Research Note (1998) 76(4) *Public Administration*, pp. 803–809.

Ramsey L. E., The Copy out Technique: More of a Cop Out Than a Solution? (1996) 17 (3) *Statute Law Review*, pp. 218–228.

Ricketson S., The Boundaries of Copyright: Its Proper Limitations and Exceptions: International Conventions and Treaties (1999) 1 *Intellectual Property Quarterly*, pp. 56–94.

Rizzuto F., The European Union law Concept of Communication to the Public and the Protection of Copyright in Electronic Transmissions (2012) 18(6) *Computer and Telecommunications Law Review*, pp. 179–197.

Ross A. and Livingstone C., Communication to the Public: Part 1 (2012) 23(6) *Entertainment Law Review*, pp. 169–173.

Schwarz M. and Hansen G., Current Misguided Developments in the Interpretation of the Term "Initial Transmission" as a Prerequisite for the Right of Retransmission by Cable: An Analysis Proceeding from Section 20b of the German Copyright Act (2011) 42(2) *International Review of Intellectual Property and Competition Law*, pp. 201–213.

Von Lewinski S., WIPO Diplomatic Conference Results in Two New Treaties (1997) 28 (2) *International Review of Intellectual Property and Competition Law*, pp. 203–208.

Legislation

Berlin Act 1908.

Berne Convention for the Protection of Literary and Artistic Works 1886.

Brussels Act 1948.

Copyright and Related Rights Regulations 2003 (SI 2003/2498).

Copyright, Designs and Patents Act 1988.

Council Directive 93/83/EEC of 27 September 1993 on the Coordination of Certain Rules Concerning Copyright and Rights Related to Copyright Applicable to Satellite Broadcasting and Cable Retransmission [1993] *OJ* L 248/15.

Directive (EU) 2019/790 of the European Parliament and of the Council of 17 April 2019 on Copyright and Related Rights in the Digital Single Market and Amending Directives 96/9/EC and 2001/29/EC [2019] *OJ* L 130/92.

Directive 2001/29/EC of the European Parliament and of the Council of 22 May 2001 on the harmonisation of certain aspects of copyright and related rights in the information society [2001] *OJ* L 167/10.
Rome Act 1928.
WIPO Copyright Treaty 1996.
WIPO Performances and Phonograms Treaty 1996.

Official documents and reports

Association Littéraire et Artistique Internationale (ALAI), *Report and Opinion on the Making Available and Communication to the Public in the Internet Environment – Focus on Linking Techniques on the Internet*, Paris, 16 September 2013: http://www.alai.org/en/assets/files/resolutions/making-available-right-report-opinion.pdf.
Bergström S., *Records of the Intellectual Property Conference of Stockholm June 11 to July 14, 1967 Volume II*, Report on the Work of Main Committee I, at para 218: http://global.oup.com/booksites/content/9780198259466/15550029.
Broadcasting and Copyright in the Internal Market. Discussion Paper prepared by the Commission of the European Communities on Copyright Questions concerning Cable and Satellite Broadcasts, III/F/5263/80-EN, Brussels, November 1990.
Communication from the Commission to the Council and European Parliament on Audiovisual Policy, COM (90) 78 final, Brussels, 21 February 1990.
Communication from the Commission to the European Parliament, the Council, the European Economic and Social Committee and the Committee of the Regions, Towards a Modern, More European Copyright Framework, COM (2015) 626, Brussels, 9 December 2015.
Department of Trade and Industry, *Review of the Implementation and Enforcement of EC Law in the UK* (London: Department of Trade and Industry, 1993).
Hansard, HL, Copyright, Designs and Patents Bill [HL], 5th Ser, Col 268 2 November 1988.
International Bureau of WIPO, *Comparative Table for the Sixth Session*, WIPO doc BCP/CE/VI/12.
International Bureau of WIPO, *Memorandum for the Fifth Session, Industrial Property and Copyright* (1995).
International Bureau of WIPO, *Report on the Seventh Session*, WIPO doc BCP/CE/VII/4-INR/CE/VI/4.
Proposal for a European Parliament and Council Directive on the Harmonization of Certain Aspects of Copyright and Related Rights in the Information Society, COM 97 (628) final, Brussels, 10 December 1997.
WIPO, *Records of the Diplomatic Conference on Certain Copyright and Neighbouring Rights Questions* (Geneva: WIPO, 1996) Summary of Minutes of Main Committee II.
WIPO, *Agreed statements concerning the WIPO Copyright Treaty adopted by the Diplomatic Conference on December 20, 1996* (Geneva: WIPO, 1978).
WIPO, *Guide to the Berne Convention for the Protection of Literary and Artistic Works, Paris 1971* (Geneva: WIPO, 1978).
WIPO, *Guide to the Copyright and Related Rights Treaties Administered by WIPO and Glossary of Copyright and Related Rights Terms* (Geneva: WIPO, 2003).

Web sources

React Native: https://facebook.github.io/react/index.html.

6 Communication to the public

Communication, transmission and the public

Introduction

Traditionally, the reproduction right has drawn more attention, but this is changing. Communication to the public is becoming increasingly important in the information society:[1] "The right of communication to the public has been transformed from a relatively peripheral right to one which is taking centre stage for the protection of works."[2]

At first glance, it might appear that communication to the public, being a more recent form of copyright protection that is used to protect works online might have cleared up some of the challenges faced in applying reproduction online. However, as highlighted in Chapter 5, the definition of "communication to the public" is a highly contentious, grey area and its meaning is uncertain.[3] As technologies continue to develop, it has become difficult to determine what constitutes a communication for the purposes of copyright infringement online.[4]

This chapter first considers what is meant by communication in light of the internet. Livingstone theorised that the internet has changed communication as a concept, as it allowed much more interaction between people. He stated: "What's new about the internet may be the combination of interactivity with those features which were innovative for mass communication – the unlimited range of content, the scope of audience reach and the global nature of communication."[5] Thus the internet has essentially created an extension to communication as a concept.[6] In many respects, the internet can be

1 Depreeu S., *The Variable Scope of The Exclusive Economic Rights in Copyright* (Amsterdam: Kluwer Law, 2014) p. 245.
2 Keane B., Ill Communication? The Concept of a Communication to the Public Under EU Copyright Law (2013) 24(5) *Entertainment Law Review*, pp. 165–171, p. 170.
3 Communication from the Commission to the European Parliament, the Council, the European Economic and Social Committee and the Committee of the Regions, Towards a Modern, More European Copyright Framework, COM (2015) 626, Brussels, 9 December 2015, pp. 9–10.
4 Depreeu S., *The Variable Scope of The Exclusive Economic Rights in Copyright* (Amsterdam: Kluwer Law, 2014) p. 265.
5 Livingstone S., New Media, New Audiences? (1999) 1(1) *New Media and Society*, pp. 59–66, p. 65.
6 McQuail D., *McQuail's Mass Communication Theory* (London: Sage Publications Ltd, 2011) p. 139.

understood as a tool for communication.[7] As a result, regulating communication online could potentially regulate all online activity. It is, therefore, essential that the perimeters of communication to the public for the purposes of copyright infringement online are clearly defined. The internet is considered itself a mass medium for communication, and the interactivity which the online technology provides has transformed the concept of communication. In light of copyright infringement, communication to the public could therefore potentially be incredibly broad.[8]

The chapter then undertakes an analysis of the case law relating to communication to the public. First, it compares the case law before and after the Copyright and Related Rights Regulations 2003[9] that amended section 20 of the CDPA 1988 from a broadcasting right to a right of communication to the public. Since the Regulations there has been an increase in the use of this section. Before the Regulations the disputes took place between copyright holding companies, but since then the majority of disputes are between copyright holding companies and individuals, and the most successful cases were brought by copyright holding companies.

The chapter then looks at the key factors in defining communication to the public, namely how the courts have defined "communication", "electronic transmission" and "the public". This jurisprudence revealed that there is no definition of "communication" as such, but that it always involves electronic transmission; but "electronic transmission" is also not defined. The discussion then considers how the CJEU case law has been applied by UK judges, through an analysis of the application of communication in UK courts.

In particular, it is clear that whilst the understanding of the internet as a medium of communication is an internal perspective, the drafting of the law is made from an external perspective. This tension is clearly highlighted in the application of the law. Whilst the judges often take considerable time to explain and understand the technical function of the online activity in their reasoning, ultimately the decision is taken from an internal perspective – that a copyright work is accessed without authorisation. This also contrasts with the approach taken in applying reproduction online.[10]

This chapter seeks to establish three key points. Firstly, that the nature of the internet as a communication device is understood from an internal perspective, which contrasts with the external drafting of copyright law. Secondly, to consider the impact of the communication to the public regulation, in particular comparing the cases before and after the introduction of the law.[11] Thirdly, how the judges

7 Berners-Lee T., *Weaving the Web: The Original Design and Ultimate Destiny of the World Wide Web* (New York: Harper Business, 2000) p. 36.

8 Ross A. and Livingstone C., Communication to the Public: Part 1 (2012) 23(6) *Entertainment Law Review*, pp. 169–173, p. 170.

9 Copyright and Related Rights Regulations 2003 (SI 2003/2498).

10 See Chapter 4, where whilst both perspectives were taken, the external perspective was more commonly applied.

11 As introduced by the Copyright and Related Rights Regulations 2003 (SI 2003/2498).

interpret and apply the law of communication to the public to online activity, looking particularly at their use of the internal and external perspectives.

What does "communication" mean online?

The first section of this chapter considers what is meant by communication in light of online technologies and how copyright infringement by way of communication to the public fits in with this understanding.

The *Oxford English Dictionary* definition of communication is "the imparting or exchanging of information by speaking, writing, or using some other medium ... a letter or message containing information or news."[12] It is a late middle English word that originates from Old French *comunicacion* and Latin *communicatio*(n-)[13] which stems from the verb "communicare" which means "to share".[14]

This is significant in light of the internet, which has been considered to facilitate the sharing economy. Internet technologies allow instant interaction and communication of an unlimited range of content to a global audience.[15] The internet therefore, created an extension to communication as a concept.[16] Furthermore, Kalyanaraman and Sundar identified that "one of the unique features of the World Wide Web as a mass medium lies in the fact that message sources are indistinct from message receivers."[17] This suggests not only an extension, but also a transformation in the meaning of communication altogether.

The creation of the internet was based on the idea of communication.[18] When designing the World Wide Web, Tim Berners-Lee specified that his goal was to link information so that it could be available to people around the world, he explained that "the art was ... to allow one computer to talk to another, in such a way that when all computers everywhere did it, the system would thrive ... There was no central computer 'controlling' the Web, no single network on which these protocols worked, not even an organisation anywhere that 'ran' the Web. The Web was not a physical 'thing' that existed in a certain 'place.' It was a 'space' in which information could exist."[19]

According to communication theory the internet is considered a *mass communication medium*, characterised as a medium of interconnectedness, accessible to

12 https://www.lexico.com/en/definition/communication.
13 *Ibid.*
14 *Ibid.*
15 Livingstone S., New Media, New Audiences? (1999) 1(1) *New Media and Society*, pp. 59–66, p. 65.
16 McQuail D., *McQuail's Mass Communication Theory* (London: Sage Publications Ltd, 2011) p. 139.
17 Kalyanaraman S. and Sundar S., Portrait of the Portal as a Metaphor: Explicating Web Portals for Communication Research (2008) 65(2) *Journalism and Mass Communication Quarterly*, pp. 239–256, p. 239.
18 Berners-Lee T., *Weaving the Web: The Original Design and Ultimate Destiny of the World Wide Web* (New York: Harper Business, 2000).
19 *Ibid.*, p. 36.

individuals as communicators, for both mass and personal communication.[20] Carey proposed an understanding of communication as transmission; a theory of communication that centralises culture as a key feature in communication and society. He defined communication as "a symbolic process whereby reality is produced, maintained, repaired and transformed."[21] Therefore, it can be understood that the internet is not a place or a thing, but a medium for communication that has expanded the concept of communication as it facilitates the ability to share anything to anyone at any time.

As explained, understanding the internet in this way, as a medium for communication, is to take the internal perspective. Conceptualising the technical functions of the hardware and software connections that create the internet as a medium for sharing or communicating information is simply a metaphorical cognitive process within the human mind that gives meaning to this otherwise seemingly abstract concept.

However, in contrast, statutory law defined the parameters of copyright infringement by communication to the public online using the external perspective. This is demonstrated by section 20(2) of the CDPA 1988, which stated its meaning as "communication to the public by electronic transmission." This was confirmed by the CJEU in the case of *TVCatchup*:[22] "The author's right of communication to the public covers any transmission or retransmission of a work to the public not present at the place where the communication originates, by wire or wireless means, including broadcasting."[23]

Therefore, in order to determine the application of the restricted act of communication to the public, the next section undertakes a consideration of the case law referring to section 20 of the CDPA 1988.

UK case law on communication to the public

In order to assess the meaning of "communication to the public" within the context of UK copyright law, all the cases referring to section 20 of the CDPA 1988 were collated and analysed.[24] There were 43 UK cases that referenced section 20, which were separated into cases that took place before the Copyright and Related Rights Regulations 2003[25] (pre-regulation cases) and after the 2003 regulations (post-regulation cases). These cases were analysed and compared in order

20 McQuail D., *McQuail's Mass Communication Theory* (London: Sage Publications Ltd, 2011) p. 41.

21 Carey J., *Communication as Culture* (Boston: Unwin Hyman, 1988) p. 23.

22 *ITV Broadcasting Ltd, ITV 2 Ltd, ITV Digital Channels Ltd, Channel 4 Television Corporation, Four Ventures Ltd, Channel 5 Broadcasting Ltd, ITV Studios Ltd v TVCatchup Ltd* (Case C-607/11) ECLI:EU:C:2013:147.

23 *Ibid.*, at 23.

24 The same methodology used for Chapter 4 was mirrored here. This part of the analysis was completed by 30 April 2016.

25 Copyright and Related Rights Regulations 2003 (SI 2003/2498), which updated the CDPA 1988 in order to transpose communication to the public into UK legislation.

to demonstrate the impact of the Regulations. Thereafter, an analysis of the post-regulation cases is undertaken in order to consider the interpretation and application of the law by the judges, particularly considering the internal and external perspectives.

The pre-regulation case law

As explained in Chapter 5, before the Information Society Directive[26] was transposed into UK law by way of the Copyright and Related Rights Regulations 2003, which came into force on 31 October 2003, section 20 of the CDPA 1988 was understood as a restriction on broadcasting. Therefore, analysis of these cases would not contribute to understanding communication to the public, and as a result cases before 2003 were excluded from the content analysis.

However, prior to the exclusion of these cases a comparative analysis was undertaken, the results of which are now briefly discussed. There were only six cases brought under section 20 of the CDPA 1988 prior to the 2003 Regulations. These were:

Phonographic Performance Ltd v Candy Rock Recording Ltd 2000 WL 331042[27]
IPC Magazines Ltd v MGN Ltd [1998] FSR 431[28]
Shetland Times Ltd v Dr Jonathan Wills and Another [1997] FSR 604[29]
Film Investors Overseas Services SA and Another v The Home Video Channel Ltd [1997] EMLR 347[30]
The Association of Independent Radio Companies Ltd (Airc) and Another v Phonographic Performance Ltd and the British Broadcasting Corporation (Intervener) [1994] RPC 143[31]
British Broadcasting Corporation v British Satellite Broadcasting Ltd [1992] Ch 141[32]

26 Directive 2001/29/EC of the European Parliament and of the Council of 22 May 2001 on the harmonisation of certain aspects of copyright and related rights in the information society [2001] OJ L 167/10 (hereafter, the Information Society Directive).

27 Phonographic Performance Ltd (PPL) appealed the Copyright Tribunal decision on 10 November 1998, against Candy Rock Recording Ltd, a background music dubbing company.

28 The plaintiff was the publisher of *Woman* magazine and the defendant was the publisher of *The Sunday Mirror* newspaper.

29 The pursuers own and publish *The Shetland Times*, a newspaper which carries local, national and international news. The defenders provide a news reporting service.

30 The plaintiffs claim to own the copyright of a number of films. The defendants operate a television broadcast service.

31 The original applications were made by 76 independent radio companies holding licences to broadcast and the defendants, Phonographic Performance Ltd (PPL).

32 This involved a copyright infringement claim brought by the British Broadcasting Corporation (BBC) against British Satellite Broadcasting for the use of the BBC's broadcasts of international football matches played in Italy in June and July 1990 in the course of the World Cup finals.

Every case involved a large or medium sized company in the field of either publication or broadcasting. Section 20 was not used to claim infringement against an individual. Equally, it was never invoked by content creators, but in each case the claimant was a copyright holding corporation.

The post-regulation case law

The key findings of the post-regulation cases are summarised in Table 6.1.

Comparing the pre- and post-regulation cases

To carry out a comparison, the cases were categorised and counted to determine: (1) the number of judgments; (2) the parties involved; (3) the copyright work subject to the claim; and (4) the successful party. Details of the six pre-regulation cases are in the footnotes to the list in the section "The pre-regulation case law", and the details of the post-regulation cases are in Table 6.1. The analysis revealed four main findings.

Firstly, the number of cases rose dramatically following the 2003 Regulations, unsurprisingly. During the 15-year period from 1988 to 2003, only six cases were brought under section 20 of the CDPA 1988. However, following the 2003 Regulations, during the 13 years from 2003 to 2016, there have been 37 cases invoking section 20. This demonstrates that section 20 has increased in importance and relevance in relation to online copyright infringement.

Secondly, 100% of the pre-regulation cases were disputes between corporations. The 37 post-regulation judgments represent 23 unique disputes (as the cases included appeals). Of these 23 disputes, nine cases were brought by corporations against individuals, only four disputes occurred between corporations and seven actions were brought against ISPs by corporations. Therefore, this demonstrates that before the 2003 Regulations, cases were only between corporations and not against individuals or ISPs; subsequently, however, since 2003 this dynamic has dramatically changed. This is significant as it suggests that the impact of the internet and online technologies has changed the way in which copyright regulation is utilised.

Thirdly, the type of copyright works subject to the disputes of the pre-regulation cases were: 1/6 football match, 2/6 news related media, 1/6 pornographic film and 2/6 musical works. In contrast, the copyright works subject the post-regulation disputes were 7/23 football matches, 5/23 musical works, 4/23 photographs, 3/23 films, 2/23 pornographic films, 1/23 TV programme and 1/23 computer software. This demonstrates an expansion in the range of copyright works being subject to dispute since the 2003 Regulations. The Online Copyright Infringement Tracker 2018 reported that when looking at the infringement levels amongst consumers of each content type, computer software declined significantly, down from 26% in 2017 to 20% in 2018. TV programmes had the highest infringement level of any content type at 23% (up slightly from 22% in

Table 6.1 Key findings of the post-regulation cases

Case name	*Party*	*Work*	*Outcome*
Polydor Ltd v Brown [2005] EWHC 3191 (Ch)	C v I	Music	Applicant C
Union des Associations Europeennes de Football (UEFA) v Briscomb [2006] EWHC 1268 (Ch)	C v I	Football match	Applicant C
Karen Murphy v Media Protection Services Ltd [2007] EWHC 3091 (Admin)	C v I	Football match	Applicant C
Football Association Premier League Ltd, NetMed Hellas SA, Multichoice Hellas SA v QC Leisure (David Richardson), AV Station Plc, Malcolm Chamberlain, Michael Madden, Sanjay Raval, David Greenslade, SR Leisure Ltd, Phillip George Charles Houghton, Derek Owen [2008] EWHC 1411 (Ch)	C v I	Football match	Referred to CJEU
Alan MacKie t/a 197 Aerial Photography v Nicola Askew, Largsholidaylets.co.uk (SA1251/08) (2009) WL 2392381	I v I	Photographs	Applicant I
Alan Grisbrook v MGN Ltd, Scottish Daily Record and Sunday Mail Ltd, Syndication International Ltd [2009] EWHC 2520 (Ch); [2010] EWCA Civ 1399	I v C	Photographs	Defendant C
Twentieth Century Fox Film Corporation, Universal City Studios Productions LLP, Warner Bros Entertainment Inc, Paramount Pictures Corporation, Disney Enterprises Inc, Columbia Pictures Industries Inc v Newzbin Ltd [2010] EWHC 608 (Ch)	C v I	Film	Applicant C
Union of European Football Associations v Euroview Sport Ltd [2010] EWHC 1066 (Ch)	C v C	Football match	Referred to CJEU
Football Dataco Ltd, The Scottish Premier League Ltd, The Scottish Football League, PA Sport UK Ltd v Sportradar GmbH (a Company Registered in Germany), Sportradar AG (a Company registered in Switzerland) [2010] EWHC 2911 (Ch); [2011] EWCA Civ 330	C v C	Football match	Referred to CJEU
ITV Broadcasting Ltd, ITV 2 Ltd, ITV Digital Channels, Channel 4 Television Corporation, 4 Ventures Ltd, Channel 5 Broadcasting Ltd v TV Catch Up Ltd [2010] EWHC 3063 (Ch); [2011] EWHC 2977 (Pat)	C v I	TV programmes	Referred to CJEU

Case name	*Party*	*Work*	*Outcome*
Media CAT Ltd v A – H [2010] EWPCC 017; *Media CAT Ltd v Malcolm Adams, Katherine Taylor, Hooper, Mitchell Chance, Miss Gonzalles Romeo, Mark Jimack, Miss Maria Shewan, Keith Wood, William Wickam, Sean Allen, Christopher Beck, Dave Cundall, Danny Cowan, Glyn Bentley, Pana Begum, Peter Armitage, Allan Billington, James Bryant, Julia Abbott, Christopher Birkett, M Brunt, Gareth Bacon, Wayne Bacon, Michelle McGlade, Elaine Cox, David Bick* [2011] EWPCC 006	C v I	Pornography	Applicant C
Dramatico Entertainment Ltd, EMI Records Ltd, Mercury Records Ltd, Polydor Ltd, Rough Trade Records Ltd, Sony Music Entertainment UK Ltd, Virgin Records Ltd, Warner Music UK Ltd, 679 Recordings Ltd v British Sky Broadcasting Ltd, British Telecommunications plc, Everything Everywhere Ltd, Talktalk Telecom Group plc, Telefónica UK Ltd, Virgin Media Ltd [2012] EWHC 268 (Ch)	C v ISP	Music	Applicant C
Golden Eye (International) Ltd, Ben Dover Productions, Celtic Broadcasting Ltd, Easy on the Eye, DMS Telecoms Ltd, Gary Baker, Harmony Films Ltd, Justin Ribeiro Dos Santos t/a Joybear Pictures, Orchid MG Ltd, Kudetta BVBA, RP Films Ltd, Sweetmeats Productions t/a SMP, Sll Films Ltd, Terence Stephens t/a One Eyed Jack Productions v Telefónica UK Ltd v Consumer Focus [2012] EWHC 723 (Ch); [2012] EWCA Civ 1740	C v ISP	Pornographic film	Applicant C
Performing Right Society Ltd v B4U Network (Europe) Ltd [2012] EWHC 3010 (Ch)	C v C	Music	Applicant C
David Hoffman v Drug Abuse Resistance Education (UK) Ltd [2012] EWPCC 2	I v C	Photograph	Applicant I
EMI Records Ltd, Infectious Ltd, Liberation Music Pty Ltd, Polydor Ltd, Simco Ltd, Sony Music Entertainment UK Ltd, Universal Music Operations Ltd, Virgin Records Ltd, Warner Music UK Ltd, Wea International Inc v British Sky Broadcasting Ltd, British Telecommunications plc, Everything Everywhere Ltd, Talktalk Telecom Group plc, Telefónica UK Ltd, Virgin Media Ltd [2013] EWHC 379 (Ch)	C v ISP	Music	Applicant C

Case name	*Party*	*Work*	*Outcome*
Football Association Premier League Ltd v British Sky Broadcasting Ltd, British Telecommunications Plc, Everything Everywhere Ltd, Talktalk Telecom Ltd, Telefónica UK Ltd, Virgin Media Ltd [2013] EWHC 2058 (Ch)	C v ISP	Football match	Applicant C
Paramount Home Entertainment Ltd, Sony Pictures Home Entertainment Ltd, Twentieth Century Fox Film Company Ltd, Universal Pictures (UK) Ltd, Warner Bros. Entertainment UK Ltd, Disney Enterprises Inc v British Sky Broadcasting Ltd, British Telecommunications Plc, Everything Everywhere Ltd, Talktalk Telecom Ltd, Telefónica UK Ltd, Virgin Media Ltd [2013] EWHC 3479 (Ch); [2014] EWHC 937 (Ch)	C v ISP	Film	Applicant C
Football Association Premier League Ltd v Anthony William Luxton, Barclays Bank Ltd [2014] EWHC 253 (Ch)	C v I	Football match	Applicant C
1967 Ltd, Dramatico Entertainment Ltd, Infectious Music Ltd, Liberation Music PTY Ltd, Simco Ltd, Sony Music Entertainment UK Ltd, Universal Music Operations Ltd v British Sky Broadcasting Ltd, British Telecommunications plc, EE Ltd, Talktalk Telecom Ltd, Virgin Media Ltd [2014] EWHC 3444 (Ch)	C v ISP	Music	Applicant C
Omnibill (PTY) Ltd v EGPSXXX Ltd (in liquidation), Mr Robert Ashley Carter [2014] EWHC 3762 (IPEC)	C v I	Photograph	Applicant I
Twentieth Century Fox Film Corporation, Universal City Studios Productions LLP, Warner Bros Entertainment Inc, Paramount Pictures Corporation, Disney Enterprises, Inc, Columbia Pictures Industries, Inc v SKY UK Limited, British Telecommunications plc, EE Ltd, Talktalk Telecom Limited, Virgin Media Ltd [2015] EWHC 1082 (Ch)	C v ISP	Film	Applicant C
Ultrasoft Technologies Ltd v Hubcreate Ltd [2016] EWHC 544 (IPEC)	C v C	Software	Defendant C

Key: C: Corporation (copyright holding corporations, collecting societies[33] and a charity)[34]; ISP: Internet Service Provider (these cases related to section 97A injunctions to block websites); I: Individual (including Newzbin, which was created by three individuals).

33 E.g. *Performing Right Society Ltd v B4U Network (Europe) Ltd* [2012] EWHC 3010 (Ch).

34 *David Hoffman v Drug Abuse Resistance Education (UK) Ltd* [2012] EWPCC 2.

2017). Infringement of sports content was 21%, which was a new question introduced to the 2018 study.[35]

Fourthly, the outcomes of the post-regulation cases demonstrate that the most successful applicant was corporations. All cases brought by corporations were either successful or referred to the CJEU. In fact, on only one occasion did a defendant succeed, and this was in the only case brought by an individual against a corporation. Therefore, the success rate of claims under communication to the public is extremely high, particularly for corporations.

Overall, the post-regulation cases were dominated by applications against ISPs (7/23), brought by corporations to block infringing websites. There was a 100% success rate for cases bought under these circumstances. In fact, the only successful cases brought by individuals related to photographs, in all instances, used on the defendant's website without permission. Although, only two out of three cases under these circumstances were successful.

The analysis now turns to consider the post-regulation cases in detail, together with the CJEU case law in order to determine the application and interpretation of communication to the public.

Communication to the public in the CJEU and UK courts

As mentioned, once the pre-regulation cases had been excluded from the data set, 37 judgments remained (from 23 disputes). The judgments were uploaded to the qualitative data analysis software Nvivo in order to be organised and coded, using the same methodology as in Chapter 4. This analysis assisted in the understanding of the body of case law, it allowed for the categorising, counting and content analysis of the judgments. Whilst this chapter emphasises the most significant cases where the judges went into detailed explanation as to what is meant by communication to the public, it also draws on the other cases where relevant.

Furthermore, communication to the public differs from reproduction in that it was developed more recently and with a clearer impact from European regulation in the form of the Information Society Directive and CJEU case law. As Rosati explained: "From recent CJEU case law it has become apparent that the InfoSoc Directive should be interpreted as leaving very limited (if any at all) room for independent national initiatives."[36] Therefore, this chapter takes the European case law into deeper consideration than in previous chapters, due to the greater influence on the meaning of the law within the UK.

35 Kantar Media, *Online Copyright Infringement Tracker* (London: Intellectual Property Office, 2018): https://assets.publishing.service.gov.uk/government/uploads/system/uploads/attachment_data/file/729184/oci-tracker.pdf, p. 5.

36 Rosati E., Neighbouring Rights for Publishers: Are National and (Possible) EU Initiatives Lawful? (2016) 47(5) *International Review of Intellectual Property and Competition Law*, pp. 569–594, p. 575.

The discussion now turns to consider the judgments of the courts of the CJEU in order to determine the interpretation of communication to the public at European level. Subsequently, the UK cases are considered in order to determine how these interpretations have been applied by the UK courts.

The broad and varied principle of "communication" in the CJEU

When interpreting and applying national law that gives effect to an EU Directive, as is the case in relation to communication to the public, UK courts must do so in light of the wording and purpose of the relevant Directive.[37] The interpretation and purpose of the Directive is determined by the CJEU[38] and therefore it is necessary to first consider the EU cases in which the CJEU provided explanations as to the intended meaning of the Information Society Directive. The application of the CJEU interpretations by the UK courts is considered thereafter.

Generally, the communication right is understood to be infringed whenever a protected work is made available to the public by any means.[39] The work need only be made available in such a way that members of the public *may* access it.[40] However, the mere provision of physical facilities is not sufficient as to constitute communication to the public.[41] Communication to the public should be interpreted broadly,[42] including covering all communication where the public were not present at the time or place that the communication originated.[43] There have been a significant number of referrals to the CJEU for clarification on the meaning of the right,[44] indicating the complexity of the regulation. Overall, the CJEU has been seen to take a broad and purpose-driven approach, ensuring a high level of protection for rights-holders.[45]

37 *ITV Broadcasting Ltd, ITV 2 Ltd, ITV Digital Channels Ltd, Channel Four Television Corporation, 4 Ventures Ltd, Channel 5 Broadcasting Ltd, ITV Studios Ltd v TVCatchup Ltd (in administration), TVCatchup (UK) Ltd, Media Resources Ltd (a Mauritian company) v The Secretary of State for Business, Innovation and Skills, Virgin Media Ltd* [2015] EWCA Civ 204, as per Kitchin LJ at [86].

38 *Ibid.*, Kitchin LJ at [86].

39 *Sociedad General de Autores y Editores de Espana (SGAE) v Rafael Hoteles SA* (Case C-306/05) ECLI:EU:C:2006:764 at 42.

40 *Ibid.*, at 43.

41 *Football Dataco Ltd, The Scottish Premier League Ltd, The Scottish Football League, PA Sport UK Ltd v Sportradar GmbH (a Company Registered in Germany), Sportradar AG (a Company registered in Switzerland)* [2010] EWHC 2911 (Ch), as per Floyd J at [74].

42 Information Society Directive, Recital 23; *Sociedad General de Autores y Editores de Espana (SGAE) v Rafael Hoteles SA* (Case C-306/05) ECLI:EU:C:2006:764 at 36.

43 Information Society Directive, Recital 23; CDPA 1988, section 20(2)(b).

44 At least 18 cases have been referred to the CJEU at the last count. For a detailed discussion, see Rosati E., *Copyright and the Court of Justice of the European Union* (Oxford: Oxford University Press, 2019).

45 *Ibid.*, p. 95.

Examples of communication to the public include linking to protected content,[46] indexing activities by a platform,[47] live streaming,[48] hyperlinking and framing,[49] and distributing a television signal to the television sets in hotel rooms.[50] In this case the CJEU commented that the hotel was "in full knowledge of the consequences of its action, to give access to the protected work to its customers. In the absence of that intervention, its customers, although physically within that area, would not, in principle, be able to enjoy the broadcast work."[51] Advocate General Sharpston explained that "the hotel owner is in the same situation as a third party who relays original programmes broadcast or transmitted by cable."[52]

This approach was confirmed in the subsequent case of *Football Association Premier League*, [53] where the CJEU held that a pub owner committed an act of communication to the public by turning on a television in a pub, stating that the owner of the "public house intentionally gives the customers present in that establishment access to a broadcast containing protected works via a television screen and speakers. Without his intervention the customers cannot enjoy the works broadcast, even though they are physically within the broadcast's catchment area."[54]

However, the CJEU has also held that television broadcasting of the graphic user interface of a website does *not* constitute communication to the public of that work.[55] The court stated that this was because television viewers receive the graphic user interface solely in a passive manner, without the possibility of intervening and therefore[56] cannot use the feature of that interface which

46 *GS Media BV v Sanoma Media Netherlands BV, Playboy Enterprises International Inc, Britt Geertruida Dekker* (Case C-160/15) ECLI:EU:C:2016:644.

47 *EMI Records Ltd, Infectious Ltd, Liberation Music Pty Ltd, Polydor Ltd, Simco Ltd, Sony Music Entertainment UK Ltd, Universal Music Operations Ltd, Virgin Records Ltd, Warner Music UK Ltd, Wea International Inc v British Sky Broadcasting Ltd, British Telecommunications plc, Everything Everywhere Ltd, Talktalk Telecom Group plc, Telefónica UK Ltd, Virgin Media Ltd* [2013] EWHC 379 (Ch).

48 *Football Association Premier League Ltd, NetMed Hellas SA, Multichoice Hellas SA v QC Leisure (a trading name), David Richardson, AV Station Plc, Malcolm Chamberlain, Michael Madden, Sanjay Raval, David Greenslade, SR Leisure Ltd, Phillip George Charles Houghton, Derek Owen* [2008] EWHC 1411 (Ch).

49 *BestWater International GmbH v Michael Mebes, Stefan Potsch* (Case C-348/13) ECLI:EU:C:2014:2315.

50 *Sociedad General de Autores y Editores de Espana (SGAE) v Rafael Hoteles SA* (Case C-306/05) ECLI:EU:C:2006:764.

51 *Ibid.*, at 40 and 42.

52 *Ibid.*, at 53.

53 *Football Association Premier League Ltd, NetMed Hellas SA, Multichoice Hellas SA v QC Leisure, David Richardson, AV Station plc, Malcolm Chamberlain, Michael Madden, SR Leisure Ltd, Philip George Charles Houghton, Derek Owen and Karen Murphy v Media Protection Services Ltd* (Joined cases C-403/08 and 429/08) ECLI:EU:C:2011:631 at 629.

54 *Ibid.*, at 195 and 196.

55 *Svaz softwarové ochrany Bezpečnostní Softwarová Asociace v Ministerstvo kultury* (Case C-393/09) ECLI:EU:C:2010:816 at 57.

56 *Ibid.*

enables interaction between the computer program and the user.[57] This reasoning is difficult to follow because it suggests that the interactivity of a graphic interface is the aspect that is protected by copyright. However, since the appearance of the interface is also protected by copyright, it is suggested that, in fact, the work was communicated to the public, subject to a sufficient part of the work having been taken.[58]

In their study of EU jurisprudence, Favale, Kretschmer and Torremens found that European judges initially took a strict approach to the concept of communication to the public.[59] Following the implementation of the Information Society Directive, the court gave a broad interpretation of the concept of communication to the public.[60] For example in the case of *SGAE* [61] the court stated: "The distribution of a signal by means of television sets by a hotel to customers staying in its rooms, whatever technique is used to transmit the signal, constitutes communication to the public within the meaning of Article 3(1) of that directive."[62] The judges drew from Recital 23 of the Information Society Directive, which stated that "communication to the public must be interpreted broadly."[63]

The study found that a narrow approach[64] was taken when the CJEU determined that it was not communication to the public to transmit radio signals in a dental practice,[65] on the basis that there was no aim to obtain profit and only a limited number of people had access to the work.[66] This narrow approach was also taken in the case of communication of a work in a place open to the public.[67] However, the broad approach was applied to retransmission of TV shows via the internet[68] and on the broadcasting of TV

57 *Ibid.*

58 Vitoria M., et al (eds), *Laddie, Prescott and Vitoria: The Modern Law of Copyright and Designs* (London: Butterworths, 2011) 17.16.

59 Favale M., Kretschmer M. and Torremans P., Is there an EU Copyright Jurisprudence? An Empirical Analysis of the Workings of the European Court of Justice (2016) 79(1) *Modern Law Review*, pp. 31–75, p. 59.

60 *Ibid.*, p. 59.

61 *Sociedad General de Autores y Editores de Espana (SGAE) v Rafael Hoteles SA* (Case C-306/05) ECLI:EU:C:2006:764.

62 *Ibid.*, 55.1.

63 *Ibid.*, 36.

64 Favale M., Kretschmer M. and Torremans P., Is there an EU Copyright Jurisprudence? An Empirical Analysis of the Workings of the European Court of Justice (2016) 79(1) *Modern Law Review*, pp. 31–75, pp. 59–60.

65 *Ibid.*, p. 59, referring to *Società Consortile Fonografici (SCF) v Marco Del Corso* (Case C-135/10) ECLI:EU:C:2012:140.

66 *Ibid.*, p. 60.

67 *Ibid.*, p. 60, referring to *Circul Globus București (Circ & Variete Globus București) v Uniunea Compozitorilor și Muzicologilor din România – Asociația pentru Drepturi de Autor (UCMR – ADA)* (Case C-283/10) ECLI:EU:C:2011:772.

68 *Ibid.*, p. 60, referring to *Svaz softwarové ochrany Bezpečnostní Softwarová Asociace v Ministerstvo kultury* (Case C-393/09) ECLI:EU:C:2010:816.

signals in spa hotel rooms,[69] whilst a narrow approach was subsequently applied to internet links on a web page.[70]

Favale, Kretschmer and Torremens highlighted that the approach taken by the court did not depend on the particular Directive or legal approaches applied within the case.[71] Ultimately, they argue, the CJEU seems to operate a broad concept of communication to the public, but this concept was applied in a balanced way, taking into account various factors relating to the facts of the case.[72]

The CJEU jurisprudence has provided some guidance to what activities do or do not constitute infringement, and determined that the law is applied broadly, although many factors are taken into consideration when determining infringement.[73] This highlights that the approach taken by the CJEU is inconsistent[74] and lacks clarity.[75] Others have argued that the CJEU approach has been an attempt to develop *sui generis* case groups, which provides a degree of flexibility that is needed due to fast-developing technologies.[76] However, this leaves room for uncertainty by creating a complex patchwork of nuances in the jurisprudence. The CJEU has sought to explain the concepts of "communication" and "public" in several cases. As such, the features of a communication can be said to include the following: a copyright protected work being made available by transmission, that may be accessed by a person but it is not necessary for them to actually do so.[77] The transmission can take place between the point at which the communication takes place and the final point of reception, and there must be a separation between these points.[78]

69 *Ibid.*, p. 60, referring to *OSA – Ochranný Svaz Autorský Pro Práva K Dílům Hudebním OS v Léčebné Lázně Mariánské Lázně AS* (Case C-351/12) ECLI:EU:C:2014:110.

70 *Ibid.*, p. 60, referring to *Nils Svensson, Sten Sjögren, Madelaine Sahlman, Pia Gadd v Retriever Sverige AB* (Case C-466/12) ECLI:EU:C:2014:76.

71 Favale M., Kretschmer M. and Torremans P., Is there an EU Copyright Jurisprudence? An empirical Analysis of the Workings of the European Court of Justice (2016) 79(1) *Modern Law Review*, pp. 31–75, p. 60.

72 *Ibid.*, p. 60.

73 *Ibid.*, p. 60.

74 Baggs S., Alexander R. and Preston E., Curtains Down on Popcorn Time: S.97A Takes Centre Stage (2016) 38(1) *European Intellectual Property Review*, pp. 56–60, p. 59.

75 Smith J. and Burke S., Record Companies Win First Round v The Pirate Bay in The United Kingdom But Pirates Remain At Large: *Dramatico Entertainment Ltd v British Sky Broadcasting Ltd* (2012) 34(6) *European Intellectual Property Review*, pp. 416–419, p. 418.

76 Clark B. and Tozzi S., "Communication to the Public" Under EU Copyright Law: An Increasingly Delphic Concept or Intentional Fragmentation? (2016) 38(12) *EIPR*, pp. 715–717, p. 717.

77 *Sociedad General de Autores y Editores de Espana (SGAE) v Rafael Hoteles SA* (Case C-306/05) ECLI:EU:C:2006:764 at 43.

78 *Football Association Premier League Ltd, NetMed Hellas SA, Multichoice Hellas SA v QC Leisure, David Richardson, AV Station plc, Malcolm Chamberlain, Michael Madden, SR Leisure Ltd, Philip George Charles Houghton, Derek Owen and Karen Murphy v Media Protection Services Ltd* (Joined cases C-403/08 and 429/08) ECLI:EU:C:2011:631 at 149 and 201.

The features of the public can be said to include: an indeterminate number of potential recipients,[79] but small groups of people may be excluded,[80] and in order to assess whether the group is fairly large, all potential recipients must be considered cumulatively.[81] The meaning of the public is also considered to be a new public, in that it is an audience not taken into account by the rights-holder. In *Svensson*, the CJEU said that the public targeted by the initial communication consisted of all potential visitors to the site concerned, since, given that access to the works on that site was not subject to any restrictive measures, all internet users could therefore have free access to them.[82] But later in *Renckhoff*, the court said that communication to the public covers the posting on one website of a photograph previously posted, without any restriction preventing it from being downloaded and with the consent of the copyright holder, on another website.[83] So, that means that if the work is online the public could mean all internet users, but reposting content that is freely available online counts as an act of communication to the public. This is contradictory and undermines the criteria of public. Indeed, it seems that this contradiction, taken together with the fact that the public have to be able only to potentially access the material, the criteria of public are essentially redundant in an online context and could be removed altogether. All the factors of the public cancel each other out when applied to the internet.

In *GS Media*, [84] the Advocate General opined that in order to establish an act of communication, the intervention of the "hyperlinker" must be vital or indispensable in order to benefit from or enjoy works.[85] The CJEU agreed that the user makes an act of communication when it intervenes, in full knowledge of the consequences of its action, to give access to a protected work to its customers, and does so, in particular, where, in the absence of that intervention, its customers would not, in principle, be able to enjoy the broadcast work.[86] Moreover, the CJEU went on to presume that when a person posts a link, they carry out the necessary checks to ensure the work is not illegally published.[87] Significantly, any element of knowledge was also

79 *ITV Broadcasting Ltd, ITV 2 Ltd, ITV Digital Channels Ltd, Channel 4 Television Corporation, Four Ventures Ltd, Channel 5 Broadcasting Ltd, ITV Studios Ltd v TVCatchup Ltd* (Case C-607/11) ECLI:EU:C:2013:147 at 32.

80 *Società Consortile Fonografici (SCF) v Marco Del Corso* (Case C-135/10) ECLI:EU:C:2012:140 at 86.

81 *OSA – Ochranný Svaz Autorský Pro Práva K Dílům Hudebním OS v Léčebné Lázně Mariánské Lázně A.S.* (Case C-351/12) ECLI:EU:C:2014:110 at 28.

82 *Nils Svensson, Sten Sjögren, Madelaine Sahlman, Pia Gadd v Retriever Sverige AB* (Case C-466/12) ECLI:EU:C:2014:76 at 26.

83 *Land Nordrhein-Westfalen v Dirk Renckhoff* (Case C-161/17) ECLI:EU:C:2018:634 at 47.

84 *GS Media BV v Sanoma Media Netherlands BV, Playboy Enterprises International Inc, Britt Geertruida Dekker* (Case C-160/157) ECLI:EU:C:2016:221, Opinion of Advocate General Wathelet.

85 *Ibid.*, Advocate General Wathelet at 57.

86 *Ibid.*, at 35.

87 *Ibid.*, at 51.

stressed: "it is to be determined whether those links are provided ... by a person who did not know or could not reasonably have known the illegal nature of the publication of those works."[88] This suggests that communication to the public is a deliberate conduct by the user. Considering the mindset of the user points to the internal perspective, in contrast to previous cases such as *Svensson* [89] where the court disregarded the user and focused on the technological process.

The profit-making intention of the alleged infringer is also a relevant factor for the court to consider.[90] This factor does not fit comfortably in the UK jurisprudence of primary copyright infringement, since it is a strict liability law which means that profit and intention are not relevant. However, it is a factor utilised by the CJEU in order to determine, from a purposive perspective, the intention of the parties, such as in *The Pirate Bay* case.[91] The fact that the website was generating revenue helped the court to determine communication to the public, to uphold the objection of the Information Society Directive; a high protection for copyright holders.

The reasoning of the cases is difficult to reconcile on any principled basis, leaving uncertainty in what actually constitutes a communication to the public. It has been suggested that any attempt to establish a unified theory from these cases is doomed to fail.[92]

This uncertainty has been problematic for the UK courts. The discussion now turns to consider the meaning of "communication", as applied in the UK courts to online activity.

The interpretation and application of "communication" in the UK courts

The UK courts have also interpreted and applied communication to the public in a broad and encompassing manner. The case law demonstrates that communication to the public online reaches further than that of copying. For example, in the matter of *Alan MacKie*, [93] the judge held that when the defendant uploaded photographs to her website, she was "linking herself into a process of communication."[94] In doing so the judge recognised that the internet as a whole is a communication process system, and

88 *Ibid.*, at 55.
89 *Nils Svensson, Sten Sjögren, Madelaine Sahlman, Pia Gadd v Retriever Sverige AB* (Case C-466/12) ECLI:EU:C:2014:76.
90 *Football Association Premier League Ltd, NetMed Hellas SA, Multichoice Hellas SA v QC Leisure, David Richardson, AV Station plc, Malcolm Chamberlain, Michael Madden, SR Leisure Ltd, Philip George Charles Houghton, Derek Owen and Karen Murphy v Media Protection Services Ltd* (Joined cases C-403/08 and 429/08) ECLI: EU:C:2011:631 at 204.
91 *Stichting Brein v Ziggo BV, XS4ALL Internet BV* (Case C-610/15) ECLI:EU: C:2017:456.
92 Davis R., Quintin T. and Tritton G, *Tritton on Intellectual Property in Europe* (London: Sweet & Maxwell, 2018) pp. 640 and 642.
93 *Alan MacKie t/a 197 Aerial Photography v Nicola Askew, Largsholidaylets.co.uk* (SA1251/08) (2009) WL 2392381.
94 *Ibid.*, as per Sheriff Principal B A Lockhart at 30.

referred to the decision of Lord Drummond Young in *Bonnier Media Ltd* who stated that: "The Internet should rather be viewed as a process of communication. It is, in essence, a system of communication which allows a verbal or graphic message to be set up on a computer, which may be situated anywhere in the world, and conveyed to another computer, which may likewise be situated anywhere in the world ... The person who creates the website is linking himself into a process of communication, with the obvious intention that communication should take place by way of that process."[95] This appears to suggest that intent is a factor when committing infringement by communication; in contrast to the previous analysis of copying, which clearly stated that this was not a principle of primary copyright infringement.[96]

In the matter of *Dramatico Entertainment*, the judge found that the operators of The Pirate Bay website had committed copyright infringement by copying and communicating to the public.[97] The Pirate Bay website hosted a BitTorrent system that allowed users to share files, the judge stated that in doing so "they go far beyond merely enabling or assisting ... they also purport to grant users the right to do the acts complained of."[98] Furthermore, in the case of *EMI Records*, the judge concluded that users of the websites also infringed the claimants' copyrights both by copying and by communication to the public.[99]

In order to arrive at these decisions, Mr Justice Arnold set out two key questions.[100] Firstly, was the copyright work communicated by electronic transmission?; and, secondly, was it communicated to a new public which was not taken into account by the rights-holders when authorising the distribution of the recordings?[101] Following Mr Justice Arnold's questions, the meaning of

95 *Bonnier Media Ltd v (First) Gregg Lloyd and (Second) Kestrel Trading Corporation* (2002) Scot CS 347 as per Lord Drummond Young at 18.

96 *Sony Music Entertainment (UK) Ltd, Sony Music Entertainment Inc, Polydor Ltd, UMG Recordings Inc, Virgin Records Ltd v Easyinternetcafe Ltd* [2003] EWHC 62 (Ch), as per Peter Smith J at [35]: "This to my mind is to introduce a *mens rea* defence when none is available."

97 *Dramatico Entertainment Ltd, EMI Records Ltd, Mercury Records Ltd, Polydor Ltd, Rough Trade Records Ltd, Sony Music Entertainment UK Ltd, Virgin Records Ltd, Warner Music UK Ltd, 679 Recordings Ltd v British Sky Broadcasting Ltd, British Telecommunications plc, Everything Everywhere Ltd, Talktalk Telecom Group plc, Telefónica UK Ltd, Virgin Media Ltd* [2012] EWHC 268 (Ch) at 68.

98 *Ibid*., Arnold J at [81].

99 *EMI Records Ltd, Infectious Ltd, Liberation Music Pty Ltd, Polydor Ltd, Simco Ltd, Sony Music Entertainment UK Ltd, Universal Music Operations Ltd, Virgin Records Ltd, Warner Music UK Ltd, Wea International Inc v British Sky Broadcasting Ltd, British Telecommunications plc, Everything Everywhere Ltd, Talktalk Telecom Group plc, Telefónica UK Ltd, Virgin Media Ltd* [2013] EWHC 379 (Ch) as per Justice Arnold at 42.

100 *Dramatico Entertainment Ltd, EMI Records Ltd, Mercury Records Ltd, Polydor Ltd, Rough Trade Records Ltd, Sony Music Entertainment UK Ltd, Virgin Records Ltd, Warner Music UK Ltd, 679 Recordings Ltd v British Sky Broadcasting Ltd, British Telecommunications plc, Everything Everywhere Ltd, Talktalk Telecom Group plc, Telefónica UK Ltd, Virgin Media Ltd* [2012] EWHC 268 (Ch), as per Arnold J at [45]–[70].

101 *Ibid*., applying the test laid down by the CJEU in *Sociedad General de Autores y Editores de Espana (SGAE) v Rafael Hoteles SA* (Case C-306/05) ECLI:EU:C:2006:764;

"electronic transmission" and "new public" is considered in the following sections.

The first question: was the copyright work communicated by electronic transmission?

Communication requires electronic transmission …

The *Oxford English Dictionary* defines "electronic transmission" as the "action or process of transmitting something" or "the state of being transmitted or a programme or signal that is broadcast or sent out."[102]

However, the preparatory documents for the WCT 1996 recognised that communication and transmission are indistinguishable "as communication always involves transmission, the term 'transmission' could have been chosen as the key term to describe the relevant act."[103] This suggests that the legal drafting intended that the words "communication" and "transmission" have the same meaning. Indeed, Arezzo argued that the connection between communication to the public with the technical notion of transmission of the work is crucial to properly understand the contours of this right.[104]

The word "transmission" leads to uncertainty because uploaders do not "transmit" material in the literal sense of the word when they upload material onto the hard drive of a computer and store it in shared folders.[105] As stated above, the definition of transmission requires something to be transmitted from one place to another. As the CJEU stated: "direct physical contact is specifically absent in the case of transmission"[106] and therefore the receiver "is not present at the place where the communication originates, that is to say, at the place of the representation or performance which is broadcast."[107] Further, in relation to making available, the law does not necessarily

Football Association Premier League Ltd, NetMed Hellas SA, Multichoice Hellas SA v QC Leisure, David Richardson, AV Station plc, Malcolm Chamberlain, Michael Madden, SR Leisure Ltd, Philip George Charles Houghton, Derek Owen and Karen Murphy v Media Protection Services Ltd (Joined cases C-403/08 and 429/08) ECLI:EU:C:2011:631 and *Airfield NV and Canal Digitaal BV v Belgische Vereniging van Auteurs, Componisten en Uitgevers CVBA (Sabam) and Airfield NV v Agicoa Belgium BVBA* (Joined cases C-431/09 and C-432/09) ECLI:EU:C:2011:648.

102 https://www.lexico.com/en/definition/transmission#transmission__2.

103 WIPO, *Records of the Diplomatic Conference on Certain Copyright and Neighbouring Right Questions*, Vol 1 (Geneva: WIPO, 1996) p. 206.

104 Arezzo E., Hyperlinks and Making Available Right in the European Union – What Future for the Internet After Svensson? (2014) 45(5) *International Review of Intellectual Property and Competition Law*, pp. 524–554, p. 532.

105 Larusson H. K., Uncertainty in the Scope of Copyright: The Case of Illegal File-Sharing in the UK (2009) 31(3) *European Intellectual Property Review*, pp. 124–134, p.125.

106 *Football Association Premier League Ltd, NetMed Hellas SA, Multichoice Hellas SA v QC Leisure, David Richardson, AV Station plc, Malcolm Chamberlain, Michael Madden, SR Leisure Ltd, Philip George Charles Houghton, Derek Owen and Karen Murphy v Media Protection Services Ltd* (Joined cases C-403/08 and 429/08) ECLI: EU:C:2011:631 at 203.

107 *Ibid.*

require that the transmission be *received* and therefore it is not actually a transmission: "There appears to be no requirement that any transmission actually takes place before the restricted act takes place: The restricted act is the making available of the work so that members of the public 'may' access it."[108]

As such, in the case of *Football Association Premier League*, Mr Justice Kitchin explained that communication to the public covers any such transmission or retransmission by wire or wireless means, including broadcasting.[109] He went on to determine from the wording of section 20 of the CDPA 1988 that this was the understanding of the drafters: "I also derive some comfort from the fact that this also seems to have been the understanding of those who framed s.20 of the CDPA. Here, it is to be noted, the requirement of communication to the public … has been transposed in s.20(2) to a definitional requirement of communication to the public as being one which involves electronic transmission."[110] Kitchin's approach demonstrates how the literal approach did not allow the law to achieve the intended outcome, so he turned to a purposive approach by considering what the drafters intended the meaning to be from the words, in line with the golden rule discussed in Chapter 1.

So, communication to the public requires an electronic transmission, and the words "electronic transmission" suggest an external perspective in that it uses technical terminology, but the law does not necessarily require that the transmission be received and therefore it is not actually a transmission, and there is no definition of what a "transmission" is. Furthermore, there is no definition of "electronic transmission", accept that it requires a communication, as explained in the following section.

… but electronic transmission requires communication

In *Dramatic Entertainment*, [111] Mr Justice Arnold considered electronic transmission by looking to the CJEU judgment in *SGAE*. [112] He noted that the CJEU had stated that "the transmission of the broadcast work to that clientele using television sets … the hotel is the organisation which intervenes, in full knowledge of the consequences of its action, to give access to the protected work to its customers. In the

108 Caddick N., Davies G. and Harbottle G., *Copinger and Skone James on Copyright* (London: Sweet & Maxwell, 2005) para 7–116.

109 *Football Association Premier League Ltd, NetMed Hellas SA, Multichoice Hellas SA v QC Leisure (a trading name), David Richardson, AV Station Plc, Malcolm Chamberlain, Michael Madden, Sanjay Raval, David Greenslade, SR Leisure Ltd, Phillip George Charles Houghton, Derek Owen* [2008] EWHC 1411 (Ch), as per Kitchin J at [285].

110 *Ibid.*, Kitchin J at [261].

111 *Dramatico Entertainment Ltd, EMI Records Ltd, Mercury Records Ltd, Polydor Ltd, Rough Trade Records Ltd, Sony Music Entertainment UK Ltd, Virgin Records Ltd, Warner Music UK Ltd, 679 Recordings Ltd v British Sky Broadcasting Ltd, British Telecommunications plc, Everything Everywhere Ltd, Talktalk Telecom Group plc, Telefónica UK Ltd, Virgin Media Ltd* [2012] EWHC 268 (Ch).

112 *Sociedad General de Autores y Editores de Espana (SGAE) v Rafael Hoteles SA* (Case C-306/05) ECLI:EU:C:2006:764.

absence of that intervention, its customers, although physically within that area, would not, in principle, be able to enjoy the broadcast work."[113]

He also considered the case of *Football Association Premier League*, where the CJEU stated that: "the concept of communication must be construed broadly, as referring to any transmission of the protected works, irrespective of the technical means or process used."[114]

Mr Justice Arnold then applied this to the current case and determined that the users and operators of The Pirate Bay website communicated the copyright works by electronic transmission.[115] He explained that this was because "they make the recordings available by electronic transmission in such a way that members of the public may access the recordings from a place and at a time individually chosen by them."[116] The judgment does not explicitly state what the electronic transmission was, so in order to understand the reasoning of this decision, it is necessary to look closer at the facts of the case, and what actions were done by the users and operators of The Pirate Bay that constituted an electronic transmission.

As part of the evidence submitted by the applicants, two expert reports by a computer networking and security specialist were prepared.[117] Mr Justice Arnold relied on the reports to explain in detail the technical function of the BitTorrent peer-to-peer protocol used by The Pirate Bay.[118] He summarised from the report that the purpose of the BitTorrent protocol was to create and distribute torrent files. This was done by enabling identification of a file, and the uploading and downloading of the file.[119]

The operators of The Pirate Bay website organised a directory of content which users could browse and then select content to download.[120] The BitTorrent software provided by The Pirate Bay then allowed the user to download "pieces" of the content from the "swarm".[121] However, the second expert report stated that The Pirate Bay also offered the option to download content through a "magnet link" which connects the user either to a BitTorrent tracker or to the "swarm" in order to obtain the torrent file rather than obtaining it directly from The Pirate

113 *Ibid.*, at 42.

114 *Football Association Premier League Ltd, NetMed Hellas SA, Multichoice Hellas SA v QC Leisure, David Richardson, AV Station plc, Malcolm Chamberlain, Michael Madden, SR Leisure Ltd, Philip George Charles Houghton, Derek Owen and Karen Murphy v Media Protection Services Ltd* (Joined cases C-403/08 and 429/08) ECLI: EU:C:2011:631 at 193.

115 *Dramatico Entertainment Ltd, EMI Records Ltd, Mercury Records Ltd, Polydor Ltd, Rough Trade Records Ltd, Sony Music Entertainment UK Ltd, Virgin Records Ltd, Warner Music UK Ltd, 679 Recordings Ltd v British Sky Broadcasting Ltd, British Telecommunications plc, Everything Everywhere Ltd, Talktalk Telecom Group plc, Telefónica UK Ltd, Virgin Media Ltd* [2012] EWHC 268 (Ch), as per Arnold J at [84].

116 *Ibid.*, Arnold J at [69].

117 *Ibid.*, Arnold J at [19] and [24].

118 *Ibid.*, Arnold J at [19]–[29].

119 *Ibid.*, Arnold J at [20].

120 *Ibid.*, Arnold J at [22].

121 *Ibid.*, Arnold J at [23].

Bay website. Mr Justice Arnold stated that "it is not necessary to go into the technical details of this. Once the torrent file has been acquired, the user can download the content to which it relates."[122]

As such, Mr Justice Arnold used the technical report to determine the activities of the users and operators of The Pirate Bay, taking the external perspective. However, he essentially drew a line at how far into the technical detail it was necessary to go. Therefore, whilst it appears *prima facia* that the judgment was made on the basis of technical function, or the external perspective, in fact on closer inspection it was not. This is clear because the change in the technical functioning of how The Pirate Bay website operated (from BitTorrent to Magnet Link) did not require further consideration. Mr Justice Arnold simply determined that copyright material is acquired by users, which was facilitated by the operators.[123] In relation to the Framework for Constructing Digital Perspectives, first the external perspective was taken but its limitations were revealed by the change in technical process of the infringing website. At which point Mr Justice Arnold changed to the internal perspective, taking a purposive approach, in order to find infringement. Ultimately, therefore, this case determined that uploading and downloading copyright material are acts of electronic transmission, by whatever technical means.

This pattern was also seen in the subsequent *BskyB* case, where Mr Justice Arnold recognised the websites as also operating using BitTorrent peer-to-peer file-sharing protocol which enabled users to download the torrent files either from their websites or through a link to another website.[124] The technological manner in which the files were located and downloaded were seemingly irrelevant, for example, some of the websites used "crawling" technology to gather links and did not store any files on their own servers.[125] Mr Justice Arnold stated that "nevertheless, the way in which the torrent files (or rather the links thereto) are presented, and the underlying technology, is essentially the same as in the cases of the other Target Websites."[126] In this case, Mr Justice Arnold again found that the operators of the websites communicated the recordings by electronic transmission, as "they intervene in an active and highly material way so as to enable users to access and to download recordings content in an easy and convenient way."[127]

Hoy et al. argued that this decision was further encouragement to copyright owners as it provided "a useful roadmap for some of the hurdles that must be

122 *Ibid.*, Arnold J at [24].
123 *Ibid.*, Arnold J at [68].
124 *1967 Ltd, Dramatico Entertainment Ltd, Infectious Music Ltd, Liberation Music PTY Ltd, Simco Ltd, Sony Music Entertainment UK Ltd, Universal Music Operations Ltd v British Sky Broadcasting Ltd, British Telecommunications plc, EE Ltd, Talktalk Telecom Ltd, Virgin Media Ltd* [2014] EWHC 3444 (Ch).
125 *Ibid.*, Arnold J at [7].
126 *Ibid.*, Arnold J at [8].
127 *Ibid.*, Arnold J at [19].

cleared to obtain such a block, and of the type and extent of evidence that the UK courts will accept as sufficient to clear those hurdles."[128]

Whilst the case law may be encouraging for copyright holders, the law remains unclear and inconsistent. The meaning of "communication" within the law is "electronic transmission", but "electronic transmission" is not defined, other than to say by wire or wireless means. However, the case law has demonstrated that whilst the technical function of the electronic transmission is considered in the reasoning of the judgments, the decision is ultimately made on the concept of *communication*, not *electronic transmission*.

The case law provides examples of what does and does not constitute a communication, but an analysis of the jurisprudence demonstrated a scattered approach with no clear parameters of the right to communication. What can be said is that the law is applied broadly, to any transmission by any means.

The second question, of whether the communication was made to "the public" is discussed in the following section.

The second question: was the copyright work communicated to a new public?

The concept of "the public" does not presume a physical gathering of people in the same place to jointly enjoy the work, but rather presupposes a fragmented notion of the "public".[129] EU jurisprudence proposed that the transmission must reach "a public which was not taken into account by the authors of the protected works when they authorized their use by the communication to the original public"[130] and be performed in such a way as to potentially[131] reach an indeterminate, but fairly large, number of potential viewers.[132] What is important is not the economic relevance of the single user but the cumulative effect[133] created by the number of people who simultaneously, or in succession, may access the work.[134]

128 Hoy R., Wilks J. and Edbrooke N., *Dramatico Entertainment v BSKYB*: Pirate Bay Runs Aground in English Waters (2012) 23(5) *Entertainment Law Review*, pp. 151–153, p.153.

129 Arezzo E., Hyperlinks and Making Available Right in the European Union – What Future for the Internet After Svensson? (2014) 45(5) *International Review of Intellectual Property and Competition Law*, pp. 524–554, pp. 533–534.

130 *Airfield NV and Canal Digitaal BV v Belgische Vereniging van Auteurs, Componisten en Uitgevers CVBA (Sabam) and Airfield NV v Agicoa Belgium BVBA* (Joined cases C-431/09 and C-432/09) ECLI:EU:C:2011:648 at 76.

131 *ITV Broadcasting Ltd, ITV 2 Ltd, ITV Digital Channels Ltd, Channel 4 Television Corporation, Four Ventures Ltd, Channel 5 Broadcasting Ltd, ITV Studios Ltd v TVCatchup Ltd* (Case C-607/11) ECLI:EU:C:2013:147 at 34–36.

132 *Sociedad General de Autores y Editores de Espana (SGAE) v Rafael Hoteles SA* (Case C-306/05) ECLI:EU:C:2006:764 at 37–38.

133 *Ibid.*, at 39.

134 *Società Consortile Fonografici (SCF) v Marco Del Corso* (Case C-135/10) ECLI:EU:C:2012:140 at 87.

Identification of the relevant public is central to the outcome of a decision on whether a work has been communicated to the public.[135] The following sections consider in more detail what is required by the public in order to fall within the meaning of communication to the public.

How many people make a public?

In the case of *Rafael Hoteles*,[136] the CJEU found that the hotel guests constituted a "public" due to the large number of potential hotel guests that could benefit from the service.[137] This suggested that a large number of people are required to accumulate a public.

This was subsequently confirmed in the case of *SCF v Marco del Corso*, which concerned the communication of copyright works via radio on the premises of a dentist. Mr del Corso, the defendant in the case, claimed that it was not communication to the public because his dental practice was not a public place. The CJEU confirmed that patients attending dental appointments did not constitute a "public" as the number of persons was not large, given that the number of persons present in the practice at any one time was very limited. In addition, since the patients enter one at a time, they do not hear the same music.[138]

In making the decision in this case, the CJEU determined the meaning of communication to the public as "making a work, performance, phonogram or broadcast perceptible in any appropriate manner to persons in general, that is, not restricted to specific individuals belonging to a private group."[139] Consequently, this suggests that the public should constitute a fairly large number of people who are "both targeted by the user and receptive, in one way or another, to that communication."[140] Alexander and Livingston found this decision troubling, as they believed it narrowed the scope by suggesting that communication to the public "must be determined by an 'individual assessment' of all the circumstances, including the type of usage, the role of the user, the number of both actual and potential listeners/viewers, and whether an element of profit is involved."[141]

In the more recent case of *Phonographic Performance (Ireland) Ltd v Ireland*, it was again confirmed that the hotel guests were a public, describing them as "an indeterminate number of potential listeners, insofar as the access of those guests to

135 Hoy R., Internet Blocking Injunctions are Alive and Well in the Post Svensson World (2015) 26(2) *Entertainment Law Review*, pp. 44–47, p. 47.

136 *Sociedad General de Autores y Editores de Espana (SGAE) v Rafael Hoteles SA* (Case C-306/05) ECLI:EU:C:2006:764.

137 *Ibid.*, at 39.

138 *Società Consortile Fonografici (SCF) v Marco Del Corso* (Case C-135/10) ECLI:EU:C:2012:140.

139 *Ibid.*, at 77 and 89.

140 *Ibid.*, at 91.

141 Alexander R. and Livingstone C., Communication to the Public: Part 2 (2012) 23(7) *Entertainment Law Review*, pp. 209–213, pp. 209–210.

the services of that establishment is the result of their own choice and is limited only by the capacity of the establishment in question."[142]

Furthermore, in the case of *TVCatchup*,[143] the CJEU defined the term "public" as referring to "an indeterminate number of potential recipients and implies, moreover, a fairly high number of persons."[144] Therefore, EU jurisprudence has suggested that there is not a specific number of people required in order to constitute a public, but that it is likely to be a high number.

It is important to consider the application of this reasoning to the internet. From an external perspective, users are likely to be individuals who access the internet from a device, simultaneously or at different times, but on an individual basis. However, from an internal perspective, it might be considered that users are a community once they are connected online.

Equally as concerning, the communication is only required to potentially be accessed by the public and, therefore, it might be suggested that any number of persons may access any material online. Therefore, any copyright material online could be subject to copyright infringement by way of communication to the public, since it is online and anyone could potentially access it. As the CJEU stated in the case of *Svensson*: "A communication made on the Internet ... and therefore by the same technical means."[145] This, therefore, suggests that any material online could potentially be subject to communication to the public, should the second criterion of the public also be fulfilled.

The second criterion for the public set out by the CJEU is that the public must be new.[146] The meaning of "new public" is considered in the following section.

The unexpected potential of the "new public"

In *SGAE*, [147] the CJEU explained that a copyright owner authorises the broadcast of his work taking into account direct users. Therefore, if the work reaches a larger audience than intended by way of an independent act of an unauthorised third party,

142 *Phonographic Performance (Ireland) Ltd v Ireland* (Case C-162/10) ECLI:EU:C:2012:141 at 41.

143 *ITV Broadcasting Ltd, ITV 2 Ltd, ITV Digital Channels Ltd, Channel 4 Television Corporation, Four Ventures Ltd, Channel 5 Broadcasting Ltd, ITV Studios Ltd v TVCatchup Ltd* (Case C-607/11) ECLI:EU:C:2013:147 at 32 citing *Sociedad General de Autores y Editores de Espana (SGAE) v Rafael Hoteles SA* (Case C-306/05) ECLI:EU:C:2006:764.

144 *Ibid.*, at 37 and 38.

145 *Nils Svensson, Sten Sjögren, Madelaine Sahlman, Pia Gadd v Retriever Sverige AB* (Case C-466/12) ECLI:EU:C:2014:76 at 24.

146 *Sociedad General de Autores y Editores de Espana (SGAE) v Rafael Hoteles SA* (Case C-306/05) ECLI:EU:C:2006:764 at 40 and 42; *Organismos Sillogikis Diacheirisis Dimiourgon Theatrikon kai Optikoakoustikon Ergon* (Case C-136/09) ECLI:EU:C:2010:151 at 38.

147 *Sociedad General de Autores y Editores de Espana (SGAE) v Rafael Hoteles SA* (Case C-306/05) ECLI:EU:C:2006:764.

the work is infringed by communication to a new public.[148] As such, a new public is "a public which was not taken into account by the authors of the protected works when they authorised their use by the communication to the original public."[149]

In *Svensson*, the CJEU held that making copyright works available by means of a clickable link did *not* lead to the works in question being communicated to a new public.[150] This was because the public targeted by the initial communication consisted of all potential visitors to the website concerned. Since the website was not subject to any restrictive measures, all internet users could have free access to the works.[151] The users who clicked the link to access the material could have also accessed the material directly from the original site. Therefore, they could be deemed to be potential recipients of the initial communication and as such where part of the public taken into account by the copyright holders when they authorised the initial communication.[152] Therefore, providing clickable links on a website to works freely available on another website does not necessarily constitute an act of communication to the public.[153]

However, the CJEU did state that this would not be the case where the link allowed users to circumvent restrictions put in place by the original site on which the protected work appeared, for example by subscription or paywall. In this event, the link would constitute an intervention by the link to access the works transmitted by a new public.[154]

Arezzo argued that the requirement of the works to be communicated to a "new public" takes an extensive interpretation of the CJEU of Article 11*bis* of the Berne Convention[155] as the provision does not literally mention a "new public" but takes into account the circumstance where a third party makes an unauthorized act of communication.[156] Keane also recognised the particular influence of the WIPO *Guide to the Berne Convention* [157] on the CJEU in creating this criteria.[158]

148 *Ibid.*, at 41.

149 *Football Association Premier League Ltd, NetMed Hellas SA, Multichoice Hellas SA v QC Leisure, David Richardson, AV Station plc, Malcolm Chamberlain, Michael Madden, SR Leisure Ltd, Philip George Charles Houghton, Derek Owen and Karen Murphy v Media Protection Services Ltd* (Joined cases C-403/08 and 429/08) ECLI:EU:C:2011:631 at 198 citing *Sociedad General de Autores y Editores de Espana (SGAE) v Rafael Hoteles SA* (Case C-306/05) ECLI:EU:C:2006:764 at 41.

150 *Nils Svensson, Sten Sjögren, Madelaine Sahlman, Pia Gadd v Retriever Sverige AB* (Case C-466/12) ECLI:EU:C:2014:76 at 25.

151 *Ibid.*, at 26.

152 *Ibid.*, at 27.

153 *Ibid.*, at 32.

154 *Ibid.*, at 31.

155 Berne Convention for the Protection of Literary and Artistic Works 1886, as amended 28 September 1979, Article 11*bis*(1)(i).

156 Arezzo E., Hyperlinks and Making Available Right in the European Union – What Future for the Internet After Svensson? (2014) 45(5) *International Review of Intellectual Property and Competition Law*, pp. 524–554, p. 535.

157 WIPO, *Guide to the Berne Convention for the Protection of Literary and Artistic Works, Paris 1971* (Geneva: WIPO, 1978).

158 Keane B., Ill Communication? The Concept of a Communication to the Public Under EU Copyright Law (2013) 24(5) *Entertainment Law Review*, pp. 165–171, p. 169.

The jurisprudence of the CJEU has determined that communication to the public will depend on the context in question and that there are several tests that a court should carry out in deciding if communication to the public has taken place.[159] Therefore, whilst the CJEU set out a number of criteria in *SGAE*,[160] it is apparent from the more recent cases that it is not strictly necessary for all these criteria to be satisfied for there to be a public.[161] Ultimately, the CJEU jurisprudence required only that the transmission of the work be performed by an unauthorised party in a way that can *potentially* [162] be *accessed* [163] by an indeterminate number of people[164] who were not taken into account by the original communication of the work.[165] The approach and interpretation of the EU law changes throughout the case law, thereby creating inconsistency and uncertainty in relation to communication to the public.[166]

The final section of this chapter turns to consider how the UK courts have implemented the law as determined by the CJEU interpretations of the law.

Communication to the public online: *TVCatchup*

CJEU case law has provided some guidance as to what does or does not constitute communication to the public. However, most of these cases refer to offline activities. As discussed throughout this book, applying the law as constructed for offline activities can create tension due to the fact that the online world can be interpreted by either the internal or external perspectives. The case of *TVCatchup* [167] exemplifies this tension as it demonstrates the UK court implementing the

159 Hoy R., Internet Blocking Injunctions are Alive and Well in the Post Svensson World (2015) 26(2) *Entertainment Law Review*, pp. 44–47, p. 47.

160 *Sociedad General de Autores y Editores de Espana (SGAE) v Rafael Hoteles SA* (Case C-306/05) ECLI:EU:C:2006:764: (1) must be accessible to a fairly large number of persons; (2) the public is "new"; and (3) the service to the public is profit-making.

161 Keane B., Ill Communication? The Concept of a Communication to the Public Under EU Copyright Law (2013) 24(5) *Entertainment Law Review*, pp. 165–171, p. 167.

162 *ITV Broadcasting Ltd, ITV 2 Ltd, ITV Digital Channels Ltd, Channel 4 Television Corporation, Four Ventures Ltd, Channel 5 Broadcasting Ltd, ITV Studios Ltd v TVCatchup Ltd* (Case C-607/11) ECLI:EU:C:2013:147 at 34–36: "it is irrelevant whether the potential recipients access the communicated works through a one-to-one connection."

163 *Società Consortile Fonografici (SCF) v Marco Del Corso* (Case C-135/10) ECLI:EU:C:2012:140 at 87.

164 *Sociedad General de Autores y Editores de Espana (SGAE) v Rafael Hoteles SA* (Case C-306/05) ECLI:EU:C:2006:764 at 37–38; *Società Consortile Fonografici (SCF) v Marco Del Corso* (Case C-135/10) ECLI:EU:C:2012:140 at 84.

165 *Airfield NV and Canal Digitaal BV v Belgische Vereniging van Auteurs, Componisten en Uitgevers CVBA (Sabam) and Airfield NV v Agicoa Belgium BVBA* (Joined cases C-431/09 and C-432/09) ECLI:EU:C:2011:648 at 76.

166 Baggs S., Alexander R. and Preston E., Curtains Down on Popcorn Time: S.97A Takes Centre Stage (2016) 38(1) *European Intellectual Property Review*, pp. 56–60, p. 59.

167 *ITV Broadcasting Ltd, ITV 2 Ltd, ITV Digital Channels, Channel 4 Television Corporation, Four Ventures Ltd, Channel 5 Broadcasting Ltd v TVCatchup Ltd* [2010] EWHC 3063 (Ch); *ITV Broadcasting Ltd, ITV 2 Ltd, ITV Digital Channels Ltd,*

CJEU jurisprudence and applying it to an online situation. It is also one of the more recent cases in the UK courts, thereby taking into account all of the cases discussed in the previous sections.

This case has been before the court since 2010,[168] and most recently in 2015 before Lady Justice Arden, Lord Justice Kitchin and Lord Justice Underhill on appeal.[169] The matter involved an internet-based live-stream service of broadcast television programmes.[170] The claimant broadcasters appealed on the basis that the judge had wrongly interpreted the word "cable" as meaning "wire" to refer only to dedicated cable networks operated by conventional cable programme providers and therefore excluded retransmissions over the internet.[171]

Lord Justice Kitchin stated from the outset that the restricted act of communication to the public was by wire or wireless means and that included communication via the internet.[172] Nevertheless, the meaning of "wire" and "cable" was unclear and therefore he decided to refer to the CJEU for clarification.[173]

The applicants argued that the legislature drew a clear distinction between "wire" and "cable" and, by the latter, meant only traditional dedicated cable systems;[174] whereas the defendants argued that there was no consistent use of the term "cable" in EU law and there was no rational basis for such an all-purpose concept to exist.[175] The Secretary of State's position was that the term "cable" had a specific technical meaning, the scope of which was and has always been limited to traditional cable systems which exclude the internet.[176] These arguments demonstrate the different outcomes possible in taking a literal or purposive

Channel 4 Television Corporation, Four Ventures Ltd, Channel 5 Broadcasting Ltd, ITV Studios Ltd v TVCatchup Ltd, The Secretary of State for Business, Innovation and Skills [2011] EWHC 2977 (Pat); *ITV Broadcasting Ltd, ITV 2 Ltd, ITV Digital Channels Ltd, Channel 4 Television Corporation, Four Ventures Ltd, Channel 5 Broadcasting Ltd, ITV Studios Ltd v TVCatchup Ltd* (Case C-607/11) ECLI:EU:C:2013:147; *ITV Broadcasting Ltd, ITV 2 Ltd, ITV Digital Channels Ltd, Channel Four Television Corporation, 4 Ventures Ltd, Channel 5 Broadcasting Ltd, ITV Studios Ltd v TVCatchup Ltd (in administration), TVCatchup (UK) Ltd, Media Resources Ltd (a Mauritian company) v The Secretary of State for Business, Innovation and Skills, Virgin Media Ltd* [2015] EWCA Civ 204.

168 *ITV Broadcasting Ltd, ITV 2 Ltd, ITV Digital Channels, Channel 4 Television Corporation, Four Ventures Ltd, Channel 5 Broadcasting Ltd v TVCatchup Ltd* [2010] EWHC 3063 (Ch).

169 *ITV Broadcasting Ltd, ITV 2 Ltd, ITV Digital Channels Ltd, Channel Four Television Corporation, 4 Ventures Ltd, Channel 5 Broadcasting Ltd, ITV Studios Ltd v TVCatchup Ltd (in administration), TVCatchup (UK) Ltd, Media Resources Ltd (a Mauritian company) v The Secretary of State for Business, Innovation and Skills, Virgin Media Ltd* [2015] EWCA Civ 204.

170 *Ibid.*, Kitchen LJ at [4].

171 *Ibid.*, Kitchen LJ at [15].

172 *Ibid.*, Kitchen LJ at [61].

173 *Ibid.*, Kitchen LJ at [79] and [96].

174 *Ibid.*, Kitchen LJ at [62].

175 *Ibid.*, Kitchen LJ at [72].

176 *Ibid.*, Kitchen LJ at [73].

approach. The applicant and the Secretary of State also argued that the term "cable" was used in a technologically specific way and that by using the phrase "access to cable of broadcasting services", the EU did not intend to provide an exception for national provisions concerning internet retransmissions.[177]

However, Lord Justice Kitchin offered his provisional view, agreeing with the defendant, that it was unlikely that the EU intended by the use of the term "cable" to exclude provisions concerning retransmissions falling within the scope of these exceptions but which are made over the internet.[178] Lord Justice Underhill agreed with Lord Justice Kitchin that the term "cable" would likely include the internet, but that it was ultimately unclear and therefore the reference to the CJEU was necessary.[179]

However, Lady Justice Arden, whilst agreeing that the answer was unclear, offered a different opinion.[180] She suggested that the word "cable" was introduced to replace the word "broadcasting" with a technologically-neutral word.[181] Furthermore, that following the implementation of the Information Society Directive, the expression "cable" had a narrower meaning and since there was no definition, the word could bear an ambulatory, or movable, meaning so that the court could interpret the phrase in accordance with the Information Society Directive.[182] Thus, in the absence of a definition, she suggested that Parliament intended that the word "cable" should bear whatever meaning it had in EU law.[183] Therefore, this case demonstrates that the meaning of the terminology used within the law to describe technology created clear tensions due to its ambiguity in scope.

Ultimately, this case demonstrated that the exact meaning of technological terminology in the law has a great impact on the application of the law to the meaning of copyright infringement online. This is true only when taking the external perspective. However, as the case law demonstrated, the courts often made the decision based on the internal perspective and not the technical function of the specific technology.

Lim and Chik suggested that courts are less likely to accept the legality of new technologies that attempt to exploit loopholes in the law. Instead, they suggested that the judges take a results-driven, or purposive, approach in order not to allow technological form to trump the true "substance" of the transmission/communication in question.[184] Giblin and Ginsburg agreed that technological design

177 *Ibid.*, Kitchen LJ at [81].
178 *Ibid.*, Kitchen LJ at [82].
179 *Ibid.*, Underhill LJ at [100].
180 *Ibid.*, Arden LJ at [104].
181 *Ibid.*, Arden LJ at [105].
182 *Ibid.*, Arden LJ at [106].
183 *Ibid.*, Arden LJ at [106].
184 Lim S. C. and Chik W. B., Whither the Future of Internet Streaming and Time-Shifting? Revisiting the Rights of Reproduction and Communication to the Public in Copyright Law after Aereo (2015) 23(1) *International Journal of Law and Information Technology*, pp. 53–88, p. 87.

should never determine legal outcome.[185] Efroni argued that the ramifications the extension of communication to the public to the internet realty has bestowed an unparalleled amount of power upon rights-holders, beyond anything the analogue past has ever seen.[186] In any event, the analysis demonstrated that the law is unclear and uncertain as to how to apply the law to such circumstances in a consistent manner.

Conclusion

This chapter investigated the meaning of online copyright infringement by way of communication to the public. It first considered the meaning of "communication" within the context of the internet, demonstrating that communication theory suggests that the internet is considered a mass medium for communication that has transformed the scope of communication as a concept.[187]

The chapter then took a comparative look at the UK case law relating to communication to the public, before and after the 2003 Regulations[188] that amended section 20 of the CDPA 1988 from a broadcasting right to a right of communication to the public. The analysis revealed four key findings. Firstly, that since the 2003 Regulations there has been an increase in the use of this section. Secondly, before the Regulations the disputes took place between copyright holding companies; however, subsequently, the majority of disputes took place between copyright holding companies and individuals. Thirdly, the copyright works subject to dispute have increased in scope. Lastly, the most successful cases were brought by copyright holding companies.

In particular, it is clear that whilst the understanding of the internet as a medium of communication is through an internal perspective, the drafting of the law was done so from an external perspective. This tension was clearly highlighted in the application of the law. Whilst judges often take considerable time to explain and understand the technical function of the online activity in their reasoning, ultimately the decision is taken from an internal perspective – that a copyright work is accessed without authorisation. The judgments demonstrate how taking a purely literal interpretation can be limited, by either creating absurdities or not achieving the remedy to the mischief it intended to address. Therefore, judges are led towards a more purposive approach in their application of the law.

185 Giblin R. and Ginsburg J., We (Still) Need to Talk about Aereo: New Controversies and Unresolved Questions after the Supreme Court's Decision (2014) 38 *Columbia Journal of Law and the Arts*, pp. 18–22.

186 Efroni Z., *Access Right: The Future of Digital Copyright Law* (New York: Oxford University Press, 2011) p. 284.

187 McQuail D., *McQuail's Mass Communication Theory* (London: Sage Publications Ltd, 2011) p. 139.

188 Copyright and Related Rights Regulations 2003 (SI 2003/2498).

Bibliography

Books

Berners-Lee T., *Weaving the Web: The Original Design and Ultimate Destiny of the World Wide Web* (New York: Harper Business, 2000).

Caddick N., Davies G. and Harbottle G., *Copinger and Skone James on Copyright* (London: Sweet & Maxwell, 2005).

Carey J., *Communication as Culture* (Boston: Unwin Hyman, 1988).

Davis R., Quintin T. and Tritton G., *Tritton on Intellectual Property in Europe* (London: Sweet & Maxwell, 2018).

Depreeu S., *The Variable Scope of The Exclusive Economic Rights in Copyright* (Amsterdam: Kluwer Law, 2014).

Efroni Z., *Access Right: The Future of Digital Copyright Law* (New York: Oxford University Press, 2011).

McQuail D., *McQuail's Mass Communication Theory* (London: Sage Publications Ltd, 2011).

Rosati E., *Copyright and the Court of Justice of the European Union* (Oxford: Oxford University Press, 2019).

Vitoria M., et al (eds), *Laddie, Prescott and Vitoria: The Modern Law of Copyright and Designs*, 4th edition (London: Butterworths Law, 2011).

Case law

1967 Ltd, Dramatico Entertainment Ltd, Infectious Music Ltd, Liberation Music PTY Ltd, Simco Ltd, Sony Music Entertainment UK Ltd, Universal Music Operations Ltd v British Sky Broadcasting Ltd, British Telecommunications plc, EE Ltd, Talktalk Telecom Ltd, Virgin Media Ltd [2014] EWHC 3444 (Ch).

Airfield NV and Canal Digitaal BV v Belgische Vereniging van Auteurs, Componisten en Uitgevers CVBA (Sabam) and Airfield NV v Agicoa Belgium BVBA (Joined cases C-431/09 and C-432/09) ECLI:EU:C:2011:648.

Alan Grisbrook v MGN Ltd, Scottish Daily Record and Sunday Mail Ltd, Syndication International Ltd [2009] EWHC 2520 (Ch); [2010] EWCA Civ 1399.

Alan MacKie t/a 197 Aerial Photography v Nicola Askew, Largsholidaylets.co.uk (SA1251/08) (2009) WL 2392381.

BestWater International GmbH v Michael Mebes, Stefan Potsch (Case C-348/13) ECLI:EU:C:2014:2315.

Bonnier Media Ltd v (First) Gregg Lloyd and (Second) Kestrel Trading Corporation (2002) Scot CS 347.

Circul Globus București (Circ & Variete Globus București) v Uniunea Compozitorilor și Muzicologilor din România – Asociația pentru Drepturi de Autor (UCMR – ADA) (Case C-283/10) ECLI:EU:C:2011:772.

David Hoffman v Drug Abuse Resistance Education (UK) Ltd [2012] EWPCC 2.

Dramatico Entertainment Ltd, EMI Records Ltd, Mercury Records Ltd, Polydor Ltd, Rough Trade Records Ltd, Sony Music Entertainment UK Ltd, Virgin Records Ltd, Warner Music UK Ltd, 679 Recordings Ltd v British Sky Broadcasting Ltd, British Telecommunications plc, Everything Everywhere Ltd, Talktalk Telecom Group plc, Telefónica UK Ltd, Virgin Media Ltd [2012] EWHC 268 (Ch).

EMI Records Ltd, Infectious Ltd, Liberation Music Pty Ltd, Polydor Ltd, Simco Ltd, Sony Music Entertainment UK Ltd, Universal Music Operations Ltd, Virgin Records Ltd, Warner Music UK Ltd, Wea International Inc v British Sky Broadcasting Ltd, British Telecommunications plc, Everything Everywhere Ltd, Talktalk Telecom Group plc, Telefónica UK Ltd, Virgin Media Ltd [2013] EWHC 379 (Ch).

Football Association Premier League Ltd, NetMed Hellas SA, Multichoice Hellas SA v QC Leisure (a trading name), David Richardson, AV Station Plc, Malcolm Chamberlain, Michael Madden, Sanjay Raval, David Greenslade, SR Leisure Ltd, Phillip George Charles Houghton, Derek Owen [2008] EWHC 1411 (Ch).

Football Association Premier League Ltd, NetMed Hellas SA, Multichoice Hellas SA v QC Leisure, David Richardson, AV Station plc, Malcolm Chamberlain, Michael Madden, SR Leisure Ltd, Philip George Charles Houghton, Derek Owen and Karen Murphy v Media Protection Services Ltd (Joined cases C-403/08 and 429/08) ECLI:EU:C:2011:631.

Football Association Premier League Ltd v Anthony William Luxton, Barclays Bank Ltd [2014] EWHC 253 (Ch).

Football Association Premier League Ltd v British Sky Broadcasting Ltd, British Telecommunications Plc, Everything Everywhere Ltd, Talktalk Telecom Ltd, Telefónica UK Ltd, Virgin Media Ltd [2013] EWHC 2058 (Ch).

Football Dataco Ltd, The Scottish Premier League Ltd, The Scottish Football League, PA Sport UK Ltd v Sportradar GmbH (a Company Registered in Germany), Sportradar AG (a Company registered in Switzerland) [2010] EWHC 2911 (Ch).

Golden Eye (International) Ltd, Ben Dover Productions, Celtic Broadcasting Ltd, Easy on the Eye, DMS Telecoms Ltd, Gary Baker, Harmony Films Ltd, Justin Ribeiro Dos Santos t/a Joybear Pictures, Orchid MG Ltd, Kudetta BVBA, RP Films Ltd, Sweetmeats Productions t/a SMP, Sll Films Ltd, Terence Stephens t/a One Eyed Jack Productions v Telefónica UK Ltd, Consumer Focus [2012] EWHC 723 (Ch); [2012] EWCA Civ 1740.

GS Media BV v Sanoma Media Netherlands BV, Playboy Enterprises International Inc, Britt Geertruida Dekker (Case C-160/15) ECLI:EU:C:2016:644.

ITV Broadcasting Ltd, ITV 2 Ltd, ITV Digital Channels, Channel 4 Television Corporation, Four Ventures Ltd, Channel 5 Broadcasting Ltd v TVCatchup Ltd [2010] EWHC 3063 (Ch).

ITV Broadcasting Ltd, ITV 2 Ltd, ITV Digital Channels Ltd, Channel 4 Television Corporation, Four Ventures Ltd, Channel 5 Broadcasting Ltd, ITV Studios Ltd v TVCatchup Ltd, The Secretary of State for Business, Innovation and Skills [2011] EWHC 2977 (Pat).

ITV Broadcasting Ltd, ITV 2 Ltd, ITV Digital Channels Ltd, Channel 4 Television Corporation, Four Ventures Ltd, Channel 5 Broadcasting Ltd, ITV Studios Ltd v TVCatchup Ltd (Case C-607/11) ECLI:EU:C:2013:147.

ITV Broadcasting Ltd, ITV 2 Ltd, ITV Digital Channels Ltd, Channel Four Television Corporation, 4 Ventures Ltd, Channel 5 Broadcasting Ltd, ITV Studios Ltd v TVCatchup Ltd (in administration), TVCatchup (UK) Ltd, Media Resources Ltd (a Mauritian company) v The Secretary of State for Business, Innovation and Skills, Virgin Media Ltd [2015] EWCA Civ 204.

Karen Murphy v Media Protection Services Ltd [2007] EWHC 3091 (Admin).

Land Nordrhein-Westfalen v Dirk Renckhoff (Case C-161/17) ECLI:EU:C:2018:634.

Media CAT Ltd v A – H [2010] EWPCC 017.

Media CAT Ltd v Malcolm Adams, Katherine Taylor, Hooper, Mitchell Chance, Miss Gonzalles Romeo, Mark Jimack, Miss Maria Shewan, Keith Wood, William Wickam, Sean Allen, Christopher Beck, Dave Cundall, Danny Cowan, Glyn Bentley, Pana Begum, Peter Armitage, Allan Billington, James Bryant, Julia Abbott, Christopher Birkett, M Brunt, Gareth Bacon, Wayne Bacon, Michelle McGlade, Elaine Cox, David Bick [2011] EWPCC 006.

Nils Svensson, Sten Sjögren, Madelaine Sahlman, Pia Gadd v Retriever Sverige AB (Case C-466/12) ECLI:EU:C:2014:76.

Omnibill (PTY) Ltd v EGPSXXX Ltd (in liquidation), Mr Robert Ashley Carter [2014] EWHC 3762 (IPEC).

Organismos Sillogikis Diacheirisis Dimiourgon Theatrikon kai Optikoakoustikon Ergon (Case C-136/09) ECLI:EU:C:2010:151.

OSA – Ochranný Svaz Autorský Pro Práva K Dílům Hudebním OS v Léčebné Lázně Mariánské Lázně AS (Case C-351/12) ECLI:EU:C:2014:110.

Paramount Home Entertainment Ltd, Sony Pictures Home Entertainment Ltd, Twentieth Century Fox Film Company Ltd, Universal Pictures (UK) Ltd, Warner Bros. Entertainment UK Ltd, Disney Enterprises Inc v British Sky Broadcasting Ltd, British Telecommunications Plc, Everything Everywhere Ltd, Talktalk Telecom Ltd, Telefónica UK Ltd, Virgin Media Ltd [2013] EWHC 3479 (Ch); [2014] EWHC 937 (Ch).

Performing Right Society Ltd v B4U Network (Europe) Ltd [2012] EWHC 3010 (Ch).

Phonographic Performance (Ireland) Ltd v Ireland (Case C-162/10) ECLI:EU:C:2012:141.

Polydor Ltd v Brown [2005] EWHC 3191 (Ch).

Sociedad General de Autores y Editores de Espana (SGAE) v Rafael Hoteles SA (Case C-306/05) ECLI:EU:C:2006:764.

Società Consortile Fonografici (SCF) v Marco Del Corso (Case C-135/10) ECLI:EU:C:2012:140.

Sony Music Entertainment (UK) Ltd, Sony Music Entertainment Inc, Polydor Ltd, UMG Recordings Inc, Virgin Records Ltd v Easyinternetcafe Ltd [2003] EWHC 62 (Ch).

Stichting Brein v Ziggo BV, XS4ALL Internet BV (Case C-610/15) ECLI:EU:C:2017:456.

Svaz softwarové ochrany Bezpečnostní Softwarová Asociace v Ministerstvo kultury (Case C-393/09) ECLI:EU:C:2010:816.

Twentieth Century Fox Film Corporation, Universal City Studios Productions LLP, Warner Bros Entertainment Inc, Paramount Pictures Corporation, Disney Enterprises Inc, Columbia Pictures Industries Inc v Newzbin Ltd [2010] EWHC 608 (Ch).

Twentieth Century Fox Film Corporation, Universal City Studios Productions LLP, Warner Bros Entertainment Inc, Paramount Pictures Corporation, Disney Enterprises, Inc, Columbia Pictures Industries, Inc v SKY UK Limited, British Telecommunications plc, EE Ltd, Talktalk Telecom Limited, Virgin Media Ltd [2015] EWHC 1082 (Ch).

Ultrasoft Technologies Ltd v Hubcreate Ltd [2016] EWHC 544 (IPEC).

Union des Associations Europeennes de Football (UEFA) v Briscomb [2006] EWHC 1268 (Ch).

Union of European Football Associations v Euroview Sport Ltd [2010] EWHC 1066 (Ch).

Journals

Alexander R. and Livingstone C., Communication to the Public: Part 2 (2012) 23(7) *Entertainment Law Review*, pp. 209–213.

Arezzo E., Hyperlinks and Making Available Right in the European Union – What Future for the Internet After Svensson? (2014) 45(5) *International Review of Intellectual Property and Competition Law*, pp. 524–555.

Baggs S., Alexander R. and Preston E., Curtains Down on Popcorn Time: S.97A Takes Centre Stage (2016) 38(1) *European Intellectual Property Review*, pp. 56–60.

Burke S. and Smith J., Record Companies Win First Round v The Pirate Bay in the United Kingdom but Pirates Remain at Large: Dramatico Entertainment Ltd v British Sky Broadcasting Ltd (2012) 34(6) *European Intellectual Property Review*, pp. 416–419.

Clark B. and Tozzi S., "Communication to the Public" Under EU Copyright Law: An Increasingly Delphic Concept or Intentional Fragmentation? (2016) 38(12) *EIPR*, pp. 715–717.

Favale M., Kretschmer M. and Torremans P., Is there an EU Copyright Jurisprudence? An Empirical Analysis of the Workings of the European Court of Justice (2016) 79(1) *Modern Law Review*, pp. 31–75.

Giblin R. and Ginsburg J., We (Still) Need to Talk about Aereo: New Controversies and Unresolved Questions after the Supreme Court's Decision (2014) 38 *Columbia Journal of Law and the Arts*, pp. 18–22.

Hoy R., Internet Blocking Injunctions are Alive and Well in the Post Svensson World (2015) 26(2) *Entertainment Law Review*, pp. 44–47.

Hoy R., Wilks J. and Edbrooke N., *Dramatico Entertainment v BSKYB*: Pirate Bay Runs Aground in English Waters (2012) 23(5) *Entertainment Law Review*, pp. 151–153.

Kalyanaraman S. and Sundar S., Portrait of the Portal as a Metaphor: Explicating Web Portals for Communication Research (2008) 65(2) *Journalism and Mass Communication Quarterly*, pp. 239–256.

Keane B., Ill Communication? The Concept of a Communication to the Public Under EU Copyright Law (2013) 24(5) *Entertainment Law Review*, pp. 165–171.

Larusson H. K., Uncertainty in the Scope of Copyright: The Case of Illegal File-Sharing in the UK (2009) 31(3) *European Intellectual Property Review*, pp. 124–134.

Lim S. C. and Chik W.B., Whither the Future of Internet Streaming and Time-Shifting? Revisiting the Rights of Reproduction and Communication to the Public in Copyright Law after Aereo (2015) 23(1) *International Journal of Law and Information Technology*, pp. 53–88.

Livingstone S., New Media, New Audiences? (1999) 1(1) *New Media and Society*, pp. 59–66.

Rosati E., Neighbouring Rights for Publishers: Are National and (Possible) EU Initiatives Lawful? (2016) 47(5) *International Review of Intellectual Property and Competition Law*, pp. 569–594.

Ross A. and Livingstone C., Communication to the Public: Part 1 (2012) 23(6) *Entertainment Law Review*, pp. 169–173.

Smith J. and Burke S., Record Companies Win First Round v The Pirate Bay in The United Kingdom But Pirates Remain At Large: *Dramatico Entertainment Ltd v British Sky Broadcasting Ltd* (2012) 34(6) *European Intellectual Property Review*, pp. 416–419.

Legislation

Berne Convention for the Protection of Literary and Artistic Works 1886.

Copyright and Related Rights Regulations 2003 (SI 2003/2498).

Copyright, Designs and Patents Act 1988.

Directive 2001/29/EC of the European Parliament and of the Council of 22 May 2001 on the harmonisation of certain aspects of copyright and related rights in the information society [2001] *OJ* L 167/10.

Official documents

Communication from the Commission to the European Parliament, the Council, the European Economic and Social Committee and the Committee of the Regions, Towards a Modern, More European Copyright Framework, COM (2015) 626, Brussels, 9 December 2015.

Kantar Media, *Online Copyright Infringement Tracker* (London: Intellectual Property Office, 2018): https://assets.publishing.service.gov.uk/government/uploads/system/uploads/attachment_data/file/729184/oci-tracker.pdf.

WIPO, *Guide to the Berne Convention for the Protection of Literary and Artistic Works, Paris 1971* (Geneva: WIPO, 1978).

WIPO, *Records of the Diplomatic Conference on Certain Copyright and Neighbouring Right Questions*, Vol 1 (Geneva: WIPO, 1996).

Web sources

Lexico, Communication: https://www.lexico.com/en/definition/communication.

Lexico, Transmission: https://www.lexico.com/en/definition/transmission#transmission__2.

7 Concluding the story

The difficulties of applying copyright infringement online

"Do not worry about the wall", replied the Woodman "when we have climbed over it we shall know what is on the other side."

The Wizard of Oz [1]

Overview of findings

This investigation has undertaken an analysis of the law in relation to copyright infringement by way of copying and communication to the public, through the lens of the internal and external perspectives.

The external perspective involved considering the technical functioning of the network in the physical world, focusing on the physical technology.[2] This concept of the external perspective was developed together with the theory of literalism.[3] It was concluded that the benefits of taking this perspective were that the law is specific, technologically accurate and could be considered as providing clarity on the legality of a particular technology.[4] However, taking the external perspective can also create challenges such as incentivising avoidance creations, developing law that is too technologically specific that becomes quickly obsolete in the face of new technological developments. As Hutchinson argued "a purely literal interpretation can lead to the law falling short of serving its purpose."[5]

On the other hand, the internal perspective involved considering the virtual reality as a legitimate construct in order to understand the online experience.[6] The concept of the internal perspective was grounded in the theory of purposivism through the devices of metaphor and skeumorph.[7] It was concluded that the

1 Baum L. F., *The Wizard of Oz* (New York: Puffin Books, 2013) p. 164
2 *Ibid.*, p. 360.
3 See Chapter 2, p. 42.
4 See Chapter 2, pp. 42–44.
5 Hutchison C. J., Interpretation and the Internet (2010) 28 *John Marshall Journal of Computer and Information Law*, pp. 251–272, pp. 259–260.
6 Kerr O. S., The Problem of Perspective in Internet Law (2003) 91 *Georgetown Law Journal*, pp. 357–405, p. 359.
7 See Chapter 2, p. 48.

internal approach could overcome some of the challenges of the external perspective, such as being so specific that it could not apply to new technology. As mentioned, the judges appear to lean towards a purposive approach, when the literal approach creates absurdities or does not allow the law to achieve the intended outcome – by way of remedying a particular mischief. However, tensions also arose when taking the internal perspective. For example, when metaphors are not recognised as metaphors,[8] the original conceptions could unknowingly transfer the meaning of the previous concept and be perceived as the only purpose of a given regulation.[9] This is particularly relevant in the use of skeumorphs because of the connotations that carry when using past concepts for understanding new technology. Due to the pace of technological development, using old concepts as a bridge from the old to the new can be incompatible with allowing copyright to fulfil its purpose in the digital age.

The analysis demonstrated that whilst the legislation was drafted from a mostly external perspective, the case law tended to start from an external perspective but move to an internal perspective in line with a metaphorical understanding of the technology and a purposive approach of legal application. This lens served as a useful tool for identifying and understanding the inconsistencies within the law of reproduction and communication to the public as applied to online activity.

The internal and external perspectives demonstrate that the human experience of new technology differs from the technological processes of online activity. As a result, the internet provides two possible set of facts to which copyright law can be applied. This creates a problem for judges in their interpretation and application of copyright law to online activity. It was seen that in taking the technological perspective, which is aligned with the literal rule in statutory interpretation, judges interpret the law literally and apply it to the technical function of the technology. However, it was clear from the judgments that this often created an absurdity in the law. As a result, judges tended to – but did not always – lean towards a more purposive approach, taking an internal perspective, in order to allow the law to fulfil its intended function. This was done, for example, by utilising the mischief rule approach whereby judges considered whether or not the online activity *should* be illegal and interpreted the law as seeking to remedy that behaviour.

The unique factor in this issue, as the internal and external perspectives illuminate, is that the consideration of the human element is lacking from the discourse in the application of copyright law to the internet. Excluding the notion of the human element in law-making, the application of the law and new technology creates technologically specific law that results in absurdities.

8 For example, use of the word "incidental storage" as discussed in Chapter 3.

9 Larsson S., Metaphors, Law and Digital Phenomena: The Swedish Pirate Bay Court Case (2013) 21(4) *International Journal of Law, Information and Technology*, pp. 354–380, p. 367.

Concluding thoughts on reproduction

The analysis of the statutory development of copyright infringement by reproduction revealed three main criticisms. Firstly, that certain areas of the CDPA 1988 were introduced without foresight or particular expertise in the understanding of computer technology or copyright law.[10] Secondly, a key aim was to simplify the legislation; this led to much of the new law being a re-statement of the old law leaving copyright in the 21st century dating back to 1956. Lastly, due to the lengthy negotiations between stakeholders and the nature of the political and practical challenges, the law became very long and complex, and potentially over-compromised in favour of the loudest voices.

The case law and focused on two key areas of copying online: storage by any technical means and transient or incidental copying. In relation to storage, it was found that both judges and counsel used both the internal and external perspectives in their interpretation and application of copyright law. In particular, the external perspective was used to understand the technical function of the network or process in question.[11] However, a metaphorical approach was often taken to map the law onto the circumstances of the case applying the law to old offline concepts to justify how it should apply to the new technology.[12] This created confusion in the application of the law by starting out with a very technically accurate approach and then attempting to understand the use of that technology by using a metaphorical approach.

The case law analysis demonstrated that the law was applied broadly and encompassed activity such as display of the work on a screen.[13] Moreover, it was deemed irrelevant if the display only lasted a few seconds and did not amount to a substantial part because, from a technological perspective, a transient copy would be made in the device used to create the display.[14] Therefore, if the display of a copyright work on a screen can amount to copyright infringement, this creates the possibility that users of the internet could be liable simply by viewing any copyright work online. This demonstrates how a literal reading of the law creates an absurdity.

10 *Hansard*, Copyright (Computer Software) Amendment Bill, HL Deb 5 June 1985 Vol 464 Cols 823–829, Viscount Colville of Culross at 824 and Lord McIntosh at 825.

11 For example, *IBCOS Computers Ltd and Another v Barclays Mercantile Highland Finance* [1994] FSR 275, in which Jacob J considered the technical function of the internet, at 285.

12 For example in the case of *Ocular Sciences Ltd and Another v Aspect Vision Care Ltd* [2013] UKSC 18 the Supreme Court considered that viewing or reading a physical book is not an act of infringement in order to understand how the law applied to viewing material online; as per Lord Sumption at [1].

13 *Christopher Paul Gilham v The Queen* [2009] EWCA Crim 2293.

14 *Ibid.*, as per Stanley Burton LJ at [27].

Concluding thoughts on communication to the public

The historical analysis of the development of the right to communication has dramatically expanded from controlling television and radio broadcasts[15] over the course of its relatively short development through international, European and UK legislation. At the stage of the Berne Convention there was a suggestion of an internal perspective as the guidance discussed the need for the work to be received by the eyes or ears of a person.[16] However, it appeared that the scope of the right has extended so far that the making available of the work is enough to constitute communication and therefore only the potential to access the material is needed, no eyes or ears necessarily need to receive it.[17]

There is no clear definition of the boundaries or meaning of communication to the public. This has enabled the law to expand and easily encompass different types of activity, and it is largely unclear as to where the boundaries of communication to the public end.[18] The case law demonstrated a complex, fragmented and inconsistent application of "communication" and "the public". As a result of the vague and broad concept of communication to the public, particularly as applied online, copyright holders have benefited from a rapid extension in their rights: "Communication rights … the ramifications of their extension to the Internet reality, and the amount of power they bestow upon rights-holders, are unparalleled by anything the analogue past has ever seen."[19]

In 1999, Russell Frame argued that "the internet is a relatively unregulated medium for communication."[20] However, as appears to be the case with reproduction, the development of the right to communication would also suggest that it is possible that once a copyright work is available online it falls within the scope of infringement.

15 Vitoria M., et al (eds), *Laddie, Prescott and Vitoria: The Modern Law of Copyright and Designs* (London: Butterworths Law, 2011) 17.3.

16 WIPO, *Guide to the Berne Convention for the Protection of Literary and Artistic Works, Paris 1971* (Geneva: WIPO, 1978) p. 68.

17 Association Littéraire et Artistique Internationale (ALAI), *Report and Opinion on the Making Available and Communication to the Public in the Internet Environment – Focus on Linking Techniques on the Internet*: http://www.alai.org/en/assets/files/resolutions/making-available-right-report-opinion.pdf, point (i).

18 Gillen M., File-Sharing and Individual Civil Liability in the United Kingdom: A Question of Substantial Abuse? (2006) 17(1) *Entertainment Law Review*, pp. 7–14, p. 11.

19 Efroni Z., *Access Right: The Future of Digital Copyright Law* (New York: Oxford University Press, 2011) p. 284.

20 Frame R., The Protection and Exploitation of Intellectual Property Rights on the Internet: The Way Forward for the Music Industry (1999) 4 *Intellectual Property Quarterly*, pp. 443–470, p. 443.

FYI – online copying and communication to the public are the same thing

It becomes apparent that many of the same issues arose in the application of copyright infringement online relating to both copying and communication to the public. In addition, in many of the cases, the claimants brought actions for both copying and communication to the public.[21]

Due to taking the external perspective in the development of the law and the focusing on the technological detail in the ways in which copyright works were used online, the distinction between copying and communication to the public is blurred. This is because of the technological developments in the way that copyright works are used online. As Depreeu stated: "In a digital online environment … a reproduction and a communication to the public in the copyright sense no longer necessarily correspond to distinct exploitation forms."[22] He goes on to recognise the overlap between the reproduction right and the right to communication to the public.[23] This is because when a communication to the public is made by way of a transmission, a copy is always inherently made in the transmission device, in the receiving device, and quite possibly in servers and systems in between. It has been recognised that "in the digital world, even the most routine access to information invariably involves making a copy."[24] Therefore, where there is communication to the public, there is reproduction. As Spoor concluded: "Every single copy, however transient it may be, during the transmission or in the end-users' computer's working memory is a reproduction."[25]

Equally, when copyright infringement by way of reproduction online occurs, the work is therefore available to be enjoyed by the public. Therefore, this would also constitute communication to the public. Efroni explained that "in the course of streaming media process, two types of temporary reproduction usually takes

21 For example in cases: *Football Association Premier League Ltd, NetMed Hellas SA, Multichoice Hellas SA v QC Leisure (a trading name), David Richardson, AV Station Plc, Malcolm Chamberlain, Michael Madden, Sanjay Raval, David Greenslade, SR Leisure Ltd, Phillip George Charles Houghton, Derek Owen* [2008] EWHC 1411 (Ch); *Alan Grisbrook v MGN Ltd, Scottish Daily Record and Sunday Mail Ltd, Syndication International Ltd*[2009] EWHC 2520 (Ch); *ITV Broadcasting Ltd, ITV 2 Ltd, ITV Digital Channels Ltd, Channel 5 Broadcasting Ltd, ITV Studios Ltd v TVCatchup Ltd, The Secretary of State for Business Innovation and Skills* [2011] EWHC 2977 (Pat).

22 Depreeu S., *The Variable Scope of The Exclusive Economic Rights in Copyright* (Amsterdam: Kluwer Law, 2014) p. 262.

23 *Ibid.*, p. 483.

24 National Research Council, Computer Science and Telecommunications Board and Committee on Intellectual Property Rights and the Emerging Information Infrastructure, *The Digital Dilemma: Intellectual Property in the Digital Age* (Washington, DC: National Academies Press, 2000).

25 Spoor J. H., The Copyright Approach to Copying on the Internet: (Over) Stretching the Reproduction Right? in Hugenholtz P. B. and Dommering E. J. (eds) *The Future of Copyright in a Digital Environment: Proceedings of the Royal Academy Colloquium Organized by the Royal Netherlands Academy of Sciences and the Institute for Information Law* (Amsterdam: Kluwer Law, 1996) pp. 67–80, p. 78.

place. First RAM buffer internal reproductions occur in the computer of the end user. Additionally, external reproductions occur on network servers ... reproduction occurs automatically and they are imperceptible to end users, who are often completely unaware of those intermediate technical steps."[26]

As the case law demonstrated, the work need not actually be consumed. There appears to be no requirement that any transmission actually takes place as the restricted act requires only that members of the public "may" access the work.[27] In other words: "The independence is lacking in the case of exploitation in a digital environment. In order to make a work available, the work needs to be stored, and in order to enjoy the work it needs to be copied and made perceptible to the end user."[28] Depreeu described this overlap as a cause for concern, as it creates legal uncertainty and further complicates copyright regulation.[29] This also demonstrates how copyright regulation has transgressed from its original intentions. The book discussed the historical context and development of both copying and communication to the public, which were distinctly different. However, in applying these legal principles online, the two have merged.[30] Therefore, it can be inferred that either one, or both, of these regulations no longer serves its purpose in relation to copyright works online.

Some argue that it is the reproduction right that has had its day: "The reproduction right belongs to the past chapters in copyright law's evolution; it has grown evidently unsuitable to usher the system into the digital future. The notion of fixation is structurally inimical to contemporary modes and methods of providing and gaining access to digital information."[31]

It seems that in the event that all activity online could constitute a reproduction and a communication to the public – e.g. loading, uploading, downloading, running, accessing, or just potentially able to access a work – then the law is not fit for purpose. It cannot be that the law intends to encapsulate everything that ever happens on the internet. The internet is a mass medium for communication that has transformed the scope of communication as a concept,[32] built with the goal to link information and people together.[33] Attempting to restrict communication on

26 Efroni Z., *Access Right: The Future of Digital Copyright Law* (New York: Oxford University Press, 2011) p. 210.

27 Caddick N., Davies G. and Harbottle G., *Copinger and Skone James on Copyright* (London: Sweet & Maxwell, 2005) para 7.

28 Depreeu S., *The Variable Scope of The Exclusive Economic Rights in Copyright* (The Netherlands: Kluwer Law, 2014) p. 485.

29 *Ibid.*, p. 484.

30 Efroni Z., *Access Right: The Future of Digital Copyright Law* (New York: Oxford University Press, 2011) p. 248: arguing that "the advent of digital transmission seriously confused the distinctions between the fixed and unfixed, the private and the public."

31 *Ibid.*, pp. 247–248.

32 McQuail D., *McQuail's Mass Communication Theory* (London: Sage Publications Ltd, 2011) p. 139.

33 Berners-Lee T., *Weaving the Web: The Original Design and Ultimate Destiny of the World Wide Web* (New York: Harper Business, 2000).

the internet in this manner is gross over-regulation that stifles the development of creativity, technology, business models, freedom of expression and the health of the public domain. As quoted at the very beginning of this book, Tim Berners-Lee reminded us that even though the internet is enabled through technology, it is really a system of connecting people.[34]

Taking a purposive approach, as has been seen by the CJEU to uphold a high protection of IP for rights-holders has proved to stretch the boundaries of infringement online to the entire internet. Therefore, simply taking a purposes approach is also inadequate as it does not protect the fair balance that copyright is supposed to uphold. It is proposed that in order for copyright to achieve its goal in the digital age it must be construed within its original intention. That is to say that the goal of copyright is to balance the rights of the creator with those of the public interest, in order that the creator be remunerated for his work and the public may access that work.[35] To achieve this goal copyright regulation, therefore, restricts the use of copyright works with limitations in scope and copyright exceptions. In dealing with copyright infringement online, this research addressed the two key ways in which copyright can be infringed on the internet: reproduction and communication to the public.

Viewed in line with the mischief rule, and from the context and background of the development of the law, it can be seen that the reproduction right was intended to regulate the act of copying of a work.[36] It can also be seen that the communication to the public right was developed as a remedy for the unauthorised sharing of digital copyright material online.[37] Accordingly, the following section suggests that these statutory provisions be interpreted in line with their intention. In order to achieve this, it is suggested that the reproduction right be applied to offline copying from an external perspective and the communication to the public right be applied to online activity from an internal perspective.

Copyright regulation for the future

In his article setting out the internal and external perspectives, Kerr suggested that a particular perspective could be identified within a particular context and thereafter be chosen and applied in those circumstances.[38] However, as has been demonstrated throughout this book, there is no clear choice of perspective evident

34 Berners-Lee T., Speech at the Newseum in Washington at the announcement of the World Wide Web Foundation, 14 September 2008, Washington, DC:: http://webfoundation.org/about/community/transcript-of-tim-berners-lee-video/

35 Vitoria M., et al (eds), *Laddie, Prescott and Vitoria: The Modern Law of Copyright and Designs* (London: Butterworths Law, 2011) 1.9.

36 Litman J., Revising Copyright Law for the Information Age (1996) 75 *Or L Rev*, pp. 19–48, p. 35.

37 Gillen M., File-Sharing and Individual Civil Liability in the United Kingdom: A Question of Substantial Abuse? (2006) 17(1) *Entertainment Law Review*, pp. 7–14, p. 11.

38 Kerr O. S., The Problem of Perspective in Internet Law (2003) 91 *Georgetown Law Journal*, pp. 357–405, p. 390.

for the application of copyright law to the internet overall, and there are limitations to taking purely one approach.

In contrast to Kerr's application of the internal and external perspectives, Frischmann argued that the courts should resist adopting a particular choice of perspective. Instead, he suggested that both perspectives of the facts should be considered, otherwise courts may only appreciate "a partial view of the underlying facts."[39] Hutchinson agreed that judges should be wary of taking a single perspective and should consider both the internal and the external perspectives in the context of the facts to determine whether there are important differences that need to be accommodated for.[40] Whilst it might seem helpful to alert the court to both perspectives, this does not provide a solution to the problem of perspective. Ultimately, in order to come to a decision, the court would have to make a choice. Therefore, simply suggesting that the courts consider both perspectives does not provide a solution.

For that reason, it is proposed that when applying copyright regulation to online activity, the internal perspective should be taken and applied to communication to the public only. Judges should do this by utilising the mischief rule which allows the interpretation of the law to remedy the behaviour intended to be prohibited. This should be done with a purposive view of the objectives of copyright to balance between the copyright holders and the public domain, not just the objective of the Information Society Directive for a high level of protection for IP.

In contrast, copyright infringement by way of reproduction should be considered from the external perspective and be applied to offline activity only. Judges should do this using the literal rule of interpretation, as is historically prevailing in this context.

As demonstrated above, when applying reproduction and communication to the public online in the way that they are currently interpreted, there is a clear overlap. However, the suggested approach of separating these sections to apply reproduction offline and communication to the public online, resolves this redundancy in the law.

Furthermore, this approach takes these offences back to their original purposes. Copyright infringement by way of copying was never designed to encompass internet technology.[41] However, communication to the public quickly adapted to encompass online activity and remedy unauthorised sharing of copyright protected material on the internet.

In addition, choosing an internal perspective for online communication to the public with a purposive approach, and an external perspective for offline reproduction with a literal approach provides consistency in the law. This means that lawyers, users and copyright holders will more easily be able to predict the boundaries of the law and act accordingly.

39 Frischmann B. M., The Prospect of Reconciling Internet and Cyberspace (2004) 35 *Loyola University Chicago Law Journal*, pp. 205–234, p. 207.

40 Hutchison C. J., Interpretation and the Internet (2010) 28 *John Marshall Journal of Computer and Information Law*, pp. 251–272, p. 268.

41 Litman J., Revising Copyright Law for the Information Age (1996) 75 *Or L Rev*, pp. 19–48, p. 19.

Taking the internal perspective in the application of communication to the public would also reduce the number of cases considering the specific technological differences in the facts of the case. As highlighted in the study, the external and literal approach to communication to the public resulted in many similar cases being heard before the courts and required the judges to consider each technical element in detail, despite eventually using a purposive approach in the end. Therefore, this suggestion would relieve the judges from this challenge and allow the law to encompass all relevant versions of technology that achieves an unauthorised use of copyright material. As Olswang suggested, continuing to distinguish between acts of infringement by way of the technological process online is ineffective because technology offers a range of means to reach the same end.[42] Therefore, this approach provides a mechanism by which the intended outcome – user experience – can be regulated as opposed to making new law every time a new technology is developed, thereby also overcoming the challenge of the law becoming obsolete in the face of technological development.

Moreover, due to the internal perspective, this would clarify the law in relation to access, a point of contention that arose frequently in the investigation.[43] The idea of regulating copyright online through an access-based approach has been suggested by other academics such as Efroni in his study *The Future of Digital Copyright Law*: "The present study endeavours to investigate precisely this fairly underdeveloped idea – that of an access-based copyright regulation … examines the idea of literally premising copyright regulation on the concept of access to digital information and the implications of such a system."[44] Whist Efroni's study did not consider the internal and external perspectives explicitly, the proposed access right was clearly defined from the internal perspective: "The concept of access implies, inter alia, cognitive processing occurring inside the recipient's mind once exposure to the message signals takes place … Human-access to information is an internal, cognitive occurrence that is to a significant degree involuntary."[45]

On this understanding of the meaning of access, Efroni's study proposed a conceptual copyright that limited the user's ability to experience or apprehend a work, as opposed to making a technical copy of it. Access online could be considered as the ability to experience or apprehend a work – in other words, to view, read or listen to it via the internet.[46] This aligns with the internal perspective as it incorporates the human experience of the interaction with the copyright work

42 Olswang S., Accessright: an evolutionary path for copyright into the digital era? (1995) *European Intellectual Property Review*, pp. 215–218, p. 216.

43 Koelman K. J., A Hard Nut to Crack: The Protection of Technological Measures (2000) 22(6) *European Intellectual Property Review*, pp. 272–288, p. 274: "the trend seems to be for copyright to slowly move in the direction of granting an exclusive right to access."

44 Efroni Z., *Access Right: The Future of Digital Copyright Law* (New York: Oxford University Press, 2011) p. xxi.

45 *Ibid.*, p. 128.

46 Besek J. M., Anti-Circumvention Laws and Copyright: A Report from the Kernochan Centre for Law, Media and the Arts (2004) 27 *Columbia Journal of law and Arts*, pp. 385–519.

online, disregarding the technological means beyond the use of the internet as a tool for access.

It may seem radical, on the face of it, to suggest that copyright should regulate the consumption of a work in this way. However, the analysis in this research has demonstrated several times that the courts are already applying the law so that it restricts access to copyright work. Additionally, as previously noted, Lessig argued that this is the future of copyright regulation: "Copyright law has got to give up its obsession with 'the copy.' The law should not regulate 'copies' or 'modern reproductions' on their own. It should instead regulate uses – like public distributions of copies of copyrighted work – that connect directly to the economic incentive copyright law was intended to foster."[47]

This idea was also approached by Fitzgerald, who argued that the concept of copyright should develop beyond its current technical boundaries to consider the human element and human consumption by way of access: "We should be moving beyond the limited conceptual framework of copyright to a legal framework that looks more closely at the relationships any individual or entity has with information, knowledge, culture or creativity … open up the politics and economy of the rights to access, reuse and communicate information, knowledge, culture or creativity."[48]

As the UK prepares to (potentially) leave the European Union, an opportunity presents itself to legislators to draft a new copyright Act. If a new copyright Act was drafted in line with this suggested proposal it would involve the following:

- *Copyright infringement regulated differently online and offline.* The nature of the internet results in unique circumstances. The application of offline copyright regulation using metaphorical understanding creates inconsistency and uncertainty in the law. Therefore, it is appropriate to regulate online use of copyright material differently to that of offline use of copyright material.
- *Offline copyright infringement regulated by way of the restricted act of reproduction.* This is in line with the historical context and intention of copyright law to regulate the copying of copyright protected works. This legislation should be drafted and interpreted from an external perspective, focusing on the physical elements involved in the copying. In addition, judges should interpret and apply the law in line with the literal rule. This enables the law to be clear, certain and consistent. The literal rule and external perspective are appropriate in this context as there is only one possible set of facts in offline copyright infringement.
- *Online copyright infringement regulated by way of the restricted act of communication to the public.* The purpose of communication to the public is to regulate the unauthorised access of copyright works on the internet. The

47 Lessig L., *Remix: Making Art and Commerce Thrive in the Hybrid Economy* (New York: Penguin Press, 2008) p. 268.

48 Fitzgerald B., Copyright 2010: The Future of Copyright (2008) 30(2) *European Intellectual Property Review*, pp. 43–49.

legislation should be drafted and interpreted from an internal perspective, focusing on the experience of the user or infringer. In addition, judges should interpret and apply the law with a purposive approach in line with the mischief rule. They should consider the mischief that the law seeks to remedy. This reduces the need for detailed technological analysis, and brings clarity to the boundaries of the law. What is regulated is what the user is doing, not how they achieve that from a technical perspective. As a result, the law is clearer, more certain and consistent.

This proposal could be a possible direction for the future of copyright regulation in the digital age. As Mr Justice Arnold advocates: "there are systemic problems in the design of the 1988 Act whose effects have become worse over time[49] … it is plain that we need a new Copyright Act."[50]

Bibliography

Books

Berners-Lee T., *Weaving the Web: The Original Design and Ultimate Destiny of the World Wide Web* (New York: Harper Business, 2000).

Caddick N., Davies G. and Harbottle G., *Copinger and Skone James on Copyright* (London: Sweet & Maxwell, 2005).

Depreeu S., *The Variable Scope of The Exclusive Economic Rights in Copyright* (Amsterdam: Kluwer Law, 2014).

Efroni Z., *Access Right: The Future of Digital Copyright Law* (New York: Oxford University Press, 2011).

Groves P., *Copyright and Designs Law: A Question of Balance* (London: Graham and Trotman Ltd, 1991).

Lessig L., *Remix: Making Art and Commerce Thrive in the Hybrid Economy* (New York: Penguin Press, 2008).

McQuail D., *McQuail's Mass Communication Theory* (London: Sage Publications Ltd, 2011).

Spoor J. H., The Copyright Approach to Copying on the Internet: (Over) Stretching the Reproduction Right? in Hugenholtz P. B. and Dommering E. J. (eds) *The Future of Copyright in a Digital Environment: Proceedings of the Royal Academy Colloquium Organized by the Royal Netherlands Academy of Sciences and the Institute for Information Law* (Amsterdam: Kluwer Law, 1996).

Vitoria M., et al (eds), *Laddie, Prescott and Vitoria: The Modern Law of Copyright and Designs*, 4th edition (London: Butterworths Law, 2011).

49 Arnold R., The Need for a New Copyright Act: A Case Study in Law Reform, The Herchel Smith Intellectual Property Lecture (2014) 5(2) *Queen Mary Journal of Intellectual Property*, pp. 110–131, p. 125.

50 *Ibid.*, p. 126.

Case law

Alan Grisbrook v MGN Ltd, Scottish Daily Record and Sunday Mail Ltd, Syndication International Ltd [2009] EWHC 2520 (Ch).

Christopher Paul Gilham v The Queen [2009] EWCA Crim 2293.

Football Association Premier League Ltd, NetMed Hellas SA, Multichoice Hellas SA v QC Leisure (a trading name), David Richardson, AV Station Plc, Malcolm Chamberlain, Michael Madden, Sanjay Raval, David Greenslade, SR Leisure Ltd, Phillip George Charles Houghton, Derek Owen [2008] EWHC 1411 (Ch).

IBCOS Computers Ltd and Another v Barclays Mercantile Highland Finance [1994] FSR 275.

ITV Broadcasting Ltd, ITV 2 Ltd, ITV Digital Channels Ltd, Channel 5 Broadcasting Ltd, ITV Studios Ltd v TVCatchup Ltd, The Secretary of State for Business Innovation and Skills [2011] EWHC 2977 (Pat).

Ocular Sciences Ltd and Another v Aspect Vision Care Ltd [2013] UKSC 18.

The Newspaper Licensing Agency Ltd, MGN Ltd, Associated Newspapers Ltd, Express Newspapers Ltd, Guardian News and Media Ltd, Telegraph Media Group Ltd, Independent Print Ltd v Meltwater Holding BV, Meltwater News UK Ltd, Public Relations Consultants Association Ltd [2010] EWHC 3099 (Ch).

The Newspaper Licensing Agency Ltd, MGN Ltd, Associated Newspapers Ltd, Express Newspapers Ltd, Guardian News and Media Ltd, Telegraph Media Group Ltd, Independent Print Ltd v Meltwater Holding BV, Meltwater News UK Ltd, Public Relations Consultants Association Ltd, [2011] EWCA Civ 890.

Journals

Arnold R., Content Copyrights and Signal Copyrights: The Case for a Rational Scheme of Protection (2011) 1(3) *Queen Mary Journal of Intellectual Property*, pp. 272–279.

Arnold R., The Need for a New Copyright Act: A Case Study in Law Reform, The Herchel Smith Intellectual Property Lecture (2014) 5(2) *Queen Mary Journal of Intellectual Property*, pp. 110–131.

Besek J. M., Anti-Circumvention Laws and Copyright: A Report from the Kernochan Centre for Law, Media and the Arts (2004) 27 *Columbia Journal of Law and Arts*, pp. 385–519.

Fitzgerald B., Copyright 2010: The Future of Copyright (2008) 30(2) *European Intellectual Property Review*, pp. 43–49.

Frame R., The Protection and Exploitation of Intellectual Property Rights on the Internet: The Way Forward for the Music Industry (1999) 4 *Intellectual Property Quarterly*, pp. 443–470.

Frischmann B. M., The Prospect of Reconciling Internet and Cyberspace (2004) 35 *Loyola University Chicago Law Journal*, pp. 205–234.

Gillen M., File-Sharing and Individual Civil Liability in the United Kingdom: A Question of Substantial Abuse? (2006) 17(1) *Entertainment Law Review*, pp. 7–14.

Hutchison C. J., Interpretation and the Internet (2010) 28 *John Marshall Journal of Computer and Information Law*, pp. 251–272.

Kerr O. S., The Problem of Perspective in Internet Law (2003) 91 *Georgetown Law Journal*, pp. 357–405.

Koelman K. J., A Hard Nut to Crack: The Protection of Technological Measures (2000) 22(6) *European Intellectual Property Review*, pp. 272–288.

Larsson S., Metaphors, Law and Digital Phenomena: The Swedish Pirate Bay Court Case (2013) 21(4) *International Journal of Law, Information and Technology*, pp. 354–380.

Litman J., Revising Copyright Law for the Information Age (1996) 75 *Or L Rev*, pp. 19–48.

Olswang S., Accessright: an evolutionary path for copyright into the digital era? (1995) *European Intellectual Property Review*, pp. 215–218.

Legislation

Copyright, Designs and Patents Act 1988.

Official documents

Hansard, Copyright (Computer Software) Amendment Bill, HL Deb 5 June 1985 Vol 464 Cols 823–829.

National Research Council, Computer Science and Telecommunications Board and Committee on Intellectual Property Rights and the Emerging Information Infrastructure, *The Digital Dilemma: Intellectual Property in the Digital Age* (Washington, DC: National Academies Press, 2000).

WIPO, *Guide to the Berne Convention for the Protection of Literary and Artistic Works, Paris 1971* (Geneva: WIPO, 1978).

Web sources

Association Littéraire et Artistique Internationale (ALAI), Report and Opinion on the Making Available and Communication to the Public in the Internet Environment – Focus on Linking Techniques on the Internet: http://www.alai.org/en/assets/files/resolutions/making-available-right-report-opinion.pdf, point (i).

Berners-Lee T., Speech at the Newseum in Washington at the announcement of the World Wide Web Foundation, 14 September 2008, Washington, DC: http://webfoundation.org/about/community/transcript-of-tim-berners-lee- video/.

Index

For Product Safety Concerns and Information please contact our EU representative GPSR@taylorandfrancis.com
Taylor & Francis Verlag GmbH, Kaufingerstraße 24, 80331 München, Germany

www.ingramcontent.com/pod-product-compliance
Ingram Content Group UK Ltd.
Pitfield, Milton Keynes, MK11 3LW, UK
UKHW011012180926
475701UK00004B/707

* 9 7 8 1 0 3 2 2 3 9 7 2 9 *